# Dangerous Theatre

George Kazacoff

# Dangerous Theatre

## The Federal Theatre Project as a Forum for New Plays

PETER LANG
New York • Bern • Frankfurt am Main • Paris

**Library of Congress Cataloging-in-Publication Data**

Kazacoff, George
   Dangerous theatre : the Federal Theatre Project /
George Kazacoff.
      p. cm
   Bibliography: p.
   1. Federal Theatre Project (U.S.)   I. Title.
PN2270.F43K39      1989      792'.0973 – dc19      88-13959
ISBN 0-8204-0752-6                              CIP


**CIP-Titelaufnahme der Deutschen Bibliothek**

**Kazacoff, George:**
Dangerous theatre : the Federal Theatre Project
as a forum for new plays / George Kazacoff. –
New York; Bern; Frankfurt am Main; Paris:
Lang, 1989.
   ISBN 0-8204-0752-6

Printed by Weihert-Druck GmbH, Darmstadt, West Germany

"The theatre, when it's good, is always dangerous."


--Hallie  Flanagan

# Table of Contents

*Altars of Steel*
Photograph
from
Library of Congress Federal Theatre Project Collection
at
George Mason University
Fairfax, Virginia

PREFACE

No formal study of the Federal Theatre Project has dealt in any significant way with it as a forum for new plays. Currently published studies make only limited reference to this major function of the FTP. Even Hallie Flanagan's <u>Arena</u>, which documents the history of the Project, barely mentions those units involved with locating, sponsoring, evaluating, and presenting new plays.[1] Most publications focus on the major and most spectacular productions--<u>Macbeth</u>, <u>Dr. Faustus</u>, <u>Murder in the Cathedral</u>, and <u>It Can't Happen Here</u>--but make few references to, say, the work of a Los Angeles Unit on a cycle of plays about theSouthwest.

Most published information focuses almost entirely on the work of the New York City Regional Unit, where the bulk of the FTP activity was centered and where most of the highly publicized controversies about censorship, radicalism, and labor strife occurred. Very little has been written about the new plays produced by the FTP outside of New York City. This study will provide a history of the various production units in each region that were involved with presenting new plays. It will delineate how each unit was organized and administered. Also described will be each unit's leadership and artistic policies. The plays produced will be described in synopses, and information regarding how the plays were directed and produced will be supplied. Critical response will be chronicled as an attempt to cover, as comprehensively as possible, reactions to the plays' dramaturgy, social, and aesthetic content.

The material will be presented so that a composite view can be obtained by observing the behind-the-scenes world of FTP in operation. Viewing the congruence or lack of congruence in opinion among the groups judging FTP--playreaders, "special readers," critics, public audiences, politicians, and other theatre professionals--provides an insight into all of the cross-currents which not only affected the Project's reputation but also contributed both to its glory and destruction.

The dissertation will describe how the Federal Theatre Project functioned as a forum for new plays during the four years of its existence, 1935 through 1939. Examined here are only those "legitimate" American and foreign plays and musicals presented for the first time to American audiences in professional productions. Excluded from consideration are revivals, classical, foreign language and stock plays, operas, pageants, puppetry, skits, and similar forms. Work done by the Living Newspaper and Negro units will not be considered since the Living Newspaper is a unique form requiring a separate, extensive examination; the Negro productions have been studied thoroughly in other publications.[2]

The dissertation will explain what new plays were presented by FTP: how they were written, evaluated, tested, and finally produced. The process involved in producing new plays--submission, readers' reports, production meetings, production, and critical reaction--will be outlined. With few exceptions, only first productions by FTP will be documented in the body of the text. Information concerning subsequent FTP presentations, including places and dates, will be included in Appendix B.[3] When a choice had to be made based upon availability of information, the most noteworthy or extensively documented production was selected even if it was in fact not the first.

The FTP Play Bureau was primarily interested in doing new plays that were contemporary, "honest," and "alive to the problems of today's world." Although a play may have had a college or little theatre production in the United States, it will still be considered new, in this study, if its first professional production was done by FTP. The same will be true for foreign plays produced outside the United States. Only when a one-act play, not fitting into the category of a new play, was presented with one that was new, will it be mentioned or discussed briefly. New play here means newly written or of recent origin.

For the first time, the new plays premiered by Federal Theatre will not only be listed and grouped in the regional areas where they were produced, but extensively described by detailing their storylines. Other publications that present critical reactions, not only do not detail the storylines, but do not discuss the specific features of the dramaturgy and how they were judged in regard to effectiveness of theme, character, dialogue, etc. The comments tend to be general and focus to a large extent on the political and social ramifications of the play without mentioning the particular techniques that gave the plays much significance, if any, as dramatic literature. The intention in this study is not to analyze plays with regard to their qualities as dramatic literature, but to reflect how the FTP Playreading Department evaluated the plays and considered them for production.

The Research Center for the Federal Theatre Project at George Mason University was an invaluable source of information which made the scope and depth of this study possible. Research gleaned from the Research Center's playreaders' reports, synopses, oral histories, production bulletins, reviews, press releases, and administrative files provided a comprehensive view of the internal workings of FTP and the productions to be discussed. All of the playreaders' reports used in this study are extant, and for the most part were done by members of the

Playreading Department in the Play Bureau of the National Service ,Bureau. Regional Play Bureau readers read and considered plays; however, very few copies of those reports exist in the files at George Mason University. All plays were selected by the regional bureaus but cleared through the National Service Bureau, although regional ,directors usually had the final say. Plays submitted this way were read by the head office's playreaders, whose job it was to consider a play's viability for inclusion in the national play list sent to all, regional directors. Playreading Department supervisors did not supply playreaders with specific guidelines which spelled out what to consider when accepting or rejecting a play. Because of this, as will be seen, readers' comments were frequently very general, biased, and lacked detailed and pertinent comments about a play's dramaturgical strengths or weaknesses. Among the playreaders hired by FTP there was a great disparity in their educational, professional, and cultural background Once a regional play bureau selected a play, it exercised a great deal of authority regarding play doctoring, which in some cases was considerable.

The WPA theatre was not a forum for new plays in the Roman sense--assembling citizens for the purpose of discussing questions of public interest--although, to a certain extent, it was that, too. It was a forum more in the sense that it gave an enormous, expanding number of venues for the production of new plays that the commercial theatre would never have produced or encouraged.

The FTP did not leave a legacy of plays considered significant as dramatic literature. It did not influence extant production styles. Federal Theatre's new plays are not known, studied, produced, or discussed. They belong to a body of work laid to rest. The single most original FTP contribution was the Living Newspaper, which is not particularly alive and well at the moment. Experimentation and originality was not abundantly evident in the new plays presented to American audiences by FTP for the first time in professional production. The tradition of realism, sometimes a muted socialist realism, was in full reign. The productions that dazzled were generally those presented in New York; they were not frequently new plays.

Reflecting how each region developed its own "indigenous drama and native expression," how well they portrayed their "regional materials" and "landscape," is the specific intention of this study about the Federal Theatre Project.

6

Notes

¹The foremost of these works is Hallie Flanagan, <u>Arena</u> (New York: Duell, Sloan and Pierce, 1940; reprint ed., New York: Benjamin Bloom, 1965). Other noteworthy works are Jane De Hart Mathews, <u>The Federal Theatre, 1935-1939: Plays, Relief and Politics</u> (Princeton: Princeton University Press, 1967); Willson Whitman, <u>Bread and Circuses</u> (New York: Oxford University Press, 1937); and John O'Connor and Lorraine Brown, eds., <u>Free, Adult and Uncensored</u> (Washington, D.C.: New Republic Books, 1978).

²The foremost of these works is E. Quita Craig, <u>Black Drama of the Federal Theatre Era</u> (Amherst: University of Massachusetts Press, 1980); and Lofton Mitchell, <u>Black Drama</u> (New York: Hawthorn Books, Inc., 1967).

³Information taken from a listing of productions at the Library of Congress Federal Theatre Project Collection at George Mason University Library, Fairfax, Virginia. Further references to materials in this collection will be noted as "George Mason University." Appendix B lists dates and performances of plays cited.

# INTRODUCTION

"Theatre, when it's good, is always dangerous," claimed Hallie Flanagan while defending the Federal Theatre Project during the investigation of its alleged subversive activity by the House Committee toInvestigate Un-American Activities in 1938.[1] What that statement meant to Senator Dirksen and other congressmen eager to demolish the FTP was--dangerous to the ruling class. After all, did not Hallie Flanagan say that one of the purposes of theatre is "giving apoplexy to people who consider it radical for a government-sponsored theatre to produce plays on subjects vitally concerning the governed. . . ."?[2]

The reasons why the Federal Theatre was dangerous are far more complex than just being a threat to the ruling class. When Harry Hopkins, Works Progress Administration Director, gave Flanagan the job as FTP Director, he told her, "Remember, whatever you do you'll be wrong." In her zeal, idealism, and passion for creating a "federation of theatres," Flanagan was wrong in dreaming that the FTP was a permanent part of American life. It was not, and that should have been clear from the beginning. With her great, abundant energy and talent, Flanagan followed her perilous course to the bitter end--right into the chambers where politicians investigated her and her theatre as "un-American." Somehow, she did not, or could not, accept the idea that the Project was a temporary measure devised to help unemployed workers in show-business. She took every risk, determined that somehow the show would never end.

But was Hallie Flanagan's theatre dangerous only to the ruling class? No! It was dangerous in every way to everyone that it could possibly benefit. Conservatives, backed by the Hearst press, found it radical, subversive, seditious, and lewd. Journals and newspapers of the far left found it dangerous because it fostered "reformist" thinking which would forestall the day when the revolution would finally come. It was in fact dangerous to the far left because it was part of an administration credited with saving the system. And while saving the system, it also helped close down the Theatre Union, New York's most radical theatre, by capturing its audiences. FTP was risky because its critics accused it of competing with private enterprise. Theatre professionals, including unionists, would never forgive the "non-professional" educational, social work, missionary zeal of all of the "amateurs" the FTP managed to congregate within its orbit. It was hazardous to insist that "socially relevant" plays about contemporary issues replace stock productions performed in the hinterlands of mainstream America. People like Eva LeGallienne, and others dedicated to "high art," felt that the "amateur" thrust of the government theatre would reduce the artistic level of theatre production in the United States to a level close to barbarism. Proponents of serious intention in art felt that art had a mission to propagate ideas and literature in the Carlos Fuentes sense.[3] The Phillistines never stopped complaining about money being spent on revolution, lewdness, and worse. The Puritan ethic was in full force, and this "boondoggling" dalliance of the Franklin Delano Roosevelt administration would never be excused. The grave where this "boondoggle" would be buried was already dug by the time Senator Dirksen railed that this dangerous theatre was not only "anti-capitalist" but also "anti-entertainment" in putting on shows like Up in Mabel's Room.[4]  Some of Federal Theatre's critics thought FTP self-destructed because of its tendency to sometimes mix art and politics.

The Federal Theatre Project was created during the Great Depression to help relieve the unemployment problem in the theatrical professions, not as a noble effort to experiment with aesthetic, theories. During the spring of 1935, counted among the fifteen million unemployed and the six million persons on relief rolls, were 40,000 show business workers who could not find even temporary jobs.[5]

As an emergency measure providing relief funds for the unemployed, Congress created the CWA (Civil Works Administration) on November 9, 1933.  This hasty measure was inadequate and was then replaced when Congress established legislation for creating the WPA(Works Progress Administration) in April 1935 to create jobs for the unemployed within their own professions or occupations.  WPA workers did everything from building dams to planting trees.  Within the larger framework of the WPA, four separate artistic projects were initiated, one each in music, writing, the plastic arts, and the theatre. According to this plan, employables were to be removed from state relief rolls, and the unemployables were to be returned to the care of the states.[6]

When Hallie Flanagan, then a professor at Vassar College, officially assumed leadership of the Federal Theatre Project in August 1935, America embarked on its first great attempt at endowing the dramatic arts and developing a national people's theatre.  Flanagan, an impassioned leader, relentlessly nourished that dream with her mandate that, "In an age of terrific implication as to wealth and poverty, as to function of government, as to peace and war, as to the relations of the artist to these forces, the theatre must grow."[7]

Although the primary aim of the FTP was the reemployment of theatre workers on public relief, Flanagan's far-reaching goal was the establishment of "theatres so vital to community life that they will continue to function when the program of the FTP is completed. These enterprises will offer entertainment free or at low cost, and encourage, whenever possible, regional theatres to develop native plays and original methods of production."[8]

Emphasizing, as a recurrent theme, one of the premises of the FTP, Flanagan stressed,

> We must see the relationship between men at work on Boulder Dam and the Greek chorus. . . . In short, the American Theatre must wake up and grow up--wake up to an age of social consciousness, an age in which men are whispering through space, soaring to the stars, and fighting miles of steel and glass in the air. . . . If the plays do not exist, we shall have to write them. We shall have to work closely with our dramatists.[9]

When Flanagan was offered the position as National Director of Federal Theatre, she was hesitant to accept. She told Harry Hopkins, WPA Director, that she was not the person for the job because her background was in educational, not commercial, theatre. Hopkins replied in a way that characterized FTP's special mission:

> It's got to be run by a person who sees from the start that profits won't be money profits. It's got to be run by a person who isn't interested just in the commercial type of show. . . .This is an American job, not just a New York job. I want someone who knows and cares about other parts of the country.[10]

The Project's organization was structured in the classic pyramid manner. At its peak was the national headquarters located first in Washington, D.C., and then later in New York. The national structure consisted of individual theatre regions, each with its own regional director. The theatre regional structure went through various organizational changes during the four years of FTP's existence, as is explained in Appendix A. By 1939 there were five regions: New York City, East, South, Midwest, and West. The regional projects were established as theatre companies attached to an existing non-profit theatre organization or as independent theatre companies (newly formed under Federal Theatre). Other units formed within each region were marionette theatres, children's theatres, vaudeville, variety and circus projects, theatre companies in CCC camps, teaching of theatre techniques units, and research and publications.[11]

The scope of the FTP plan to provide a wide spectrum of performing arts units was best exemplified by the New York City region, which established the greatest number of producing organizations. In addition to the units established for the specific purpose of presenting new or original plays given their first major production in the United States, several other performance groups were set up in New York City, including the Gilbert and Sullivan, vaudeville, marionette, and minstrel show units which were organized to perform at settlement houses, schools, clubs, and churches. Also created were other units devoted to the performance of classical plays, one-act plays, and poetic drama. A children's theatre and a "negro" youth theatre headed by Venezuella Jones were also formed. Ethnic theatre groups performed in native languages. John E. Bonn headed a German group, and there was a Yiddish vaudeville troupe in addition to an Anglo-Jewish Theatre sponsored by the Jewish Welfare Board and directed by Boris Tomashevsky. Eventually, the highly noted 891 unit headed by Orson Welles and John Houseman was established.[12]

With Hopkins's inspiration, Flanagan established her "Plan for the Organization of Regional Theatres":

> To set up theatres which have the possibilities of growing into social institutions in communities in which they are located . . . and to lay the foundation for the development of a truly creative theatre in the United States with outstanding producing centers in each of those regions which have common interests as a result of geography, language, origins, history, traditions, customs, occupations of the people.[13]

As Flanagan conceived it, the Federal Theatre would allow, for the first time, professional theatre to be considered regionally in a way that would encourage the commercial, educational, and community theatres in the various regions of the country to work collaboratively. Each region could develop its own indigenous drama and native expression.[14] It would be a drama "reflecting its own landscape and regional materials, producing plays of its past and present, in its own rhythm of speech and its native design, in an essentially American pattern."[15]

These dreams for a national theatre, although Flanagan preferred to say, "federation of theatres," were just dreams. The story of FTP is to a large extent a story about dreams because its short life hardly allowed the groundwork to be laid before its demolition was underway. However, if the dream had ever been fully realized, it would have created:

> A theatre speaking for the Eastern cosmopolis, for the West, the Midwest, and the South, . . . [Such a theatre is] increasingly necessary not only for the few who can afford it but for the many who cannot. Such a theatre can interpret region to region, emphasizing the united aspect of the states, and illuminate the United States for the other Americas. Such a theatre can oppose destructive forces without and within, a positive, creative force,

a formidable upthrust of power against the death force of ignorance, greed, fear, and prejudice. Such a theatre is a life force, creating for our citizens a medium for freedom such as no other form of government can assure and offering people access to the arts, and tools of civilization which they themselves are helping to make. Such a theatre is at once an illustration and a bulwark of the democratic form of government.[16]

While organizing, Federal Theatre sought the advice and counsel of many significant figures in the various realms of professional theatre. Several critics, including Brooks Atkinson, Burns Mantle, and Barrett H. Clark, served on the Federal Theatre Advisory Board; as did producers Herman Shumlin and Maurice Wertheimer (of the Theatre Guild Board of Managers); playwrights Sidney Howard and George Sklar; and actors Burgess Meredith, Cornelia Otis Skinner, and Blanche Yurka. Irene Lewissohn of the Neighborhood Playhouse, Helen Hall of the Henry Street Settlement House, and Elias M. Sugarman, Editor of Billboard also served. The FTP Advisory Board was augmented by the Federal Theatre Committee which included producers Cheryl Crawford, Teresa Helburn, and Lee Shubert; and playwrights Albert Maltz, Marc Connelly, and Clifford Odets. Also serving were Heywood Broun, Jo Mielziner, Martha Graham, Ralph Steiner, and Herbert Kline, of the New Theatre League.[17]

Hallie Flanagan's sight was on creating FTP as a permanent enterprise. She insisted that the Project would have to build audiences and gain their support not by competing with commercial theatre but by contributing to it the work of unknown playwrights who would emphasize regional and local material and experiment with new techniques and ideas. Flanagan stressed that Federal Theatre would have to be "free, adult, uncensored theatre," relevant to modern life, experimental artistically, reflecting the social and economic forces of the contemporary world. The workers on the stage would be united with workers in the audience in common belief.

The immediate need to offer economic survival to the unemployed clashed with the drive to create a dynamic contemporary theatre organization. Relief and popular appeal competed with the goal of training actors, improving public taste, and the writing of relevant and meaningful new plays dealing with contemporary issues. The conflict intensified when dismissals caused by budget cuts forced administrators to make relief their priority; therefore, the most competent workers were frequently the first to be released. The fact that this contradiction hampered FTP's long-range plans at every turn and still allowed it to function creatively, and sometimes memorably, was one of FTP's great achievements, and part of its drama.

Although ten percent of FTP's new plays were in the category of "social dramas," Flanagan insisted that FTP would not be fundamentally a social theatre.[18] Plays produced by the Federal Theatre included plays in the following categories: new plays, Broadway successes, minor stock plays, foreign plays, classical plays, children's plays, Living Newspapers, marionettes, dance drama, American pageants, social dramas, musicals, vaudeville, religious plays, negro plays, Yiddish plays, early American plays, one-act plays, plays written by Project workers on their own time, and plays written by Project workers on government time.[19]

Gerald Rabkin observed in Drama and Commitment that critics of social dramas failed to notice that 90 percent of Federal Theatre productions included "cycles of plays by Shakespeare, Shaw, and O'Neill; the presentation of a classical repertory that ranged from Aeschylus to

Sheridan; the organization of units which presented European classics in their native tongues . . . Gilbert and Sullivan . . . regional plays . . . and puppet shows for children."[20] Investigating FTP, the Dies Committee selected 81 plays out of a list of 830 titles for official castigation. Of these 81 titles, 29 originated with Federal Theatre. The other 51 titles represented: 32 standard stock or revival productions; five plays that were never produced by the Project; seven plays that originated with community drama groups, not with the Project; one children's play; one Yiddish play; one Italian translation; two pieces of Americana; and two classics.[21]

The dramas found objectionable by the Dies Committee were grouped into four categories: 1) the Living Newspapers; 2) new plays by American authors; 3) plays by three European authors: Bernard Shaw, Ernst Toller, and Friedrich Wolf; and 4) other forms of performance: a dance drama based upon Euripides' Trojan Women, a children's play, and a very unsuccessful musical.[22]

The "dangerous" new plays produced by FTP and officially criticized by the Dies Committee include the following, which will be documented in this study: Around the Corner; Chalk Dust; Class of '29; Created Equal; It Can't Happen Here; No More Peace; Professor Mamlock; Prologue to Glory; The Sun and I; Woman of Destiny; Help Yourself; Machine Age; On the Rocks; and the musical, Sing for Your Supper. Ironically, two of the most "revolutionary" new FTP plays not censured and to be examined were Dance of Death and Battle Hymn.

Flanagan emphasized that FTP would not do just new social plays, but she still argued for socially relevant scripts while WPA officials wanted safe shows. Regional Directors soon learned that their function was creating relief employment, not new or relevant theatre. The attempt to create a permanent, artistic national theatre was under constant scrutiny by congressmen not sympathetic to anything FTP represented. These politicians did not want to be Federal Theatre's benefactors in helping to produce new socially relevant plays. The contradictions cast a lingering dark cloud over all of the Project's efforts. Relief as a stop-gap measure and theatre as Hallie Flanagan envisioned it never became a "marriage made in heaven," and the conflict was one of the causes of FTP's demise. Flanagan indicated that she wanted FTP plays to reflect a variety of social experience and theatrical expression. However, she also felt that Federal Theatre should earnestly reflect the "changing social order" and critical social issues. This was always one of her paramount concerns; she expressed it in one of her editorials for Federal Theatre Magazine, the magazine of the Federal Theatre:

> In [the] attack on injustice, poverty, and despair, so graphically described by President Roosevelt in his second Inaugural, what part can the Federal Theatre play? It can make it part of its theatre business to show what is happening to people, all sorts of people in America today. Not that our plays should be restricted to a study of the one-third of our nation which is ill-housed, ill-clad, and ill-nourished, though these millions are so inescapably a part of America today that they are subjects for drama with the militant ring of the Second Inaugural. Even more potently, perhaps, our plays can concern themselves with conditions back of the conditions described by President Roosevelt.[23]

Despite her penchant for social relevance in FTP scripts, Flanagan warned her administrators: "It need not be Lenin's blood streaming from the firmament."[24]

Morgan Himmelstein points out in <u>Drama Was a Weapon</u> that Flanagan did not want FTP to present communist dramas depicting "the oversimplified collision of workers and bosses." Federal Theatre would produce social plays that reveal "rather the struggle of many different kinds of people to understand the natural, social, and economic forces [for] a better life for more people."[25]

Although the percentage of new social plays presented (very few in the regions) by FTP was small, they were a large part of the New York production and led eventually to allegations that FTP was controlled by Communists for the purpose of promoting Marxist ideology. Eventually, when the FTP was investigated by the Dies Committee on Un-American Activities in 1938, an onslaught of attacks came from various quarters equating the reforms of the New Deal with Communism. As an example, Representative J. Parnell Thomas of New Jersey viewed E.P. Conkle's <u>Prologue to Glory</u>, a play of benign political content portraying Abraham Lincoln as a young man, as a propaganda play conceived "to prove that all politicians are crooked."[26]

Himmelstein indicated that some FTP plays did reflect the Marxist viewpoint, but that this criticism was overstated. Flanagan defended Federal Theatre plays as, for the most part, either classics or native American drama.[27] Despite the fact that a few Marxist plays were produced by the Project, the number was not significant enough to label all of the new FTP social plays communistic.[28]

The new plays produced in the various regions ran the gamut from light comedies written by Northwest authors for the Tacoma Playwrighting Unit to John Dunne's work on the folklore of the Southwest. The collaborative process utilized by Virginia Farmer and her

Southwest Unit in developing new scripts and the work done on musicals in California were vital and creative ventures proving that not everything noteworthy was happening in New York. However, the enormous attention given to New York productions overshadowed work done in the regions. Productions mounted in regional theatres were virtually neglected in any meaningful research or publicity.

Very few of the new plays produced in the regional theatres were in the social protest category. The great majority were plays written to entertain local audiences.

In assessing responses given to FTP plays by Play Bureau readers and critics, it is necessary to establish a framework in which to group judgments according to contemporary, social, political, and aesthetic perspectives. Because Federal Theatre could not advertise its productions, opinions expressed in newspapers and journals were important links between FTP and the audiences it wished to attract.[29] In New York City, opinions expressed by journals and newspapers of the far and center left were as significant to FTP as reactions given by mainstream critics because New York was now attracting a new working class audience that was politically motivated and involved. Articles appearing in trade papers such as Variety informed FTP how it was viewed by the commercial theatre. Phillip Barber, a New York City Administrator, indicated that critics in New York reacted to FTP productions based upon the editorial policy of the papers for which they were writing. The conservative Hearst papers were categorically against most of FTP's new plays. Hearst reviewers in New York were Gilbert Gabriel of the New York American and Robert Coleman for the Daily Mirror. The New York Evening Journal, the Sunday American, and the American Weekly were also generally negative in their reviews. Barber refers to Percy Hammond of the New York Herald Tribune as "controlled" by the Tribune and Richard Lockeridge as somehow escaping the editorial influence of the Sun, which was always "belaboring or beating our brains out." The other "mainstream" critics, particularly Brooks Atkinson of the New York Times, were favorable to FTP. Also complimentary were John Mason Brown, New York Post, Burns Mantle of the Daily News, and sometimes John Anderson of the New York Evening Journal. According to Barber, five or six daily reviewers in New York and just a few periodicals had influence upon the way the work of the FTP was viewed. He placed the Nation, the New Republic, and Theatre Arts Monthly in this category.[30]

Reviewers of regional productions were generally not very searching or revelatory regarding play content or form, but generally, the Hearst press exercised the same type of influence nationally that it did in New York.[31] Rosamond Gilder, head of FTP Research and Publication, concurred with Barber that, with the exception of the Herald Tribune, the newspaper and journal critics were generally sympathetic.[32]

During the period of the Popular Front, the Daily Worker began, in the fall of 1935, to change its function and image as the newspaper representing the American Communist Party as its official organ, to become a popular "mainstream" leftist newspaper reflecting varied subjects including culture and sports instead of only politics. The Popular Front comprised socialists, liberals, "fellow travelers," and non-communist sympathizers regardless of "class character," joined in a common struggle against war and fascism. Previously the Daily Worker focused mainly on social and political issues related to strikes, labor disputes, and the continuing "class struggle." With its new emphasis on art, culture, and entertainment, the Worker wanted to attract a wider readership and take advantage of Popular Front sympathy for the Communist Party's role in fighting the forces of "reaction." In 1935 the Worker began publishing a weekly edition (the Sunday Worker), and in 1938 its circulation reached 30,598. American Communist Party national membership reached 55,000 in 1938. Forty-seven percent of its 1938 membership was in New York City. These figures, added to the growing membership of the Young Communist League and the various socialist parties, gave New York a large base of a Marxist-oriented potential audience for FTP's new plays, particularly those dealing with "relevant social themes." The Daily Worker was the Party paper published in New York and sold in other American cities. Other leftist journals influencing "progressive" opinion regarding theatrical performances were the New Masses, Nation, and New Republic. New Theatre was a leftist journal reporting about theatre and politics. These periodicals, although not following the Party Line, generally adhered to a Marxist interpretation of history, culture, and society.[33]

Radical journals and newspapers did not exert much influence in the regions. This is perhaps reflected by the fact that while the FTP Research Center has numerous reviews of New York productions appearing in leftist periodicals including the Daily Worker, very few are available for regional productions.

The Communist Party press was not always pleased with the FTP's social plays because they were "reformist" and did not adhere to the doctrinaire formula of the "conversion ending" requiring that workers come to a radical, revolutionary consciousness. In general, the Marxist press gave the Federal Theatre support because the period of the Federal

Theatre was the era of the Popular Front. Despite the fact that the Party could not give FTP its full endorsement because of the reformist character of most of the New York productions, it at least recognized that FTP was attempting to fulfill social needs; thus, frequently it was concilliatory when indicating the ideological, "politically unreliable" drawbacks of several of the FTP plays.[34] The support given the Project by the Daily Worker, New Masses, New Theatre, and other leftist journals and newspapers was used as a weapon against Federal Theatre, as purportedly indicating its radical bias.

As a Federal agency, the FTP was forbidden to exclude from its ranks any workers on the basis of his or her political affiliation. Therefore, Flanagan admitted that there probably were Communists working in the New York Project, as there were Democrats, Socialists, and Republicans.

Some New York commercial producers, including Eva Le Gallienne, Brock Pemberton, and John Golden, were afraid that the FTP's emphasis on providing jobs for the unemployed would reduce the quality of theatre work to a low amateur level.[35] Amateurism was a charge frequently leveled at the work of the Project by the Hearst press and the trade papers such as Variety. The covert fear was the fear of competition with the commercial theatre. This fear was not general among Broadway producers. Lee Shubert saw the FTP as a force that would create audiences and produce plays that would fill dark theaters. For this reason, the League of New York Theatres signed an agreement with FTP allowing it to operate within a restricted area around the Broadway theatre district.

For all the claims made by staunch FTP supporters who have said that the FTP launched writing careers for many during a "golden age" of opportunity destroyed by fascist forces, the list of names of those who went on to become professionally known is not very long. Fascist or Communist conspiracy theories of the Federal Theatre's downfall may provoke controversy but hardly tell the whole truth about this dynamic enterprise. The truth is that the FTP is important in American cultural history because it was an extraordinary effort to organize the arts within the context of a gigantic, complex network of government services which are still a part of American life. Federal Theatre is unique because structurally there is nothing with which to compare it in American theatre history.

Generally considered now by theatre historians mainly as a noble but pathetic failure, the FTP's demise was inevitable. The tragic flaw of the protagonist in this drama, Hallie Flanagan, was that she dreamed too big, too much, and too hard. When considering the accomplishments of Federal Theatre as a whole, not just the new plays it produced, the tragedy and greatest danger for America was that it created a false hope, and a haunting vision of what could be when a government commits its resources to nourishing the human spirit.

The Federal Theatre Project existed during the "fervent years" of the Great Depression, and as that economic catastrophe resolved, a new drama was already shaping to take its place. National energies and resources were preparing to perform on the world stage of World War II, and as the workers entered the factories to lend their force to the war effort, somehow the FTP affair became a mini-drama in all of its comedy of errors, factional disputes, self-delusion, and little power-games being fought by careerists at cross-purposes. The "Red Decade" ended just as the FTP was ending--one-and-a-half years before the bombing of Pearl Harbor.

That is probably why, now that the FTP has just celebrated its fiftieth anniversary in 1985, a backward glance into the 1930s does seem "like a bittersweet indulgence in discovering that life is ironic."[36]

24

## Notes

1John Cambridge, Daily Worker, undated. Billy Rose Collection, Performing Arts Research Center, The New York Public Library. Further references to material in this collection will be noted as "Billy Rose Collection."

2Federal One, A Newsletter of the Institute on the Federal Theatre Project and New Deal Culture (December 1985), IO-2: 5. George Mason University.

3Carlos Fuentes quoted by Eric Bentley, "Writing for a Political Theatre," Performing Arts Journal 26/27: 48.

4Bentley, "Writing for a Political Theatre," p. 48.

5Dixon Wecter, The Age of the Great Depression, cited in Gerald Rabkin, Drama and Commitment (Bloomington: Indiana University Press,1964), pp. 97-98.

6Flanagan, Arena, p. 16.

7Hallie Flanagan addressing Federal Theatre Regional Directors, 8 October 1935, in Flanagan, Arena, pp. 45-46.

8Instructions for Federal Theatre Programs of Works Progress Administration, 10 October 1935, p. 5. George Mason University.

9Hallie Flanagan, "Federal Theatre Tomorrow," Federal Theatre Magazine (May 1936): 6.

10Rabkin, p. 105.

11Hallie Flanagan, "Federal Theatre Instructions," October 1935, pp. 5-6. George Mason University. Appendix A will list FTP organizational structure, listing regional divisions, major units of the Project, and managerial personnel for each year of Federal Theatre's existence (1935-1939).

[12]Flanagan, Arena, p. 60.

[13]Ibid., p. 23.

[14]Ibid.

[15]Ibid., p. 371.

[16]Ibid., p. 373.

[17]With the exception of Burgess Meredith, who headed the Advisory Committee in 1937, the membership in both organizations changed during FTP's existence. Lists compiled from undated lists in Billy Rose Collection. Cited in Malcolm Goldstein, The Political Stage (New York: Oxford University Press), p. 249; see also Flanagan, Arena, pp.284-285.

[18]Flanagan, Arena, pp. 183-184.

[19]Emmet Lavery to Converse Tyler, a Memorandum about FTP productions, 17 August 1938. George Mason University.

[20]Walter Pell, "Which Way the Federal Theatre," New Theatre, April 1937, cited in Rabkin, p. 104.

[21]Rabkin, p. 104.

[22]Flanagan, Arena, pp. 432-435.

[23]Flanagan, Federal Theatre Magazine, n.d., n.p., cited in Goldstein, p. 251.

[24]Ibid.

[25]Morgan Himmelstein, Drama Was a Weapon (New Brunswick: Rutgers University Press, 1963), p. 86.

[26]Ibid., pp. 86-87.

27Ibid., p. 87.

28Ibid.

29Rabkin, p. 101.

30Interview with Philip Barber conducted by members of the George Mason University Federal Theatre Collection staff, 11 November 1978. Tape at George Mason University.

31A complete list of the Hearst Corporation papers published in the various regions is as follows: Atlanta Georgian, Albany Times Union, Baltimore American, Baltimore News, Baltimore Post, Boston American, Boston Daily Advertiser, Boston Herald, Boston Record, Chicago American, Chicago Herald, Detroit Times, Fort Worth Record, Los Angeles Express, Los Angeles Herald, Milwaukee Sentinel, Omaha Bee, Omaha News, Oakland Post, Oakland Enquirer, Pittsburg: Sun, Chronicle-Telegraph, Post, Gazette-Times; Rochester Journal, Syracuse Telegraph, San Antonio Light, San Francisco Bulletin, San Francisco Call, San Francisco Examiner, Seattle Post-Intelligencer, Syracuse Journal, Syracuse Telegram, Washington News, Washington Times, Wisconsin News, Washington Herald. King Features division of the Hearst Corporation was the syndication service.

32Interview with Rosamond Gilder conducted by John O'Connor, 16 March 1975. Tape at George Mason University.

33Joseph R. Conlin, The American Radical Press (1888-1960), Vol. I (Westport, CT: Greenwood Press, 1974), pp. 227-228); Nathan Glazer, The Social Basis of American Communism (New York: Harcourt Brace and World, 1961), pp. 92-93.

34Himmelstein, p. 89.

35Flanagan, Arena, p. 40. Actors only had to prove membership in Actors Equity and former professional employment.

36Famous American Plays of the 1970s, The Laurel Drama Series, with an Introduction by Theodore Hoffman (New York: Dell, 1981), p. 10.

# PART I

## NEW YORK CITY UNITS

Popular Price, Manager's Try-Out, Experimental
Specialized Theatres, and Independent Productions


Thus the New York City Project became the best
and the worst of Federal Theatre. It presented
the widest range of productions, tastes, attitudes,
races, religions and political faiths. It was
everything in excess. In short it reflected its
people.

Hallie Flanagan

# CHAPTER I

## THE NATIONAL SERVICE BUREAU

In 1935, to facilitate its aims as a forum for new plays, the FTP created the National Service Bureau, originally called the Bureau of Research and Publication and later the National Play Bureau. Various regional bureaus were also established. Despite some changes, the basic policies of the National Service Bureau remained essentially the same throughout its existence:

> To recommend and test plays for the use of the Federal Theatre Project, inaugurate rental agreements for the use of plays and radio broadcasts, arrange for loan of actor and directional personnel, provide advice and suggestions on various technical matters, and clear music; edit, and publish bulletins, play scripts, etc. which are intended for national distribution, initiate research into important theatrical problems and to make the findings available to our Federal Theatre organizations and to community groups, schools, etc., throughout the country.[1]

The Reference Department of the National Service Bureau had as its specific purposes:

> a. To record and collate data pertaining to Federal Theatre presentations throughout the United States and to make sure material is available to other divisions of Federal Theatre. Also to maintain a library of general dramatic material for the use of Federal Theatre units.
> b. Within the limitations of our budget and personnel, to prepare and disseminate recommended dramatic material essential to community groups.[2]

To implement the aims of the Reference Department, the National Service Bureau compiled a large number of lists and bibliographies related to theatrical history and productions, including about 25 playlists ranging from "Jewish Plays," "Catholic Plays," "Labor Plays, "Anti-War Plays," to "American Folk Plays" and "Rural Plays." The lists included such essential production information as a brief synopsis, the number of roles in the play, set and technical requirements, and the particular audience for which the play was intended. The lists also included information on length of run, box-office re-receipts, and statistics about audience attendance. In addition, lists contained historical information about early productions in various cities. A researcher named Catherine Henry, using 15,000 playbills in the New York Public Library's Theatre Collection, created a separate list of New York City productions, including their literary sources.[3]

There were also bibliographies about motion pictures, puppetry, theatre techniques (design, lighting, costumes, and make-up), as well as a number which provided material to be used in the creation of documentary plays. These bibliographies concerned such topics as medicine, housing, American Indians, and a "famous lives" series of books for children, as well as folklore material from Appalachia, Oklahoma, and Iowa. Numerous lists of legends intended for dramatization were compiled.

There were reports about theatre in various parts of the world, including Java, Poland, Russia, Ireland, Germany, Spain, China, and Japan. Reports also listed material about early American theatre, ethnic theatre in America, and "American Social Drama." There were historical accounts of theatre in Chicago and Seattle, as well as profiles of individual theatres such as the Ritz and Adelphi in New York City, the Copley in Boston and the Goodman in Chicago. Also included in these reports was historical data about American opera, circus, caravan theatre, CCC camp entertainment, vaudeville, comic monologues, minstrel sketches, and variety skits. The intention of such research efforts was to stimulate and revitalize popular entertainments as well as to encourage FTP units throughout America to understand and to produce foreign theatre.[4]

A great deal of research was conducted on potential subjects for future plays, such as the lives of historical figures, important women, and noted black Americans such as Booker T. Washington. Other subjects thought worthy of future dramatization were topical novels and such historically, politically, socially, and economically varied subjects as the American city, the Boulder Dam, and the lumber and cotton industries. Notable examples of work begun on these topics were Norman Rosten's Iron Land, which focused on the steel industry and the immigrants working in it, and Frank Silvera's Liberty Deferred, about black history. Unfortunately, due to the FTP's early demise, neither was ever produced.

Before becoming an arm of the National Service Bureau, the Playreading Bureau went through various incarnations. Initially a part of the Bureau of Research and Publication, it became an autonomous unit in May 1936 under Francis Bosworth; next, during the early part of 1937, it was re-formed as the Play Policy Board. In July 1937 the Play Bureau and the Play Policy Board merged due to budget cuts and thus became the National Service Bureau. In the new organization, Emmet Lavery became director, Converse Tyler headed the play-reading staff, Ben Russak supervised playwriting, and Benson Inge coordinated play translations.

When the Playreading Bureau was established in 1936, headed by Converse Tyler and Ben Russak, its purpose was to read and provide written reports on the scripts sent to FTP and perhaps eventually acquired by the Project. Many of the readers were new or unproduced writers earning a bare livelihood while working on their scripts. Readers were required to read a script a day, working five days a week, and to submit weekly reports. These reports generally contained a detailed synopsis, one or two paragraphs of comments, and a place for the reader's overall reactions, indicated with one of four symbols:  R=recommended, R/R=recommended with reservations, Rej.=rejected, and Rej./R=rejected with reservations.

Three readers studied each script. If the script was rejected by all three, it was either returned to the author or, in some cases, held for future consideration. A script recommended by at least one reader would be considered further. If there were conflicting opinions or if the material was too "controversial," it was read by Playreading Department Supervisors Converse Tyler or Ben Russak, who made the final decision. Readers often discovered scripts on their own, suggesting classics or successful modern plays as possibilities for revivals. Friends of readers freely offered plays which would have been rejected in the commercial theatre because of the young playwright's lack of a "name" or because the material was considered too "experimental" or too "politically controversial."

In studying the reports, one eventually begins to recognize the names of the readers, their biases and idiosyncracies. Because the reports were so subjective and uninhibited, reading them offers an endless source of amazement and amusement. It also provides a glimpse into the "behind the scenes" world of FTP, where individuals known as readers (in fact, "unemployed" writers) passed judgment on other writers' work, revealing through their candor, naivete, and subjectivity much about the dramaturgy, social issues, politics, and the mores of the time. Frequently the reactions were not without malice. In their zeal, some readers rhapsodized for pages about a play rather than following instructions that a synopsis be written on a single page. Sometimes nothing more than "dump it" or "trash" would be written in the space for recommendations.

The list of readers employed by the Playreading Bureau includes several names that have become known in the theatre, including Norman Rosten, Arthur Miller, and John Silvera. The names of all three of these readers were on a list of "playwrights of ninety best new plays" compiled by Bosworth and Tyler in 1938.

An early director of the Play Bureau, Katharine Clugston, developed a set of guidelines for her unit to follow. Her objectives included the record-keeping of all plays and other performance material produced by the various WPA units and the negotiating, contracting, and registering of all scripts when copyrighted. The Play Bureau would also conduct a search for, and recommend, not only plays, sketches, and musicals already published but also unpublished material such as legends and stories which would then be filed for future reference. Clugston urged her Bureau to give experimental productions to plays written by Bureau members and others, with minimal production costs and utilizing actors loaned from the various projects. These experimental productions would be given in conjunction with various FTP groups for the purpose of testing a play's suitability for particular Federal Theatre units. In addition to play production, the Play Bureau would conduct research into the literature and history of the performing arts with a special concentration on those with American origins. A special emphasis would be placed upon fostering the writing of plays, sketches, and pageants for use by Federal Theatre organizations. This writing would be done as work of the Play Bureau, or as the leisure-time activity of Bureau workers and others not a part of Clugston's unit.[5]

In addition to the activities already discussed, the Play Bureau included in its objectives the reading, recommending, and translating of foreign plays and of American musical comedies, vaudeville, and similar material.[6] Alfred Kuttner, supervisor of the Translation Department, listed several translations his group was working on in September 1936, including four modern Greek plays and several Russian and Rumanian scripts. Additionally, Kuttner's staff translated Lope de Vega's "Peribanez" or "The Commander of Ocana," some Commedia dell 'Arte scripts, and several other early Spanish and French plays. Kuttner indicated his intention to translate outstanding foreign plays after contracting European publishers, agents, lawyers, and booksellers handling foreign plays in the United States. The Translation Department would make a special effort to familiarize itself with good foreign scripts that could be considered for FTP production.[7]

The philosophic stance that the FTP assumed regarding play selection was delineated by Katharine Clugston, who, while director of the Play Bureau in September 1936, described the type of play the Play Bureau was seeking. Clugston stressed that promising playwrights with something to say but lacking in technical facility would be nurtured to master their craft and encouraged to write honest plays, "alive to the problems of today's world." These writers would be inspired to "build a new school of playwriting for tomorrow that will have vigor and vision." For these playwrights "there would be no taboos on subject, form, or theme." The only restrictions to be placed upon the FTP writers would be those prohibiting "bad taste." Opportunities for free expression would be open: "We believe in an experiment of ideas, forms and technical expression." The FTP would "work through accepted tastes of the community, rather than attempt to foist our opinions of plays upon them." Further elaborating on the type of play the FTP would seek, Clugston stressed:

> Our greatest hope is to get plays which represent a wide variety of subject matter, seen with a fresh point of view and told in a new and exciting manner. We should like our plays to portray every class of society and probe every problem of contemporary life. The phrase "contemporary life" is not limited to "current happenings." History is rich in artistic invention and social philosophy, from which may be drawn sharp analogies and shrewd commentaries on "contemporary life" in the true and broad meaning of the phrase.

In addition to plays about contemporary life, the Play Bureau would make a special effort to search for "educational dramas, light comedies, children's plays, new adaptations of classic dramas and plays in verse."[8]

Also in September 1936, a Playwriting Department was formed as a section of the Play Bureau. Harold Berman, named supervisor, outlined the goals of his department, which was established to provide opportunities for playwrights to write, individually or in groups, plays suitable for FTP production. The playwrights would be encouraged to do original creative work and to write new plays, in forms to be tested experimentally in the Play Bureau. Berman's group would examine "social material" and do original research on subjects suitable for production. Writers would also read novels and stories, evaluating them for possible adaptations. They could also "collaborate with other theatre groups and writers in New York and, as far as possible, throughout the country."[9]

In September 1936, Francis Bosworth, supervisor of the Play Bureau, developed a plan for a Playwright's Laboratory Theatre. However, the proposals were not implemented until 1938, when Halsted Welles incorporated them in his concept of "Test Productions."[10] The plan for the Playwright's Laboratory Theatre was to provide playwrights an opportunity to perfect their craft in a "laboratory" and to then showcase and market their plays. The "laboratory" would help FTP directors select intelligent scripts worth producing "in keeping with a sane experimental point of view." These "test productions" would give young promising playwrights an opportunity to work in, and study, every phase of theatrical production.[11]

The 1936 working plan devised by Bosworth, and later fully implemented by Halsted Welles, would give all playwrights hired by FTP in any capacity the right to constitute a "corporate voting body." This corporate body would select seven members to serve as a playreading board for a two-month period. It would also select a production manager who would serve for an indefinite tenure. The production manager and the playreading board would comprise the executive committee. After each two-month period, the playreading board would elect two of its own members to serve for an additional two months, while the voting body would elect five new members to replace those whose tenure had terminated. When four members of the playreading board voted affirmatively, a script would be deemed worthy of production. The author would then be placed in charge of producing the play, casting the "actors" selected from members of the Play Bureau, along with volunteers from other FTP projects. Actors not officially a part of the Project would sometimes be used. A staged reading would be presented before one or two invited audiences. Notes and criticism would be carefully compiled and released to "the field" by the Play Bureau at the discretion of the author.[12]

In April 1938 Halsted Welles indicated a desire to form the "test production" unit, tentatively to be called a "work-out-theatre. "The unit would follow Bosworth's original plan, and its purpose would be to test, during three-week workshop periods, promising plays submitted by FTP producers. If the script continued to seem promising, the producer would then work with the author to prepare it for a complete production. The same would hold true for scripts already held by the National Service Bureau and considered ready for production.[13]

Commenting further on the work of the Test Productions unit as a kind of precursor to what would be referred to today as a staged reading, director Halsted Welles recalled that he called it the "Test Theatre" because he wanted a modest name, not something that would sound pretentious or grandiose. Norman Rosten was one of the early participants who, along with 20 other writers, worked on plays in a workshop setting by presenting "works in progress." Sometimes only scenes were performed, and at other times the members of the workshop just read plays to each other to test dialogue.[14]

Emmet Lavery praised the unique contribution that Welles made to the work done by the Test Theatre and stated that some of the best direction ever done by FTP was in these workshop presentations. He remembered the intense theatrical excitement created by Welles directing new scripts: "On the dim stage of the Maxine Elliott one afternoon, with very few lights, no props and no costumes, he [Welles] evoked a singular beauty of feeling in Everywhere I Roam which was never recaptured later in Marc Connelly's more elaborate production [on Broadway]." Lavery recalled the sensitive way Welles retrained actors and his special talent for directing poetic drama. This was particularly evident when Welles presented in workshop a "breathtaking" production of Spender's Trial of a Judge: "The unity, dignity, and terror of the performance were magnificent. It was not a play which the Project was in a position to present for public performance, but it was one of the best productions I have ever seen in Federal Theatre."[15]

Lavery asserted that the real value of the Test Theatre was not so much in the quantity of the plays tested for the purpose of showcasing new work for regional directors but in the pride and feeling of unity which the workshop inspired throughout the Project. Regional directors were not always excited about every new play that the National Service Bureau recommended, but once the test unit was established, "the field had a different feeling about the Bureau. It was no longer an ivory tower at the corner of Broadway and 53rd Streets, dreaming great dreams high above the clouds. It was a hard-headed realist as much at home in production as it was in research."[16]

Recalling some of the writing done in the workshop, Lavery remembered in particular Norman Rosten's scripting of Iron Land and Arnold Sundgaard's Everywhere I Roam.[17]  Other noteworthy productions were Morning in America, a play about General Lee by Willard Wiener, and A. Simkovitch's Garment Center.[18] During January 1937, the Test Theatre rehearsed Trial of a Judge, to prepare it for three demonstration performances at the Ritz Theatre February 22 through 24. Three one-acts were also prepared for performances to be given at the Maxine Elliott the week of March 13th.[19]

When the demise of Federal Theatre occurred, many Play Bureau projects were in the developmental stage: Norman Rosten's Iron Land, Arthur Miller's Conquistador; Hughes Allison's Panyared, a trilogy tracing slavery from its origins in Africa; Frank Silvera and Abram Hill's Booker T. Washington; Arthur Vogel's Army Without Banners, an adaptation of the novel The Dark Fleece by Joseph Hergesheimer; and Edward Riley's adaptation of Father McGlyn, a dramatization "of the man who championed Henry George against his own archbishop and who was finally vindicated by the church." Also being developed were Clown's Progress, a Living Newspaper musical treatment depicting the history of vaudeville, Anthracite Ballet by William Dorsey Blake, and "Cavalcades" of Pennsylvania and New Jersey.[20]

Ben Russak, the first director of the Playwriting Department, recalled in 1976 how writers Arthur Miller and Norman Rosten worked on projects. About Miller and his work on Conquistador, a script suggested by the Southwest region, Russak stated that at the beginning, Miller did not want to write for the Playwriting Department because he was "far-sighted" in knowing that any play he wrote would not be his but owned by the government and in public domain, "So he decided to read plays and bring in a report every day. . . . He very quickly realized that he could use-- he could use it to earn enough to live on. I think it was $22.50 a week."[21] Despite Miller's hesitancy to write scripts for Federal Theatre, one of his plays, They Too Arise, was produced by FTP in Detroit for one performance, October 23, 1937.

Russak recalled that there was a great deal of excitement generated when writers gathered to criticize each other's work. These sessions inspired writers to revise and re-write their plays. The group was intimate because the Playwriting Department attempted to limit its membership to 25 writers. Sometimes when a writer complained about an assignment he was given, he would be given another assignment or transferred to the Playreading Department. The Playwriting members were privileged in that they were given an opportunity to write about things which interested them, and not forced to work on an alien subject. Russak recalled Norman Rosten's disinterest in Iron Land because he felt that he could not shape it into a play. However, as was the case with other writers, Rosten had an opportunity to work and not be fired. Like other playwrights, he would just be transferred to another project.[22]

Remembering his days as a writer in the Playwriting Department, Norman Rosten said that Ben Russak made sure that work was submitted and developed into a workable form. Rosten stated that, once writers agreed to write about a particular topic, they were not forced to write in a pre-determined manner. Writers researched topics, developed their work plans and managed to "look busy." Discussing the difficulties experienced by writers when they are obliged to write in a prescribed fashion, Rosten reflected:

> Now it's tough writing according to subject unless you are impassioned. . . . I don't think the public would have liked it if you just paid writers $23 a week and said, "Just dream up a play." You know, you would have probably got some good writing or maybe--and you know that would take weeks or months of doing nothing, and it would have been tricky.[23]

Reflecting on the topics and themes writers dealt with in the Playwriting unit, Rosten stated that they were generally "historical" rather than "sociological." "History is the best and safest place to go," according to Rosten, who considered himself a budding poet while working on Iron

Land. He attempted to give the script a poetic quality, but was never pleased with the results. According to Rosten, the lack of time was the reason. He reiterated a familiar lament that this was one of the many scripts never completed due to the FTP's brief existence.[24]

Nostalgically recounting his times with Federal Theatre and the camaraderie shared by the young writers, Rosten recalled,

> We all would wait around outside the building to wait for Arthur Miller to roll in from Patchogue where he lived on Long Island-- he was out there somewhere writing. He'd be rolling in in an old beat-up car just to make it on time to sign in. And I remember we all used to wait and cheer, "Here comes Miller and on time." . . . Of course nobody was known then at all.[25]

According to Rosten, the atmosphere in his unit was special and emotionally charged. It reflected the times: "So it was different. Then it was full of--everything was idealism, a kind of purity of political thinking and feeling. Well, they were starting something new, and when you start something new, you know it's got all that fervor. And that crept into the passion of the theatre."[26]

By the end of 1936, the Play Bureau published its first major summary of the activities of the Playreading Department. During the period from January to December 1936, the Bureau had contacted thousands of authors and their representatives and eventually procurred 7,000 plays, for the most part by unknown authors. These plays were analyzed, synopsized, and catalogued. A selective list of 90 new plays was published. Four plays from that list had been selected and produced; eight were negotiated for production. All of the recommended plays were cross-indexed to enable directors to locate plays that would suit their particular interests and needs. Augmenting the "90 New Plays" list, was a supplemental list of original one-acts and commercially produced plays suitable for revivals.[27]

Another report of the activities of the Playreading Department was published for the period October 1937 through April 1938. The list of new plays had risen to 115, and the work completed by the department during that 18-month period was summarized:

1. 4,000 plays read and analyzed as follows:
   2,386 New Scripts, submitted for routine reading
   378 Plays submitted to Dramatist Guild Contest after
   October 1, 1937
   250 Irish Plays surveyed for Irish List
   1,000 (approx.) Published Plays and Old Scripts surveyed for
   Negro List, Labor List, American Frontier & Historical
   List.[28]

To test the playwriting abilities of applicants to the Play-writing Department, Ben Russak, supervisor, devised various tests in dramaturgy which were put into use during June 1938.[29] Twenty-three writers applied, including Theodore Brown, Abram Hill, and Frank Silvera. They were to select from six "themes," or briefly stated plots and storylines, one which was to be developed into a play format, hopefully revealing skill in structuring material, developing characters, and writing dialogue.

The FTP also sponsored play contests to discover writing talent. In the fall of 1937, in conjunction with the Dramatists' Guild, which offered a cash prize of $250, the FTP sponsored the American Play Contest, guaranteeing a professional production in New York City for a run of at least two weeks. The judges were Richard Lockridge, drama critic of the New York Sun; Lloyd Lewis, drama critic of the Chicago Daily News; and W.E. Oliver, drama critic of the Los Angeles Herald Express. George

Savage, an English instructor at the University of Washington, was the winner for his play See How They Run. After the New York presentation of the play, the FTP produced it in San Francisco and Seattle.[30] (See Chapter X for a discussion of this play.)

The Federal Theatre also sponsored a playwriting contest during 1938 in the 2,000 Civilian Conservation Corps camps throughout the United States. These camps housed youths who were employed by the government to work on various WPA construction projects. The three winners, chosen from 400 entries, were awarded New York City productions by the Federal Theatre, and spent 30 days in the city under the tutelage of an important playwright. The winners were P. Washington Porter, whose Return to Death dealt with the conditions of the Negro in the South, and Bernard and Gill Winstock, whose CCC treated life in the Civilian Conservation Corps.[31] Further information is not available concerning the production of these plays.

Emmet Lavery indicated that not all of the new plays produced by the FTP were of equal quality. He further stated that of the 1,200 productions given by FTP, approximately 240 were of new plays. Of the number of new plays, 10 percent were considered exceptional and 10 percent were of inferior quality. The remaining 80 percent were only average. However, according to Lavery, the figure of 240 plays is significant: "It represents the greatest diversity of new thought and action that has ever poured into the theatre by any single organization at any given period in the history of the theatre."[32]

Lavery emphasized that the FTP gave many of the new plays productions more significant than the plays themselves and that the productions would probably be remembered longer than the writing of some of the plays. With the possible exception of the writers working on the Living Newspapers, Federal Theatre never launched playwrights who were undeniably products of the FTP. Lavery cited two reasons for this: Federal Theatre had to employ writers who were on relief roles because they could not get writing jobs. Occasionally a writer not on relief could be employed but only in an "executive" position, since the Project could hire 10 percent of its workers as "non-relief administrative personnel." The other problem was that when an FTP employee wrote plays, his work became the property of the government and was considered in the public domain. Unless the work was later revised in a significant manner, it remained in that category. The writer working for the government could not claim a copyright or an equity in his script other than the wages he was paid for writing it. Therefore, writers usually preferred to do anything but write plays for the WPA.[33]

Lavery stressed that, since the government owned the rights to the plays written on Project time and writers were not interested in working for the government, the FTP had to contract for new plays and revivals from other sources as any commercial producer would do. The sliding royalty scale (usually $50 the first week, $75 the second, $100 the third and subsequent weeks), while not overly enticing, was generous enough to gain the Federal Theatre access to most of the plays in which it was interested. Although the FTP worked on a plan to grant copyright to playwrights writing plays for the government, it was never implemented. Because writers were not motivated to create plays for the FTP, a feeling of cohesiveness and unity never developed among writers and the various units. With the exception of the Living Newspaper, writers were not hired to write for particular producing organizations. The Living Newspaper writers were excited about their work because the form challenged them and because they were committed to the ideas the Newspapers expressed. For this reason, Lavery stated, "It was only in the Living Newspapers that project production was blended with project writing to such a degree that the result was something inevitably and exclusively Federal Theatre."[34]

It should be indicated that the FTP was basically an actors' project; therefore, writing was not a top priority, nor were the needs of writers. The FTP, however, had numerous producing advantages not afforded the commercial producer. New plays, for example, could be tried in one region and then produced in others, having been improved upon and altered according to regional needs. A major disadvantage was that quantity was more important than quality, and since taxpayers expected a steady stream of openings, there was little time for experimentation. Thus, revivals were often preferred over new plays. All plays were selected by regional play bureaus and then cleared through the National Service Bureau.[35] Despite the preference regional directors had for the tried and tested, some experimentation was attempted when feasible. Lavery indicated, however, that regional directors were not always interested in experimentation or anything new. These regional directors were usually very conventional and old-fashioned, having spent most of their time doing stock productions. Lavery pondered: "We used to wonder on the Project, what would have happened, if there had been a work rule from the beginning that said, 'You have to do all new plays, or at least 80 percent of the productions have to be new plays.' It would have been an interesting concept. It would have been a different theatre."[36]

Converse Tyler stated that the final decision about play selection rested with regional directors and that they often had their own favorite playwrights, whom they would promote for "political" reasons. Tyler, who headed the Playreading Department, stressed that because writers were not interested in writing plays for the government, the Play Bureau obtained scripts by non-project authors, who submitted scripts personally or through agents whose opinions were respected by the Bureau.[37] Tyler indicated that there was wide diversity in the backgrounds and ages of the Bureau's readers and that some were more qualified than others.[38] Since many of the readers were themselves aspiring playwrights, Tyler said, their comments frequently treated material in a subjective manner.[39]

Irwin Rhodes, Counsel for FTP, observed that the difficulty in getting good plays for Project producers was a constant problem. Important playwrights were not giving FTP the rights to do their plays unless the plays were so old that stock companies had already been doing them for years. The main problem according to Rhodes was that well-known playwrights were reluctant to give FTP their plays for $50 a week.[40]

Rhodes recalled that FTP successfully negotiated with Sinclair Lewis to have him adapt his It Can't Happen Here to be done in 21 cities at one time, guaranteeing Lewis $1,000 in royalties. At the time, the idea struck him and Hallie Flanagan that perhaps other well-known playwrights such as Eugene O'Neill and George Bernard Shaw could be persuaded to offer production rights to their plays if FTP could assure them that some 20 productions would be running at one time. But Flanagan dropped the idea of another It Can't Happen Here experiment because the 21 productions of that play created enormously exhausting, tangled administrative problems. In fact, Shaw and O'Neill agreed to offer FTP the rights to produce their plays according to this plan, and other playwrights such as

Sherwood Anderson and Elmer Rice were approached. When they agreed, Rhodes indicated that it became very easy to get other playwrights to do the same.[41]

The National Service Bureau, embracing the Play Bureau, was set up to service a gigantic organization that seemed built to last for what was hoped to be an endless period of time. That was not the case, and the problems plaguing the Play Bureau in finding, nurturing, and utilizing talented or successful writers to produce highly significant plays for FTP, prevented one of Federal Theatre's dreams from fully materializing.

48

## Notes

[1]Memorandum from Emmet Lavery to all supervisors of the National Service Bureau, "Redefinition of Policies--Procedures," 10 January 1939, n.p., at George Mason University.

[2]"Resume of Policies and Objectives of the National Service Bureau," n.d., n.p. Manuscript at George Mason University.

[3]Mary Henderson, "Federal Theatre Project Records," Performing Arts Resources (Theatre Library Association, 1980), Vol. VI, p. 24.

[4]Ibid., p. 25.

[5]Katharine Clugston, "Reorganization of the Play Bureau," September 1936, p. 2. Manuscript at George Mason University.

[6]"Resume of Policies and Objectives," n.p.

[7]Alfred B. Kuttner, "Translation Department," in Clugston, p. 11.

[8]Clugston, pp. 4-5.

[9]Harold Berman, "The Playwriting Department," in Clugston, n.p.

[10]Halsted Welles, Memorandum to Reference Department, 5 April 1936, at George Mason University.

[11]Francis Bosworth, "Playwrights Laboratory Theatre," in Clugston, pp. 22-23.

[12]Ibid.

[13]Welles, Memorandum.

[14]Interview with Halsted Welles conducted by John O'Connor, 17 November 1975. Tape at George Mason University.

[15]Emmet Lavery, "The Flexible Stage," p. 60. Unpublished manuscript at George Mason University.

[16]Ibid.

[17]Ibid., p. 9.

[18]Ibid., p. 63.

[19]Halsted Welles, Memorandum to Joseph Moss, 15 February 1939, at George Mason University.

[20]Lavery, "The Flexible Stage," p. 67.

[21]Interview with Ben Russak conducted by Lorraine Brown, 19 February 1976. Tape at George Mason University.

[22]Ibid.

[23]Interview with Norman Rosten conducted by John O'Connor, 14 January 1977. Tape at George Mason University.

[24]Ibid.

[25]Ibid.

[26]Ibid.

[27]"A Review of the Productivity and Services of the Play Bureau from January 1936-December 1936," Play Bureau publication number 9, n.d., p. 2. Manuscript at George Mason University.

[28]"A Report of the Activities of the Playreading Department for the period October 1, 1937-April 1, 1938," Memorandum signed by Converse Tyler, Supervisor, Playreading Department, n.d., p. 1. Manuscript at George Mason University.

[29]Test samples taken from "Dramaturgy Tests for Playwrights," at George Mason University.

[30]Press Release, National Service Bureau, n.d., at George Mason University.

[31]New York Telegraph, 27 March 1937.

[32]Lavery, "The Flexible Stage," p. 49.

[33]Ibid., p. 50.

[34]Ibid.

[35]Ibid., p. 56.

[36]Interview with Emmet Lavery conducted by John O'Connor and Mae Mallory Krulak, Encino, California, 5 January 1976. Tape at George Mason University.

[37]Interview with Converse Tyler conducted by John O'Connor, 15 December 1975. Tape at George Mason University.

[38]Ibid.

[39]Ibid.

[40]Interview with Irwin Rhodes conducted by Lorraine Brown, 26 February 1977. Tape at George Mason University.

[41]Ibid.

CHAPTER II


THE POPULAR PRICE THEATRE


The New York unit, called the Popular Price Theatre, was established in 1935. Once Elmer Rice, then the New York City Regional Director, created the general organizational and administrative structure for his unit, he and Hallie Flanagan concerned themselves with the rental of theatres. There were a number of unused theatres in New York. Flanagan urged managers to supply "dark" theatres for "try-outs" of new plays but was discouraged by union groups fearing that successful FTP productions would draw crowds away from commercial productions.[1] She then negotiated with the League of New York Theatres to permit the FTP to stage productions in theatres outside the Broadway area. According to this agreement, the FTP could not rent theatres in the area between Fortieth and Fifty-Second Streets, the East River and Hudson.[2] These negotiations proceeded as the FTP conducted other conferences with Actors' Equity regarding wages, and after weeks of conferencing, all parties in the negotiations reached a compromise. Equity actors would receive a WPA salary of $23.86 instead of the union's minimum of $40 per week. However, in return, Equity actors would only have to give six performances a week and rehearse only four hours a day. Equity was successful in getting a closed shop; FTP considered the compromise severely limiting to the preparation of new plays for opening night.[3]

Irwin Rhodes, Counsel for FTP, recalled rental negotiations with theatre owners as favorable to Federal Theatre. Rhodes claimed that because most Broadway theatres at the time were dark, he could make advantageous deals with owners, particularly the Shuberts, who were "the heart of the producing theatre and delighted about Federal Theatre. . . . [because] I think we did create audiences."[4]

As Hallie Flanagan had stated, the FTP would have to create audiences "not by competing with commercial theatre but by supplementing it--by specializing in plays of unknown dramatists, emphasizing regional and local material, experimenting with a rapid, simplified, vivid form of stage expression," new techniques, and ideas.[5] Above all Flanagan wanted to offer the American people a "free, adult and uncensored theatre."[6]

Ultimately, the FTP established five major producing units to do new plays in their own theatres: The Living Newspapers, sponsored by the New York Newspaper Guild and supervised by Morris Watson; the Popular Price Theatre, headed by Edward Goodman, created to present original plays by new authors; the Experimental Theatre, to do "experimental" plays both in form and content, under the direction of Virgil Geddes and James Light; the Negro Theatre, under John Houseman and Rose McLendon; and the Managers' Try-Out Theatre, sponsored by the League of New York Theatres, headed by Otto Metzger for the purpose of trying out plays for Broadway. These companies were established to charge $.25 and $.50 admission prices, hoping to reach a larger audience unable to pay for tickets to see plays done in commercial theatres.

The goal of the Popular Price Theatre was stated in all of the playbills for its productions:

> The aim of the Popular Price Theatre will be to present plays of
> intrinsic merit or potential importance, particularly the works of

American authors, which because of their character, experimental or otherwise, may contribute to the development of American dramatic art and would not ordinarily be produced by the regular commercial theatre. These plays will be presented at popular prices and later in a repertory in order to keep plays alive while the demand for them lasts.

The Popular Price Theatre, housed in the Manhattan Theatre, listed several accomplishments during the first six months of its existence. By the end of July 1936, an audience of 100,000 had attended the first four productions: American Holiday by Edwin and Albert Barker; T.S. Eliot's Murder in the Cathedral; Class of '29 by Orrie Lashing and Milo Hastings; and Paul Vilpius's Help Yourself. During the initial six-month period of the theatre's tenure, more than 100 actors were employed, and an additional 200 persons were employed in technical, clerical, administrative, and personnel categories. The productions were presented at the Manhattan Theatre until it was "restored to private enterprise on a long-term lease."[7]

Goodman stressed that the first three plays presented were by native Americans whose work would not have been produced in the commercial theatre. He also emphasized that although most of the new playwrights were generally unknown, their work was worthy of being seen by large audiences. As an example, Goodman indicated that the production of Murder in the Cathedral played to an audience of 48,000, and, according to Goodman, this proved that his theatre was developing an audience for new plays and creating a genuine demand for theatre at low-price admission.[8]

The first production, American Holiday, opened February 21, 1936, and ran until March 14.[9] The play relates how an average American town attains national notoriety during the sensational trial of a young man accused of murdering his unfaithful lover. The peacefulness of the town is transformed as scandal mongers, reporters, photographers, and publicists converge to exploit the scabrous affair. The carnival atmosphere eventually causes the victim's father to die of a heart attack in a hotel lobby telephone booth while guests blithely comment on the trial in process. A reporter in love with the victim's sister publishes the murdered woman's diary, and the townspeople urge a new trial in order to escalate the level of excitement. When the trial ends, the sleepy town returns to its ordinary way of life.[10]

FTP recommended American Holiday as a satire on American justice "with a vengeance."[11] The action of the play was compared to the Bruno Hauptman trial involving the Lindberg kidnapping.[12] American Holiday would not have been considered for a commercial production, mainly because of its enormous cast. A reviewer writing in Variety indicated attitudes shared by many in the commercial theatre regarding WPA productions. One would have to "accept them for what they are," which was a typically patronizing way of characterizing FTP productions as necessarily inferior or "amateur." Or if one did not accept them on their own terms, one would have to dare the show "to be any good."[13] Initial FTP efforts frequently met with this disdainful attitude.

Variety said that American Holiday would be "ready for a Broadway production" after the "excessive talkiness" and "weak orchestration of scenes" were eliminated--this despite the fact that the reviewer stated very appologetically that although the play was not perfect, it was "pretty good," with "some fine writing, some good acting, a splendid set, excellent staging, a lot of excitement and novelty."[14]

After American Holiday, the Popular Price presented T.S. Eliot's Murder in the Cathedral, which opened March 20, 1936, and ran through May 2, 1936. Halsted Welles directed the cast of 80. It was a great hit and one of the crowning achievements of the FTP. Eliot's poetic drama was originally presented in Canterbury Cathedral in June 1935 and later at the Mercury Theatre in London. A non-professional production of the play had been presented during the 1935 season at Yale University.

Murder in the Cathedral is a dramatization of the martyrdom of Thomas Becket, Archbishop of Canterbury in the twelfth century. It depicts the Archbishop's temptation by ambition and his obsession with the thought that in his martyrdom he could find his greater glory. The issue of Becket's assassination in 1170 is dealt with so that the event is seen not just as a piece of historical drama but as a searching study of the occurrence from various points of view. The conflict between Becket and Henry II of England stemming from King Henry's attempt to use his friend, Thomas Becket, to reduce the power of the church, is the pivotal point of the story upon which the play is based. Becket, not conceding to Henry's powerful influence, staunchly defends the church and, as a result, is forced to escape to France, where he remains for seven years. The play begins at the point when Becket returns to England in 1170.

The play opens with a chorus of women who, in expectation of Becket's arrival in England, express the desire that his return will not create disharmony. When he lands, Becket faces four tempters. He is first tempted with all of the worldly pleasures he has shared with King Henry. He is then tempted with the political power accorded him as a friend of the King. The third temptation offers Becket a new conspiratorial joining of forces with the barons against the King. The last temptation is the most threatening--Becket is tempted to seek glorification through martyrdom.

During the second act, Becket is confronted by four knights, who accuse him of not submitting to the King's authority. When several priests attempt to protect Becket from another confrontation with the knights, he refuses their offer and is murdered. After the murder, the knights face the audience and address it in the language of modern prose, strongly justifying their act. The play ends as the chorus and the priests laud and praise Becket's martyrdom.

The leftist press criticized <u>Murder in the Cathedral</u> as a play chosen under right-wing pressure, claiming that the Catholic play was selected to appease those who were critical of FTP's "radical" leanings. However, the production gave Federal Theatre an opportunity to demonstrate its creativity.[15] FTP had a big advantage since it did not have to produce commercial hits and could utilize large casts and rehearse shows for long periods. It was disadvantaged because 90 percent of the money allocated for its productions had to be used to pay salaries and only 10 percent of a show's budget could be spent on the physical production. FTP compensated for its budgetary shortcomings by being resourceful in staging shows. As revealed in <u>Murder in the Cathedral</u>, lights had to be used to create "abstract space" and "symbolic realism," rather than lavish sets which could only be used one time.[16] Using the Manhattan Theatre because of its "gothic-like" structure--"high arches framing a wide proscenium [creating] the impression that the play was taking place in a cathedral"--the designer for <u>Murder in the Cathedral</u> created an "abstract quality that widened the scope of the action and mood . . .[giving] the play a timelessness and universality."[17] With a cyclorama and minimal use of props, the designer was able to give the staging a plasticity that made the static drama come alive.[18]

The director had to be extremely resourceful in other ways. The verse form in Murder in the Cathedral was influenced by the medieval morality play Everyman. Church rituals and Greek tragedy influenced the play's dramatic construction. The verse form in particular challenged the director because he had to devise ways to creatively stage the production to keep it from becoming static and declamatory. The results were impressive. In his review, "Some of the Last Act Causes Which Have Turned T.S. Eliot's Undramatic Tragedy into a Hit," John Mason Brown described how Eliot's "problematic" poetic drama was eventually saved by Halsted Welles's expert direction. He characterized the poetry as wavering between "austere beauty" and "sudden spurts of doggerel and dramatic wastelands of obscurity." Although Brown complimented Eliot on writing sermons which could serve eloquently as ministerial models, he saw the author as not making "concessions to the theatre's needs." However, he described the striking contribution of the director in saving the script in the following manner:

> Abruptly and without warning [Eliot] turns into a dramatist, almost in spite of himself, in the hugely impressive final portion. . . . A static drama is here metamorphosed into an active one. The dark shadows of a Gothic cathedral are pierced by the brilliant illuminations of the stage. A script which has been relaxed and almost oppressively dull becomes taut, nervous, vibrant and exciting. . . . No production of recent memory stands more in the debt of its director and designer than does Murder in the Cathedral.[19]

Also praising the direction, Brooks Atkinson, writing in the <u>New York</u> <u>Times</u>, stated that the director avoided giving the choral chants an "audible monotony" by dividing the longer passages and giving individual actors specific lines so that the "variegated color of their voices heighten the frightened comments they make." Commenting further on the direction, Atkinson said:

> Mr. Welles has also released the tension of the text by violent groupings, and using the unobtrusive rhythm of choral masses. The murder of Thomas in the text is so barely chronicled that it might pass almost unnoticed. . . . But this bloody climax to a long and poignant martyr's meditation Mr. Welles has powerfully expressed by bringing in, on a strange incline, an impersonal line of lancers which slowly encircles Thomas like the shrouding wings of death, and, although the murder is not painful, it is terrifying--a cardinal sin, deliberately performed.[20]

By the time it reached its twentieth performance, crowds numbering 23,000 saw <u>Murder in the Cathedral</u>, and the run was extened for a third time until its final closing date, May 2. The production was then loaned to the Music Project for festival presentations.[21]

When the Living Newspapers's <u>Triple--A Plowed Under</u> and <u>Injunction Granted</u> were presented in 1936, some congressmen criticized their political bias as radical. <u>Murder in the Cathedral</u> was widely hailed as an artistic and commercial success, and also as a production which tended to diffuse somewhat the clamorous charges that the FTP was a seething hot-bed of radicalism. The fading of the outcry was only temporary because the Popular Price's next production, <u>Class of '29</u>, was almost withdrawn during rehearsals while stories in the press labeled it "red propaganda," fueling more the growing criticism of the FTP's alleged "radical slant." That play deals with unemployment among college-educated youth. It tells the story of a group of college students who, despite being graduates of good schools and fully prepared to meet the pre-depression world full of optimism, are crushed by a failure to find employment in their chosen professions. They are forced to resort to other pursuits to support themselves: Tippy launders dogs; Martin embraces communism; Ted, a rich man's son, sponges off his friends. Several other characters make different adjustments, complicating their lives even further. The climax occurs when Ted, distraught, humiliated, and frustrated in his attempt to get a relief job, jumps into the path of a subway train.[22]

Produced with moderate success and a run that lasted from May 15 to July 4, 1936, Class of '29 was the type of social drama that could be presented under WPA aegis. Since Federal Theatre did not have to worry about the box-office, it could risk presenting plays which were perhaps not expertly crafted dramas but thought-provoking as a forum for the discussion of contemporary social problems. The ironic title reflects how the optimism of the twenties turned to despair when the Depression began after the stock market crash in 1929. Class of '29 was typical of social dramas of the thirties in the way it faithfully recorded the struggles of a younger generation coming to terms with the catastrophic events of the decade after the Wall Street collapse. The story was told by reflecting in personal terms the ways lives of individuals changed as a result of economic calamity. Class of '29 also depicted the trend of youth in the thirties to seek social change, via the Marxist path.

Written by Orrie Lashin and Milo Hastings, the play was generally viewed as not being of great consequence, either in regard to its politics or its dramaturgy. It was significant more in the way it evoked the atmosphere of the Depression and as an authentic documentation of a particular crisis period. However, during rehearsals, reports circulated indicating that one of the characters was a communist and that there was a scene in which young people ran around a table waving the red flag. Based upon these reports, some congressmen and members of the conservative press viewed the play as revolutionary. As a result, changes were made in the script before the show opened.

Burns Mantle differed with other critics on the play's social and artistic significance. After praising the show as "interesting" and "intelligently produced," Mantle, in the New York Daily News, discounted the "red scare" stigma of the play in his story "The People's Theatre Grows Stronger." Commenting on how some members of Congress reacted to reports published during rehearsals that in the play communistic students paraded around a table carrying a red flag, he wrote that in the version finally presented:

> The parade around the table is still used, but it is not communistic and there is no flag. . . . As it turns out, it is no more communistic than any published "whither-are-we-drifting" editorial query. It presents sketchily the case histories of certain graduates of the depression who find themselves unemployed and unable to adjust themselves to the situation, must less understand it.[23]

Brooks Atkinson found the play and production mediocre, the acting "no more than competent," and the writing not flowing "naturally out of its theme." However, he stressed that despite artistic mediocrity, the social drama was topical and valid. Atkinson also emphasized in the New York Times:

> Not that these jobless college students are communists at heart, but that the bleak world into which they have been disgorged makes communism look to them like a way out. To a man who can make no impression on an apparently self-contained social system, who is "out" while millions are so comfortably "in," a state that provides every one with work looks attractive.

Regarding reports made about the play while it was in rehearsal, Atkinson wrote, "As usual, the spread eagle Congressmen have misunderstood a play they have not seen, but that is the prerogative of petty bureaucrats in an election year."[24]

Rebounding from the ideological attacks leveled at it by antagonistic critics for its production of Class of '29, the Popular Price next presented Help Yourself, a Viennese farce by Paul Vilpius, adapted by John J. Coleman. Presented first in Vienna, then in London, it was performed by the Hampton Players, Southampton, New York, in 1934 in the new Americanized Coleman adaptation. It opened at the Manhattan for a three-week run on July 4, 1936.

To counteract the critics and reviewers who labeled Federal Theatre a radical organization, FTP chose a script which broke two theatrical traditions of the thirties. It presented a play which treated the unemployment problem in a light comedic manner and opened it during a very hot week in July. FTP wanted to dispel the notion that it was only interested in doing serious, somber treatments of social problems. Also during this period, it occurred to observers and audiences of Federal Theatre that FTP was doing a fine job of offering good entertainment at low admission prices. Again, a play having notable weaknesses was welcomed by enthusiastic audiences who were laughing and being entertained despite the script's "frailties." They enjoyed being able to see a show for about the price of a movie admission. Critics who were not always supportive were giving grudging compliments to FTP's ability to attract popular audiences.

While poking fun at big business and spoofing the unemployment problem, the farce deals with the play's destitute and jobless hero, Christopher Stringer, and his strategy for getting a job. This involves getting a job in a bank, claiming for himself a "special" desk and then declaring himself an expert on the "Kubensky" matter, all the while continuing the hoax that he is a valued member of the organization. None of the bank officials know of the "Kubensky" matter, but they are too embarrassed to admit their ignorance and challenge the credibility of the super-confident young man. In the tradition of the Horatio Alger story, Stringer succeeds in fooling everyone, gains the bank president's daughter and is rewarded with a happy ending for his bizarre efforts.[25]

Richard Watts in the New York Herald Tribune emphasized the contribution of comedian Curt Bois, a German exile, in the leading role and suggested that the play's value derived from its being a vehicle for Bois's talent. Watts saw the play as a "sort of slapstick satire on the bluff and mental confusion of big business." He felt that the play provided enough material for a one-act play but not for a full-length entertainment because,

> It begins to wheeze and creak considerably, until the chief suspense to be found arises from wondering how the author, actors and director can spin it out to the required length. As a matter of fact, they fail to keep it going with any startling resourcefulness, but, despite its frailities, Help Yourself contains its share of laughter for those who are not too critical, and certainly it is a more interesting bit of theatrical trade-goods

than many farces that have found customers hereabouts at considerably higher scale of prices.[26]

Help Yourself was followed by The Sun and I, an historical play by Barrie and Leona Stavis which ran at the Adelphi Theatre from February 26, 1937, through May 1937. The Sun and I is a gently satirical treatment of the famous Biblical legend of Joseph and his brethren, and Joseph's rise to power in ancient Egypt. The dramatic action implies a similarity between the contemporary problems of the 1930s and those of ancient Egypt, and the play makes its points by employing wit and style rather than propaganda. Joseph, the favorite son of Jacob, antagonizes his stupid and crude brothers with his bravura display of superior wit and intelligence, and as a result is sold into slavery and taken to Egypt where he is imprisoned and sentenced to execution. Vashnee, Potiphar's wife, impressed by Joseph's superior accomplishments, decides to save him. Joseph then becomes Governor of Egypt, initiating many necessary social and economic reforms. Vashnee desires Joseph sexually but is rejected in her attempts to seduce him. Rebuked, she accuses Joseph of rape and strips him of his power and wealth. After many years, Egypt is once again on the verge of famine. The Pharoah, haunted by disturbing dreams, consults his soothsayers, who do not give him satisfying answers. The Pharoah summons Joseph to his aid and is also impressed by his wit. Joseph is once again made ruler in Egypt but this time enters into conflicts with the priests when he tries to establish a system for flood control on the Nile. Although the Pharoah cautions him not to combat religious feeling, Joseph ignores his pleadings and sadly learns that it is the people who desire his removal from power. He realizes that his error was his exercise of autocratic dictatorial power without any attempt at educating the people, who eventually grew to despise him. Joseph leaves Egypt, prophesying that some time in the future another leader will emerge who will create the perfect state.[27]

   The Sun and I was the type of play for which FTP had a particular affinity because it used legend and historical material to cast light on contemporary problems. It generated controversy and much commentary regarding the many implied parallels and allusions to modern times, the world of the 1930s. Because these parallels were not clearly defined, debates were waged over whether The Sun and I was an attack on Fascism, Communism, or the New Deal. Critics and audiences pondered whether Joseph, a rebelious, idealistic reformer who finally realizes that power corrupts even when it seems benevolent, was Hitler, Stalin, or Franklin Delano Roosevelt. The play was seen by many as an optimistic prophecy of the coming of a form of government reflecting American democratic values. In this sense, it was viewed as singing songs of praise for FDR and his slogans insuring that good, happy times were ahead.

   As Morgan Himmelstein observed, the satire was very general and open to varying interpretations according to personal beliefs, but that ultimately, for a non-partisan observer, "The Sun and I was simply an amusing and colorful narration on a Biblical theme, with incidental jabs at all authoritarian government."[28]

   Critics of the left were generally pleased with the production. Charles Dexter, writing in the Daily Worker, liked the way the techniques of burlesque were used along with the eclecticism and artistic realism of Max Reinhardt and the critical realism of Robert Sherwood, stating that the play and production combined "Reinhardt, Minsky and [Robert] Sherwood." He was pleased about the way history was depicted: "This

Joseph and this Potiphar are not stodgy and tiresome ranters of blank verse. . . . The Sun and I veered away from weary history and created comedy drama." The conclusion appealed to Dexter because in it Joseph came to realize that his mistake was believing in individual rather than in collective effort to solve social problems.[29]

The director's approach rejected the realistic mode of interpreting history by conveying photographic replications of daily life during a particular period, and instead used modern stage-craft to depict life in an original, personal, and strikingly theatrical manner. The highly theatricalized presentation was described by Hallie Flanagan as a "coat of many colors," in which the audience sees: "pits of snakes, a palace, peacock fans, a dungeon, a slave gang, a beautiful woman tearing off her clothes. . . ."[30]

The Sun and I, which reflected upon the uses and abuse of power, as did Robert Sherwood in The Road to Rome, ran successfully for three months, managing to please some of FTP's severest critics. FTP critics and supporters began to see the possibilities afforded Federal Theatre in producing plays of such grand spectacle and artistry.

The Popular Price Theatre's next production was Prologue to Glory, the first production to be selected and supervised by the Project's new production board. It began functioning when the FTP moved its operations to the Chanin Building at Forty-Third Street and Lexington Avenue.[31] During this period, January-March 1937, due to budget cuts, the FTP created the new board in order to have a more centralized, economically viable administrative structure. In New York City, Philip Barber, who administered 12 units including the Popular Price and the Experimental, was still in charge, but the units under his authority no longer controlled their own personnel and publicity. Casting was now done by a central office headed by Madolyn O'Shea. The units continued to operate for a while, retaining only nominal administrative control and continuing to perform at the same theatres.[32]

Prologue to Glory by E.P. Conkle was the last "straight" play produced by the Popular Price. One of the FTP's greatest achievements, Prologue to Glory was a dramatization of the youth of Abraham Lincoln and his romance with Ann Rutledge.[33] It opened March 17, 1938, closed January 9, 1939, and pleased everyone but some Marxist critics who did not like the fact that the story of Abraham Lincoln's early life was presented basically as a love story and not as a cogent political drama about the battle against slavery and secession. Following FTP's trend in using popular historical figures as protagonists in plays adapted to the present, Lincoln was selected because he had become a newly discovered cult hero in the 1930s. (Other FTP plays about historical figures, including Lucy Stone, Jefferson Davis, and Ballad of Davy Crockett, will be studied later. A regional show to be reviewed will be the noted Chicago production of Howard Koch's Lonely Man in which a "reincarnated" Lincoln is the protagonist.)

Written by E.P. Conkle, author of 200 Were Chosen and professor of drama at the University of Iowa, Prologue to Glory was given an experimental production at the university theatre where Conkle was the director. George Kondolf, New York City's newly appointed FTP Regional Director, selected Prologue to Glory as a "fresh," "searching," and "realistic" depiction of Lincoln's early life as a small-town lawyer. It was Kondolf's specific intention that the "glamour" of Lincoln's later life should not "blur and overshadow the picture of Abraham Lincoln as a boy and man beset by problems and work-a-day conflicts common to all of us."[34]

In avoiding Lincoln's later life and all of the political implications inherent in that story, Kondolf chose to present a play glorifying a young Lincoln overcoming obstacles and rising above hardship. Some critics viewed this as a message related to the American population of the thirties attempting to rise above the poverty and hardship of the Depression. Burns Mantle was one critic who viewed the play as a patriotic portrayal of an American hero overcoming obstacles in hard times to realize the American dream. Mantle considered seeing the play an educational experience and a patriotic duty. He gave it unqualified raves, countering criticism that the play sentimentalized the youthful Lincoln, and claimed, "If the Federal Theatre had produced no other single drama, this production would doubly justify its history and all its struggles." He also stated, "No citizen of these United States . . . should be permitted to miss seeing Prologue to Glory."[35]

Other critics were not as glowing in their appraisals of the production. They were less inclined to accept the sentimental portrait of Lincoln and found fault with the reverential, episodic, and static treatment. These critics saw the portrayal of Lincoln as not realistic and faulted the playwright for not dramatizing the full power of Lincoln's personality. Richard Lockridge, in the New York Sun, reported that the play lacked dramatic fire and that although often "poignant," it remained a play yet to written because several of the episodes containing good possibilities for vivid dramatization remained static due to the author's "suspicion of the theater's showy fireworks"--his inability to create lively and striking images on the stage. Some images were life-like but also listless and "vague."[36] John Anderson, in the <u>New York Journal American</u>, agreed, stating that the play was only a "series of reverential snapshots" and that the scenes lacked "variety and vigor." Because the incidents were portrayed so undramatically, none of Lincoln's lustiness and power wasrevealed.[37]

The FTP production of <u>Prologue to Glory</u> was a very good example of a play that would not have been produced on Broadway because of its very large cast, utilizing 62 actors.

The last production to be presented by the Popular Price Theatre was the musical, <u>Sing for Your Supper</u>. George Kondolf was the Director of the Chicago Project when that city did its noteworthy musical, <u>O Say Can You Sing</u>. Hallie Flanagan appointed Kondolf as Director of the New York Project specifically because of his success in Chicago with <u>O Say Can You Sing</u>. With the publicity generated by musicals being done in Los Angeles, Kondolf decided it was time for New York to do a musical. This was a risky choice since New York was the home of the musical, and it was chancy for the FTP to venture into direct competition with Broadway's greatest single contribution to the American theatre.

The formats of <u>O Say Can You Sing</u> and <u>Sing for Your Supper</u> were similar. They were both satires on Uncle Sam as a show business angel, and presented in revue the government employing the talents of a large group of actors, dancers, and singers. <u>Sing for Your Supper</u> was a topical revue which blended in its production numbers a running commentary on the vital social issues of the time as well as a portrayal of the daily struggles of the artists working to put on the show.

The musical was produced by Robert Sour and Harold Hecht. Hecht, who also directed the show, had been a director in Hollywood for five years, producing shorts and directing musical scenes in feature films. The songs were by Ned Lehac, lyrics by Robert Sour, production numbers by H. Gordon Graham, with choreography by Anna Sokolow.

Many of the production numbers reflected sharp political, satire. There were numbers satirizing the military and Grover Whalen, in addition to popular cartoon scenes like "Leaning on a Shovel." The best remembered number in the show was the first act finale involving the entire 178 member cast (including 50 "Negro" performers), "Papa's Got a Job." This number dramatized a scene in which an evicted family sits dejectedly on a sidewalk surrounded by all its possessions. The family's spirits are buoyed when the oldest daughter hurries in with the happy news that her Papa found a job. Neighbors happily congregate to show their joy at hearing the good tidings. Another highly noted production number was the finale for the show, "Ballad of Uncle Sam," offering a patriotic confirmation of the blessings America bestows upon its citizens.

Sing for Your Supper was frought with difficulties from the moment of its inception. Rehearsed for one and a half years, the most promising performers were constantly being replaced because they had found employment in the commercial theatre. This constant rearrangement necessitated a re-writing of the material to suit the talents of new members joining the cast. During the long rehearsal period, material was constantly being changed to accommodate one expediency after another. These problems were compounded because FTP actors could only work 24 hours a week according to the agreement made with Equity. Many of the performers had to be taught new skills with which they were totally unfamiliar. The actors rehearsed in a number of rehearsal studios and lofts throughout the various boroughs of the city, and during the lengthy rehearsal period, the notion generally held was that the show would never open, due to the seemingly insurmountable problems. Doing a musical was new for Federal Theatre, which soon discovered that performers with the necessary ingredient of "star quality," in addition to experienced writers and composers, were not available to FTP.

The extravaganza finally opened April 15, 1939, to mixed reviews, and capacity audiences. The show ran until FTP folded June 30, 1939. Although the reviews were generally somewhat favorable, some critics felt that it was a mistake for FTP to attempt to do a copy of a Broadway musical. They concurred that several factors mitigated against a success for FTP in the field of musical revues. The list of misgivings concerning FTP's insistence on opening Sing for Your Supper, despite the interminable delays, were best reflected by Brooks Atkinson:

> Probably it is a mistake for the Federal Theatre to imitate so
> closely in form the splendor and smartness of the big Broadway
> revue. It is hard enough for a Broadway producer with the best
> show talent at his command to recruit a flamboyant cast and fit
> it to exuberant material. The Federal Theatre has no principals
> to lead a revue of those dimensions. Much of the material is
> third-rate stuff with songs that are frequently lost in the tumult
> of a noisy orchestra and to lyrics that can hardly be heard. For
> the dynamic direction that brings all the details of a Broadway
> revue into focus is wanting in the staging of Sing for Your
> Supper. Pins Are Needles in a small theatre makes a virtue of
> the amateurishness of the performing. In an enormous theatre
> Sing for Your Supper offers no protection to actors who are not
> up to this sort of thing.[38]

John Mason Brown did not excuse FTP for its lack of success in attempting to be both a theatre and a relief agency. He found the production to be "dull," "amateurish," "poorly sung," and "inefficiently danced." He also said that the show lacked any genuine talent.[39] Richard Watts found it a "remarkably dreary affair" and "rehearsed to death."[40]

Along with <u>Life and Death of an American</u> and <u>Revolt of the Beavers</u>, <u>Sing for Your Supper</u> was one of the three FTP shows playing on Broadway when the Project was terminated. During the investigations by the Dies Committee into the alleged subversive activities of Federal Theatre, <u>Sing for Your Supper</u> was the focus of some of the most intense and virulent attacks. To members of the Dies Committee and other congressmen, the show represented all that was reprehensible about FTP: disorganization, waste, and satire with a left-leaning thrust. Like the FTP itself, <u>Sing for Your Supper</u> had neither a happy history, nor a happy ending.

The Popular Price Theatre was one of the FTP organizations which best represented the aims of Federal Theatre. As reflected by statements made by Hallie Flanagan and information regarding the theatre's purpose in the playbills for its productions, the Popular Price introduced new work by little known American authors at prices affordable to a mass audience. The Popular Price did not compete with commercial theatre, but offered productions which the commercial theatre would not attempt, and in the process helped build audiences for theatre in the Broadway district. <u>Murder in the Cathedral</u> was the best example of a play which "contributed to American art" by offering "a rapid, simplified, vivid form of stage expression, new techniques and ideas." The Popular Price was most successful when it attempted to be "experimental" and least successful when it attempted to imitate Broadway as it did in <u>Sing for Your Supper</u>.

Notes

[1]New York Times, 2 October 1935; 30 October 1935; 31 December 1935; Variety, 23 October 1935, cited in Jane De Hart Mathews, p. 50.

[2]New York Times, 13 November 1935; 14 November 1935; 13 October 1935; 17 December 1935; 31 December 1935; Elmer Rice, The Living Theatre (New York: Harper and Brothers, 1959, p. 156), cited in Mathews, p. 51.

[3]New York Times, 18 October 1935; 21 December 1935; Irving Kolodin, "Footlights, Federal Style," Harpers CLXXIIII (November 1936): 623, cited in Mathews, p. 52.

[4]Interview with Irwin Rhodes.

[5]"Spirit of New York Workers Praised by the National Director," Federal Theatre, 25 November 1935, p. 2; Hallie Flanagan, "A Report of the First Six Months," Federal Theatre, March 1936, pp. 8-9, cited in Mathews, p. 61.

[6]Harry Hopkins, WPA Administrator, addressing the United States Conference of Mayors, Washington, D.C., 16 November 1937, cited in Flanagan, Arena, p. 27.

[7]"Popular Price Theatre Reviews Six-Month Career," New York Post, 4 August 1936.

[8]Ibid.

[9]Synopsis at George Mason University. Unless otherwise indicated, all synopses or readers' reports and comments will be assumed to be furnished by the National Service Bureau, Federal Theatre Project collection at George Mason University. Unless synopses are quoted directly, they are summaries of play synopses grouped either with playreaders' reports, or are official synopses in the Play Bureau or Bureau of Information files.

[10]Synopsis at George Mason University.

[11]Readers' Report by Alexander Kuttner, 21 September 1936. At George Mason University.

[12]New York World Telegram, 22 February 1936.

[13]Variety, 26 February 1936.

[14]Ibid.

[15]Tony Buttitta and Barry Witham, Uncle Sam Presents: A Memoir of the Federal Theatre 1935-1939 (Philadelphia: University of Pennsylvania Press, 1982), p. 46.

[16]Ibid.

[17]Ibid., p. 47; O'Connor and Brown, p. 7.

[18]O'Connor and Brown, pp. 7-8.

[19]New York Post, 30 March 1936.

[20]New York Times, 29 March 1936.

[21]New York Times, 14 April 1936.

[22]Synopsis at George Mason University.

[23]"The People's Theatre Grows Stronger," New York Daily News, 24 May 1936.

[24]New York Times, 16 May 1936.

[25]Synopsis at George Mason University.

[26]New York Herald Tribune, 15 July 1936.

[27]Synopsis at George Mason University.

[28]Himmelstein, p. 101.

[29]<u>Daily Worker</u>, 1 March 1937.

[30]Flanagan, <u>Arena</u>, p. 186.

[31]Press Release from the Department of Information, FTP Records of WPA. Federal Theatre Project Record Group 69, United States National Archives.

[32]Flanagan, <u>Arena</u>, pp. 190-191.

[33]Synopsis at George Mason University.

[34]George Kondolf, Press Release for <u>Prologue to Glory</u>, Department of Information, Federal Theatre Project, 10 November 1937. At George Mason University.

[35]<u>Daily News</u>, 18 March 1938.

[36]<u>New York Sun</u>, 18 March 1938.

[37]<u>New York Journal American</u>, 18 March 1938.

[38]<u>New York Times</u>, 25 April 1939.

[39]<u>New York Post</u>, 25 April 1939.

[40]<u>New York Herald Tribune</u>, 25 April 1939.

CHAPTER III

THE MANAGERS' TRY-OUT THEATRE

The Managers' Try-Out Theatre was a FTP venture in the Broadway arena that quickly revealed the frailties of Federal Theatre as a Broadway angel doing a juggling act. FTP's most important aim was to employ unemployed actors. Therefore, it was only as a secondary aim that the Try-Out Theatre was set up to introduce new plays to American audiences for the first time in professional production. The Broadway "standard" in writing and directing was crucial to the success of this theatre, which attempted to test try-out plays with a potential commercial appeal, however borderline.

In December 1935 the Managers' Try-Out Theatre began, announcing its plans and intentions. The FTP had leased the Willis Theatre in the Bronx and the Symphony Theatre in Brooklyn for the try-out of plays with commercial potential submitted by Broadway managers through the League of New York Theatres. Lee Shubert submitted for the theatre's first production, Woman of Destiny, an anti-war play by S.K. Lauser. S.M. Chartock sent Top Dog by Georgette Corneal and Burnet Hershey, however, it was not produced. Try-out productions were to open simultaneously, running three weeks before changing theatres, thus insuring each play a run of at least six weeks.[1] The plan allowed managers to use FTP actors and to retain the rights to the plays.

Woman of Destiny opened March 2, 1936, at the Willis, which had been "dark" and not used as a try-out theatre for years. The play is a dramatization of the author's novel, The Heart Is Compelled. The plot involves the ascendency to the presidency of the United States of a Mrs.

Goodwin, whose son was blinded and shell-shocked in World War I. Projected into a "future" time frame, Mrs. Goodwin becomes a vice-presidential candidate on a controversial Republic ticket against the wishes of Roger Harmon, a munitions king who dominates the party. Harmon manages to maneuver the successful presidential candidate, Cumberland, into a war with the "Eastern Alliance," composed of Japan and Russia. President Cumberland dies as Congress votes for war. Succeeding to the presidency, Mrs. Goodwin manages to out-smart the "war mongers" and negotiates an armistice which provides world peace.[2]

During the period of the development of the Managers' Try-Out Theatre, pacifist plays were popular on Broadway, and producers were eager to follow the trend. If This Be Treason, produced by the Theatre Guild in September 1935, was an example of the plays that presented anti-war stories with clear pacifist themes. Woman of Destiny was considered a good risk for a producer on Broadway because it did not take radical positions. As the New York World Telegram observed, it was a play "admirably suited to the principles of the Federal Theatre aims." It was suited because it made its point, "Without blazing forth in fierce denunciations, which some may rightly feel a play of this nature should do."[3]

Although FTP executives and some critics saw Woman of Destiny as a suitable Broadway peace-play, other reviewers did not agree with the premise of the script and found its resolution too facile and "dangerous"-- tending to give its audience a false sense of security. The New York Morning Telegraph indicated that it would lull its audiences "into a beautiful Pollyanish dream of peace."[4]

Woman of Destiny turned out to be a good choice for FTP to make since it ended up pleasing its try-out audiences and the other critics who saw it as a valid peace-play for Broadway. However, in this case, the try-out process served to dissuade Lee Shubert from producing it on Broadway because of weaknesses in the writing. Thus, the Try-Out Theatre accomplished its purpose in determining a play's commercial viability.

The New York Home News reported that Lee Shubert attended the premiere but would probably not undertake a Broadway production unless the script was considerably revised and strengthened. However, the reviewer also indicated that the play had many qualities that appealed to the neighborhood audiences:

> Last night's spectators, only a few hundred people who seemed lost in the big playhouse, gave long and vigorous applause to the melodramatic highlights. . . . Many . . . were witnessing a play for the first time in years, attracted by the low price scale, which ranges from 15 to 55 cents. Apparently they were amazed that a venture billed as a "try-out" could prove as exciting as a movie thriller.[5]

Less than a month after Woman of Destiny opened at the Willis, the lease on the theatre was dropped. However, the Willis housed the Managers' Try-Out Theatre's second production, In Heaven and Earth, scheduled to open March 26 as the last FTP play to be presented at the Bronx theatre. When the lease for the theatre was dropped, the reason given was that the theatre was located in one of the poorest sections of the Bronx where many of the residents were themselves on relief and not able to afford even the low admission price. The conclusion drawn was that the many poor residents in the neighborhood could not constitute a large enough audience.[6]

Woman of Destiny moved March 23 to the Symphony Theatre in Brooklyn. Formerly the Shubert-Teller, this theatre was retained for all future try-outs. After being dark for many years, the structure (considered then to be a landmark) was completely renovated with its stated purpose "to employ theatre people, to establish a community theatre which will continue to function after the Federal program is completed and serve as a try-out theatre for managers and producers who are doubtful as to the value of a new play, with no loss or expense to them."[7]

The Try-Out Theatre was very useful to Broadway producers who were interested in a particular property because of its intriguing story, but were not certain of its wide appeal due to various intellectual aspirations in the writing. The theatre's next show, In Heaven and Earth, proved to its producers that the material was either too intellectually challenging, or too intellectually pretentious, for a mass audience. It did not pass its try-out test. In Heaven and Earth, by Arthur Goodman and Washington Pezet, opened at the Willis on March 26. A psychological melodrama, the play is a mingling of the Berkeley Square and Elektra motifs and deals with reincarnation. The story revolves around a psychiatrist's obsessive love for his deceased wife and how the doctor's daughter attempts to replace her departed mother. Dr. Littlefield, the psychiatrist, posits the theory that multiple personality disorders are a result of repressed personalities incarnating an individual from past lives. While treating an amnesia patient, Littlefield affects a cure which awakens the patient to the realization that she is the doctor's dead wife, Leonore. The patient assumes Leonore's persona and even recalls numerous past events.

Littlefield's son, also a doctor, insists that the patient's behavior is a result of his father's unconscious hypnotic suggestion. The son brings Claire, the amnesia victim, back to normal consciousness; however, now all of her memories are those gained during her "Leonore" existence. Angry and jealous about the turn of events, Judith, Littlefield's daughter, savagely attacks Claire, shocking her back to her "real" personality. Heartbroken and remorseful, Little-field prepares to end his life.[8]

The New York Times characterized In Heaven and Earth as a "learned bit of hocus pocus" and "routine theatre," combining mysticism, Freudianism, and touches of "Pirandello"--because characters leave their real selves.[9] Variety stated that it lacked "punch" even though it was well written and acted.[10] Many managers saw the production but decided against producing it. After running for three weeks at the Willis, In Heaven and Earth opened at the Symphony in Brooklyn for an additional three-week run.

The next show was selected because of its clear commercial appeal. The final, and most successful, production of the Managers' Try-Out Theatre, Backwash, a campus mystery-comedy-drama by Edwin Harvey Blum, opened at the Symphony on May 15. The reaction of the Brooklyn Times Union was favorable: "Campus crimes are analyzed by the author and his actors with considerable skill in Backwash, a play that is far better than its uninviting title." The action of the play revolves around the solution of a campus murder. One of the professors at the university, a criminologist, places one of his colleagues, Professor Mark Adams, under general suspicion until the identity of the killer is disclosed. The Times Union reviewer felt that the "play indulges in a good deal of gentle spoofing of college life. The playwright shows himself to be expert in the fashioning of brisk dialogue even though his knowledge of dramatic construction is not overpowering."[10]

The Brooklyn Eagle was equally enthusiastic, saying the play was "equipped . . . with literacy and considerable grace," and that the actors were "more skillfully professional" than they were in other Federal Theatre productions.[12] This review, and the one in Variety, gave credit to the FTP actors, who generally were not complimented on Broadway, as "rising above the material."[13] The pervasive opinion about Managers' Try-Out Theatre productions was that plays would not be given good hearings because of the poor quality of FTP acting. This was in contrast to reactions outside of New York City in the various other regions, where the opinion frequently held was that the acting and physical aspects of the productions were usually superior to the plays.

Based upon the success accorded Backwash, the play was optioned for a Broadway production. Scheduled for a tentative June 15 opening, the show was moved from the Symphony Theatre to the Majestic on Fulton Street, in downtown Brooklyn, for a six-night run beginning June 1. After a delay, the play--produced by Paul Grole and George Hiller, redirected by Carl Hunt, and re-titled Kick Back--finally opened at the Ritz Theatre June 22, 1936, with the original cast.

While negotiations were under way for a Broadway transfer of Backwash, the discontinuation of the Managers' Try-Out Theatre was announced. Philip Barber, the new New York City Regional Director, made the announcement May 20, indicating that all actors affiliated with the theatre would be absorbed by other FTP units.[14] The unit closed after Backwash ended its run at the Majestic.

The FTP indicated that the Managers' Try-Out Theatre failed because managers felt their plays would not be presented effectively enough by the federal actors.[15] Variety suggested that there was a scarcity of scripts, although the unit indicated 21 scripts were available for production. The Try-Out Theatre also claimed that it was placed at a disadvantage having to use neighborhood theatres while other units were on or adjacent to Broadway. The business set-up required the Try-Out to make enough profit to pay the rent, which it never could, while other shows more advantageously located managed to pay rental fees.[16]

Perhaps the demise of this unit was forseen in March when the Cincinnati Enquirer predicted that the Try-Out was doomed from the beginning:

> [The Managers' Try-Out Theatre is] probably destined to be the least popular of the Federal projects, because producers will consider that a play tried out in New York in this manner might spoil its chances for Broadway, and because they will be disinclined to risk a script in which they have some faith without the benefit of carefully chosen principals of established reputation.[17]

The story of the brief life of the Try-Out Theatre illustrates how tenuous the FTP enterprise could be in serving many, sometimes conflicting, purposes. Its one success, Backwash, was successful mainly because it was a play with clear commercial appeal, and defied no Broadway formulas for success. Playwriting was only part of the issue in whether Try-Out plays would be successful. In no other venture was the quality of the acting so crucial an issue to FTP than in the operation of the Try-Out Theatre. Writing was important but only if the other criteria for success were all but guaranteed. The unit was set up to employ FTP actors as it main purpose. Its next most important task was pleasing Broadway producers who might be interested in producing what FTP was showcasing. The acting and productions given plays were very important, and the writing had to meet the "Broadway" standards; however, the single most important criterion was potential commercial appeal, as viewed by producers. Ultimately, the theatre could not survive the alleged lackluster performances given by FTP actors who were in the productions only because they happened to be on relief. However, the viewpoint expressed by <u>Variety</u> seemed to indicate that the common cry heard by producers, "Where are the good Broadway plays, where are the good Broadway plays," was perhaps an issue in why the Try-Out terminated so soon after its beginnings.

Notes

[1]New York Times, 17 December 1936.

[2]Synopsis at George Mason University.

[3]New York World Telegram, 3 March 1936.

[4]New York Morning Telegraph, 4 March 1936.

[5]New York Home News, 3 March 1936.

[6]Variety, 25 March 1936.

[7]The Chat [Brooklyn], 27 April 1936.

[8]Synopsis at George Mason University.

[9]New York Times, 27 March 1936.

[10]Variety, 1 April 1936.

[11]Brooklyn Times Union, 20 May 1936.

[12]Brooklyn Eagle, 18 May 1936.

[13]Variety, 20 May 1936.

[14]New York Telegraph, 21 May 1936.

[15]Motion Picture Herald, 6 June 1936.

[16]Variety, 27 May 1936.

[17]Cincinnati Enquirer, 8 March 1936.

# CHAPTER IV
## THE EXPERIMENTAL THEATRE

When proposals for FTP were being formulated, one of the first concrete suggestions made was that an experimental theatre should be formed and operated as a major unit of Federal Theatre. The FTP therefore created the Experimental Theatre under the direction of Virgil Geddes, who outlined his goals for a unit devoted to encouraging new writing talent, fostering experimentation in acting, directing, scene design, and in other related performance forms "which will contribute to the realization of genuine theatre and drama." The Experimental Theatre would also make a concerted effort to build a "larger, more intelligent audience."[1]

Geddes was concerned about building large audiences and emphasized that theatre should be popular, tickets low-priced, and that plays reflect the concerns of the audiences, which should be encouraged to go to the theatre regularly as a "steady indulgence, a personal habit . . . as the Saturday afternoon ball-game or Wednesday night movie." Geddes also stressed that theatre be just as available as "books are made available to everyone at the public library, . . . the public library is always there."[2]

Geddes indicated that the Experimental Theatre was not interested in runs or commercial exploitation of plays. Its major function would be to work first in conjunction with the author. Plays would be produced during the initial period and would be optioned for a brief period of three weeks. The theatre would be a try-out theatre for the author, allowing a producer to contact an author to offer another production in another theatre. The distinct emphasis would be on developing new writing talent for the theatre.[3]

Regarding his definition of experimental, Geddes explained:

"Experimental," of course, covers a wide range of errors and possible virtues. But today when the drama more and more is concerning itself with contemporary thought and controversy, there is no reason, in our opinion, why it need carry merely an arty connotation as if often did a decade ago. In a society that is still in a transitional stage, the most vital dramas of the day are bound to be of an experimental nature also.[4]

The New School of Social Research and the United Neighborhood House of New York, Inc. jointly sponsored the Experimental Theatre, which formed an acting company of 60 and a large staff, 90 percent of whom were on relief rolls. A list of 50 "experimental" plays constituted the initial group used for play selection. The intended admission price for productions ranged from $.15 to one dollar.[5]

Virgil Geddes, the Managing Producer, was formerly a lecturer with the Brookfield Players, Brookfield, Connecticut. He wrote The Earth Between, and then Native Ground, produced by the Experimental unit. James Light, the Managing Project Supervisor, was associated with the Provincetown Players and directed the early works of Eugenè O'Neill. He is credited with contributing strongly to O'Neill's success.[6]

Addressing a personnel meeting of the Experimental Theatre, noted scene designer and member of the theatre's Board of Directors Mordecai Gorelik spoke "On the Meaning of Experimental Theatre":

The quality that is outstanding about the art of the theatre is that it is a synthetic art. The different elements of production if they are to have artistic form, must have an organic, necessary relationship: they must not merely be added together

Our theatre, which is named the Experimental Theatre, is particularly concerned with this question. Our policy states that we wish to "produce plays distinguished by artistic and social clarity." Structurally, the Experimental Theatre shall combine centralized artistic leadership with democratic participation of all members. Technically it shall attempt a new synthesis of artistic elements of production based upon the social themes of the play...

I think it can be shown that our practice can and, in fact, must differ materially from the practice of the New York commercial theatres.[7]

Continuing to differentiate between the practices of commercial theatre and the proposals for the Experimental Theatre, Gorelik emphasized that his unit was striving for a permanent company rather than the "casting-office type of production practiced in New York." Another difference indicated in the address was the need for a protracted rehearsal process rather than one limited by the time constraints of the commercial theatre. Also cited as a goal of the unit was the discarding of the commercial procedure of advertising. Instead shows would be promoted by a concerted effort to involve various community groups in all phases of production, seeking their opinion and advice even to the point of asking them to serve on the production board. As an example, Gorelik indicated that the first production, Chalk Dust, a play about teachers and students, would be enhanced by approaching student and teachers' organizations for critical and informative input Gorelik illustrated how this would be done: "We will go even further than this, and in planning Chalk Dust, our directors, actors and designers will ask scene by scene 'What effect will this scene have upon our specific audience of teachers and students? Will the stylization of this scene seem real in the eyes of teachers and students?'"[8]

The Experimental offered as its first production Chalk Dust by Harold Clarke and Maxwell Nurnberg. The play in 14 scenes opened March 4, 1936, at the Daly Theatre on 63rd Street, renamed the Experimental. Running for 51 performances, Chalk Dust was a big success, bolstering the FTP season. The play deals with the issue of politics in the large metropolitan high schools and examines the problem of the suppression of academic freedom. The action takes place in a modern high school where Rogers, a young idealistic teacher, has written an article appearing in Harpers magazine condemning conditions in the public schools. Miss Sherwood, another teacher who is competent and experienced, respects Rogers and his views. Through a bizarre misunderstanding, Rogers is locked in the women teachers' room with Miss Sherwood. This creates an enormous amount of gossip and speculation that the two have behaved "unprofessionally" and "compromisingly." The principal is informed of this and also about the article Rogers has written. As a result, Rogers is dismissed with the real reason never clarified. Sherwood resigns but later decides to remain because teaching has become her entire life.[9]

In producing Chalk Dust, FTP began its "commitment to produce new, socially relevant drama. . . . typical of the 'social drama' of the thirties with its realistic setting, sympathetic protagonist (a young teacher battling the system), romantic interludes, and a cautiously upbeat ending."[10]

Critical response to the production was generally favorable. Some critics questioned whether the play was truly "experimental." These critics were not convinced that the issue of academic freedom was examined boldly enough. The reviewer writing in the New York Post expected something "daring" and "revolutionary" and regretted that the authors did not come forth with a "genuine indictment of political influence, inefficient management and simple-minded pussy-footing in a big city's public school system." He stated that the play was "very feeble" and would never be touched by the "crude commercial fellows." The feebleness resulted because the writers "approach the matter from various angles in scene after scene, then shy away like frightened rabbits and hastily change the subject."[11] The New York Sun agreed, saying, "It is simply an amateurishly overwritten, badly constructed play, which makes a feeble attack upon the evils of . . . public schools." The characterizations were seen as obvious "caricatures."[12]

The contention that Chalk Dust was not experimental enough was not shared by the reviewer in the New York World Telegram, who in one of the most supportive statements about FTP work said, "To venture the statement that Chalk Dust . . . is indeed in the nature of a noble experiment is to hope that the term will not be loosely construed. For no more simple-hearted, moving play of a social phase . . . has been seen in that extreme Broadway district for many a moon."[13]

Henry Senber's review in the New York Morning Telegraph was glowing, indicating that the production and the play "sent the WPA dramatic standards soaring to a level far above the Broadway average." Senber saw the play as an indictment of an educational system that should be seen by every teacher and administrator for its subject matter, and by every theatre-goer for its theatrical viability. Insisting that it was a play first and secondarily good propaganda, Senber indicated that its content should inspire everyone to fight for freedom from political meddling in the schools and grant the right of all students to free discussion in discussion clubs, allowing schools to be a "seething cauldron of American Democracy." Senber was very complimentary to the FTP work in this production:

> Heretofore, it has been the habit of reviewers to be lenient with the Federal Theatre productions on the basis "that what the hell they've done pretty well considering everything!" But no apologies are needed for Chalk Dust. In direction, casting and production it was superb. It has done for the theatre what its authors would do for the schools, fit them to the times. . . . It takes its place as one of the finest plays of the season.[14]

Evidently critics viewed the work of the Experimental Theatre with the same set of criteria used by Geddes, that contemporary drama "is concerning itself with contemporary thought and controversy" and, because of this, experimentation did not necessitate "merely an arty connotation as it often did a decade ago." Experimental meant to Geddes and many of those evaluating his work that plays would be experimental to the extent that they dealt in a daring manner with themes and subject matter, rather than only with methods and styles of production

Commenting very favorably upon the work of the Experimental Theatre in reflecting Geddes's views about experimentation were the statements made by Henry Senber in the New York Morning Telegraph That assessment also revealed the type of ongoing comparison made between the work done by the FTP and the "Broadway standard." Regardless of how the work of the Experimental Theatre was viewed by mainstream theatre critics, experimentation, as Geddes defined it, seemed appropriate for the time and place he was working. What was questioned was not whether Geddes's theories were appropriate but to what extent the work done by his theatre reflected those theories. What was important was that FTP gave Geddes the opportunity to test his theories, which in some ways, to a certain segment of the general theatre-going population, could be considered "dangerous." Geddes used theatre as a forum to discuss issues of importance to his audience. After performances of Chalk Dust, audiences remained to discuss the play and the issues raised in it with the actors in an open forum discussion. Rehearsal process information is not available.

Battle Hymn by Michael Gold and Michael Blankfort, the second production of the Experimental, opened May 23, 1936, and ran for 56 performances, closing July 25. The play deals with John Brown's efforts to free slaves during the Civil War. Blankfort recalled that the script evolved from a 50-page sketch given him by the journalist Michael Gold during the period 1933-34. Based upon this sketch, Blankfort continued to research the subject and eventually developed the script presented to the FTP.[15]

Battle Hymn reveals John Brown as a religiously fervent, pacifist Ohio farmer helping slaves escape from the South. Bitterly opposed to slavery, Brown does not own firearms and is against violence. When Brown's son is killed helping slaves escape to Canada, Brown moves to Kansas and becomes involved in the conflict between the abolitionists and the slave-owners. Terrorizing those against slavery for months, the Doyles finally kill another of Brown's sons. In vengeance, Brown, with his other sons, cuts the throats of the Doyles and then initiates an active drive against slavery. After raising money and outfitting some recruits, Brown plans to establish an abolitionist colony in Maryland. While attempting to take the U.S. arsenal at Harper's Ferry, Brown is captured and executed for high treason.[16]

Commenting on John Brown as subject matter for a play, Blankfort stated: "I think what interested Gold and . . . me was the attitude of people like Emerson and Thoreau and others, the so-to-speak fellow travelers of the left at that time and their attitude toward Brown, those who went all the way with him, those who felt he was too bloody and withdrew from support and so on."[17] Continuing, Blankfort indicated why left-wing writers during the thirties were interested in looking into aspects of American history to find material relevant to contemporary society:

> It seemed to us that we had to find our own revolutionary past in literature or history. . . . So the charge that we were simple reflections of a European radicalism would be invalidated because we had our own tradition of radicalism in this country. Names like Crispus Attuck were revived and the early revolutionaries [like] Tom Paine.[19]

Reviewers in general did not regard the play as having a revolutionary message--a message relevant to the circumstances of the present (1936). The New York Times specifically indicated that the "similarity" conclusions would have to be inferred since they were not clearly stated in the play:

> Theirs is a fair portrayal, avoiding alike the Thoreau deification of Brown and the reverse theory that he was simply insane. Before each act is a prologue, with speakers and chorus, and if the audience wishes to conclude that the events of 1936 are not dissimilar from those of 1856, that is their own affair. The authors don't say it in so many words."[19]

In Battle Hymn, the Experimental Theatre attempted to experiment with dramatic construction and stagecraft. Burns Mantle found the play's structure experimental:

> It is an interesting dramatic form the playwrights have adopted, even though it does slow up the action. There is a prologue for each act in which the temper of the times about to be disclosed is revealed, and a narrator speaks for the troubled soul of America and the hope of her defenders.

Mantle continued, praising the scenography: "With skeletonized settings . . . by Howard Bay, considerable authentic atmosphere is created."[20]

Following the general policy of the Experimental Theatre, Battle Hymn was analyzed and then given a promotion campaign to highlight the theme of the play. Based upon the assumption that many "Negroes" would be interested in the work of John Brown as a pre-Civil War crusader for equality, "Negro" organizations in Harlem were contacted to gain their support in promoting the show. Numerous articles appeared in newspapers and magazines, including one with an interview with Michael Blankfort appearing in The Crises, the monthly publication of the National Association for the Advancement of Colored People.[21]

Critics who were not hostile to the FTP on principle frequently were encouraging to the Experimental Theatre, even when the plays were viewed as having dramaturgical weaknesses, accepting the premises of Geddes's theatre and evaluating his work on the basis of how effectively the dramas' messages were projected in performance. Richard Lockridge cited inferences that could be drawn from the John Brown story as told by Gold and Blankfort, and from circumstances in the thirties. He frankly referred to the purpose of the play as propaganda and stated that its most vivid scenes were those in which the propaganda was most "direct and explicit." He wrote, however, that the play's dramaturgy was deficient:

> Here Mr. Blankfort and Mr. Gold take a shrewd and eloquent advantage of evident parallels, showing how battle cries now rising were raised then when armed men turned against constituted authority in the name of freedom. . . . But the play itself is, on the whole laborious. It is cluttered with detail and so weighed down with words that the drama almost never lashes through.[22]

The Experimental Theatre sought to examine ideas and social issues as its major goal. Removing weaknesses in writing was a secondary aim--to be done after a play had been rehearsed and eventually performed.

Sometimes critics asked that the message be stronger, more powerfully dramatized. Richard Lockridge's review typifies this tendency. What was becoming more and more apparent was the notion held by certain critics that plays could be experimental by dealing aggressively with relevant social issues. Critics did not question the validity of theatre being used as a forum for new plays reflecting upon those concerns. They also did not dismiss the idea of theatre being used as a public forum in the literal sense, as was the case with Chalk Dust.

The Experimental Theatre's third production was Path of Flowers, a satire on the meanderings of a "pseudo communist" by the Russian playwright Valentine Kataev, hailed as the Noel Coward of the Soviet Union and its finest satirist. His Squaring the Circle had been seen on Broadway during the previous season. Translated by Irwin Talmadge, Path of Flowers opened September 17, 1936, and ran for 57 performances.

In "An Exclusive to Sunday Worker," a press release sent from the FTP's Department of Information described the play:

Zavyalov continually harps on the man and woman of the future, who he claims will be free from all restrictions in the future society. Love, he says, will be liberated from marriage and other shackles, and there will be no responsibilities under his Communist Utopia. To justify illicit love affairs, he misquotes Marx. In fact, he is forever misquoting Marx, mixing him with Engles and Nietzsche in one breath, injecting this remarkable potpourri into his lectures, as well as into his lengthy conversations with his wife and mother-in-law.

Katayev [Kataev] has created Zavyalov as a lazy lout who shuns responsibility but who commands enough shrewdness to employ his glib tongue and Marxist reasoning as a means of escape. Does he love a woman other than his wife? Then the latter must realize that for a man to be tied down to one woman is to be bourgeois. One must love everyone, Zavyalov reasons, especially the attractive and buxom females. Does his mistress expend money entrusted to her by fellow workers in an effort to make him happy and face expulsion and disgrace? Then it is time for Zavyalov to take his leave. Such concern for money is stifling to an artistic soul.[23]

Although FTP strongly endorsed production of American plays, some foreign plays were also presented to American audiences for the first time in professional performance. Usually the choices were motivated by some desire on the part of FTP to reflect the times and also to create certain good public relation's images. Always sensitive to being too closely allied with anything suggestive of an alliance or sympathy with the Communist Party or the Soviet Union, the FTP chose Path of Flowers to appease Federal Theatre critics on both ends of the political spectrum. In choosing this friendly satire, Federal Theatre revealed a Moscow that conformed more to the way the Hearst press would depict it. Excusing the picture of Russia as presented in the play, the Daily Worker stressed that the impression given in Path of Flowers was of a Russia still in the initial stages of creating a better future, not yet reaching a communist utopia.

FTP's decision to do Path of Flowers did not please playreaders and critics as was intended. Some observers, including certain FTP playreaders, viewed the play as ridiculing the Soviet Union and not related enough to similar problems in the United States. Louis Vittes stated:

> The theme lacks relevance to the American scene (the nearest analogue we have to a Zavyalov is a parlor revolutionary stemming from the village) and taken apart from its context, which is the Soviet scene as a whole, it tends to distort conditions in the Soviet, and to give the wrong emphasis to cognate problems here.[24]

Francis Bosworth, Supervisor of the Playreading Department, strongly endorsed Path of Flowers and explained the reasons why FTP finally decided to do this foreign play that allegedly did not have much to do with the American experience. He referred to the play as a:

> . . .fine satire of a man of many words, whose head is stuffed with many self-made theories. Zavialov [sic] is a symbol of the super-intellectual the world over. The play is well constructed. The characters have an overwhelming human appeal, and some of the scenes are hilariously comical. The social problems touched upon are very significant.[25]

When the play opened, an apology for the less-than-flattering view of life in the Soviet Union was voiced in the Daily Worker. Charles Dexter was very enthusiastic about the production and explained how the left-wing saw Path of Flowers as a reflection of current Soviet history and past revolutionary plays. He stated that it was necessary to place Kataev's portrait of Soviet life into an historical perspective. Kataev's plays were seen as depicting different periods of social development in the USSR. He indicated that Kavaev's Squaring the Circle was a play dealing with the goals of the Soviet Union's first five-year plan fostering the discipline necessary to build heavy industry and that Path of Flowers dealt with the second five-year plan, during which many great victories had been won, leaving, however, the ultimate goals of the plan seemingly unattainable. Dexter characterizes Zavyalov as:

... a fervent preacher of the new order of things. He converts every act into a homily on the future world, the Communist world Glibly from his tongue spring all the familiar phrases; he paints in glowing colors the future of mankind when Communism shall have been maintained, when man's path shall be strewn with flowers.[26]

This was how left-wing critics and audiences viewed the play: as a glimpse of the Soviet Union still in the developmental stage.

Dexter acknowledged that Path of Flowers was more appropriate for Soviet theatre-goers, but that the play was still significant to Americans because of the vivid way it depicted life in modern Russia. Dexter saw Zavyalov carried away by dreams while the Moscow of 1934 still struggled for existence, building factories, apartment houses, and collective farms. Dexter concluded that, "Decidedly, Path of Flowers is for Moscow audiences. It attacked a valid and dangerous problem, the readjustment of the petty-bourgeois intellectual vulgarian of the great struggle for a new world." He found the production smooth, and the plot simple and "old-fashioned." He added that Kataev with his "masterful brush paints-in a thousand and one details . . . the living Socialist world of the U.S.S.R."[27]

Main-stream critics were always comparing FTP productions to those on Broadway. They continually held the assumption that FTP acting must, by virtue of the fact that the Federal performers were on relief, be very inferior. However, the Experimental Theatre continued its commitment to presenting "experimental" plays reflecting boldly the social conditions of the times, or issues relevant to the world scene. Geddes's unit did not deviate from its intention to not try for the commercial hit; it did not wait for the perfect cast before experimenting with a particular play. The review in the Herald Tribune typified the reaction of critics comparing FTP shows with those on Broadway. Very complimentary to the play, Herbert Drake felt that it was poorly performed by the FTP actors:

> The construction of situation and plot manipulation is so obviously good that the spectator wishes for a nice capitalistic production with the best actors so that the values of this excellent show might be exhibited in their proper light. Even so, there are plenty of laughs. . . . If there had been six acts instead of three, it would have been a hit.[28]

Native Ground by Virgil Geddes was the fourth production of the Experimental Theatre. According to Geddes, Native Ground intended to portray archtypical American farmers who live lonely and desolate lives on the prairies and vast plains of the mid-west. The play reflected a calm stoicism covering up an undercurrent of hysteria and restlessness. It attempted to raise to tragic proportions the devastating consequences of lives lived in futility and with a total lack of communication. The action centers on Milton Rogers, who returns to Nebraska seeking a new wife with whom to share a new life in South Dakota. After returning to his former employer, the Bentley farm, he decides to take Bentley's daughter as his new wife. However, Bentley's wife believes that the daughter was actually fathered by Rogers. Despite Mrs. Bentley's pleadings, Rogers leaves the farm with his wife. However, mental confusion and guilt prevent Rogers from assuming either the role of father or lover. Eventually his wife turns to a farm hand, Oscar Holm, for love and has an affair with him. Unable to hold Holm's interest, she is eventually forced to accept responsibility for the care of a child Holm has fathered as a result of a sexual relationship with a servant girl. The play ends with Rogers's wife resigning herself to "fate."[29]

Discussing Native Ground, Geddes indicated,

> The play takes place against the background of Nebraska and Dakota at the time this country was expanding and growing richer, both in regard to the soil and economic prosperity. The play deals with problems which are very acute today, seen, however, through characters developed under the philosophy of individualism.[30]

Born on a Nebraska farm, Geddes was writing about "native" material he knew. He began his playwriting career while working in Paris as Financial Editor for the Paris edition of the Chicago Tribune. During the 1920s, Geddes wrote prolifically; however, his plays were not produced because producers found them too "risky." As a result, he built the reputation of being "America's greatest unproduced playwright."[31] Returning to the United States, Geddes started the Brookfield Players in Brookfield, Connecticut.

He was always a maverick, devoting himself to writing revolutionary pamphlets expressing lofty ideas about what a "socially engaged" theatre should be. However, his plays usually dealt with the loneliness of Midwestern life. Commercial producers were hesitant to produce Geddes's plays because they dealt with a subject matter foreign to a general audience.

Geddes gained notoriety when he and Paul Sifton, co-author of 1931, protested the Theatre Guild's practice of buying options on American plays and holding them unproduced for years. Calling themselves "The Provisional Committee For Unproduced Theatre Guild Playwrights," Geddes and Sifton picketed Guild productions such as Escape Me Never, distributing handbills while marching from one Guild theatre to another.[32]

The production of Native Ground was one of the curious episodes in the FTP's career. This was an instance when the views of FTP playreaders, including the head of the Play Bureau, and critics were congruent. Both groups focused in similar ways on the play's major weakness. It was a case in which one could speculate a great deal about why the play was selected when the critical response given to the production was so negative. One can assume that the play was produced because Geddes was the Director of the Experimental Theatre and, since he set the artistic policy, was in an especially good position to select one of his own scripts.

Playreaders and critics agreed that the play was a self-conscious attempt to be "folksy" and regional. They saw the play as one written by an academic, full of good ideas, but too cerebral to create characters and dialogue that had the capacity to move an audience. Native Ground was considered derivative in certain ways, and eventually inauthentic. Its long and laborious plot construction seemed excessive and episodic. Francis Bosworth's report reflected this view and was curious in the sense that he, as a supervisor, had approved a play which he himself had found so inept. He had characterized it as a,

. . . terse, sometimes mordant play that seems peculiarly inactive dramatically. Dialogue stretches over three well organized acts, but nothing seems to "happen" . . . until the final curtain. The characters are fashioned magically out of clipped speeches (that sometimes are too uniform in manner) and develop to inner emotional climaxes which are not suited to the theatre. There are faint overtones that seem to mingle with Desire Under the Elms, but they are superficial.[33]

Another report focused on the play's academic, self-conscious attempt to imitate Greek tragedy. John Rimassa commented:

Incest, almost the sole theme of Greek tragedy, furnishes a legitimate dramatic theme. But here Mr. Geddes has harped badly and at length upon an unusual incestuous situation, and has failed to evoke horror, pity or a feeling of universality. Though well written from an academic standpoint, the play lacks dramatic climaxes, lacks any pitch or action.[34]

Reader Nicholas Andromedas concurred that the characters were not authentic: "It has the style of a lyric pastoral, but . . . the author must dig into his characters and develop them as real people. I honestly feel that when put on the stage it will be quite anemic."[35] Fanny Malkin agreed and was also moralistic:

Traditions and moral codes mean nothing to these simple farmers, who, by the way, talk most artificially--matter-of-fact- -of [the] most blood-curdling affairs of daughter and father. . . . The indifference of the author to his characters is most shocking. . . Farmers do not talk, nor act, according to the play.[36]

FTP readers frequently dismissed a play if it did not conform to the reader's particular value system. Malkin's report typifies a tendency to reject a play because of its lack of appropriate "moral outlook." Sometimes a rejection was based on lack of "social significance." In some reports, comments on plays were favorable if the play construction appealed to the reader, even if the over-all effect was less than impressive. Charles Feinberg reflected this tendency:

> Mr. Geddes has written an interesting drama, frequently absorbing because of the pattern of its ideas, less often because of the suspenseful coversation between its principal figures. Deliberately Geddes writes with great restraint, for he has apparently striven for the most difficult quality in the theatre, known as suppressed emotion. Not a little of the power of Mr. Geddes's play comes from his brief, unadorned scenes.[37]

Feinberg's report represented a dissenting opinion and was the most enthusiastic in its recommendation.

Despite the negative, rejecting comments made by the playreaders, Native Ground was accepted for production. An eight-act trilogy, it began rehearsal in July 1936 and finally opened at the Majestic Theatre in Brooklyn on January 27, 1937; it was withdrawn February 13 due to the cool critical response. The presentation at the Majestic was given with two casts (32 actors), performing on alternate evenings. Variety's comments on the opening at the Majestic were typical of how proponents of the commercial theatre responded. The fact that the Experimental Theatre was dedicating itself to a philosophy and way of working different from the commercial theatre, as defined by Geddes and Gorelik, made hostile critics scornful of the Experimental's intentions. They dismissed, as ineptitude, FTP's attempt to reflect ideas and circumstances relevant to regions in America outside of New York City. Variety commented:

> This is a bad play, poorly acted and staged, has nary a laugh and nothing to recommend it. It is about the supposed cockeyed morals of our own farm folks of the Middle West. If the play is

intended as a preachment, it misses by considerable. Sets are like crossword puzzles. They've got to be figured. It's a bucketful of neuroticism and looks to be a good demonstration of the ineptitude of the FTP.[38]

Geddes revised the script, omitting the last section of the trilogy. The new version was presented March 29 at the Venice Theatre, the largest theatre ever rented by FTP, with a seating capacity of 1,746.[39] Critical reactions to the revised version were not much more favorable. They very closely resembled observations made by the original playreaders.

Richard Watts agreed with FTP's playreaders who dismissed the play as false "folksy," "earthy" type of playwriting. He found it "a tedious, pointless and clumsy drama of the earthy school . . . never so far from burlesque. . . . It merely goes to show that Mr. Geddes, who is an earnest and argumentative debater on drama and dramatists, is a more skillful propagandist than he is a playwright."[40]

Brooks Atkinson was the most critical of Geddes's lack of resources as a writer. His review agreed with those playreaders who considered Geddes's play academic, cerebral, "anemic," and lacking in emotional power to adequately portray his tragic themes. Atkinson was not at all encouraging to the author, calling the play "monotonous" and "feeble." He agreed that Geddes was not an authentic playwright but a thinker with "a good deal of intellectual vision" and a writer with a talent for inventing "solid dramatic themes." However, Atkinson viewed Geddes as a writer without the "emotional resources that make a playwright out of a thinker." According to Atkinson, the cumulative effect of Geddes's writing added up to very little:

By the end of the evening, his theme, astringently worded, begins to seem sillier than it probably is. His bare style of writing sounds barren, which is not precisely what he intended. Native Ground is just the sort of theme O'Neill might turn into a macabre and harrowing drama. The sheer excess of the O'Neill style of tragic writing could crowd the night with black shapes of death, and give Native Ground dramatic significance.

Atkinson finally concluded that "Mr. Geddes is a pedantic writer, overfastidious about the use of words and lacking in theatre invention . . . Native Ground is only a hackneyed and humorless studio exercise."[41]

Burns Mantle found Native Ground episodic and improbable; however, he commented favorably on the physical aspects of the production in a way that was typical of many critics who found FTP plays lacking strength in playwriting but creatively produced:

As drama it is discursive, episodic and largely unpleasant. It possesses the virtue of simplicity in writing, but misses conviction by a persistent dependence upon the improbable. . . . The real stars of the evening are Howard Bay, . . . and Feder who did the lighting.

Mantle described the visual effect of the scenography: "You see right through the Bay houses, and across the fields beyond. And you stand close to some very real sunlight and moonlight in plowed fields and shadowed corners that are impressively atmospheric."[42]

Mantle's review conforms to a general opinion that the FTP productions were frequently better than the new plays. This view also held that the acting was generally not up to Broadway standards, and that the plays, if they were new plays by American playwrights, were generally inept or lacking in significant playwriting skill. However, the sets and lighting were usually considered to be of a very high quality.

As reported in the New York Herald Tribune, Geddes offered various complicated explanations for the play's poor showing. He indicated that Equity rules prevented him from rehearsing the play "appropriately," so that the plot and theme could be developed organically during the rehearsal period.[43]

One of the ironies of the FTP enterprise was the publicity Geddes received when his play was published by Samuel French several years prior to its FTP production. He and his play were lauded. Comments made by Samuel French's publicists to promote the play's publication seemed embarrassing after the way it was received in its premiere production. Perhaps the very laudatory publicity made Geddes and the Experimental Theatre confident about it as a successful venture. Virgil Geddes had been hailed as a second Eugene O'Neill ten years prior to the production of Native Ground. Horace Gregory, in reviewing the play, published in book form by Samuel French, wrote: "The publication of Native Ground will I think, establish Mr. Geddes as the most important figure on the American stage since the arrival of Eugene O'Neill."[44] Maxim Gorky read the play and wrote to the author: "I haven't read anything in five years over which I have ever been more enthusiastic."[45]

Native Ground was important as a FTP production for several reasons. It was written by a Midwesterner writing about his "native" landscape in a very self-conscious manner. However, one could speculate about whether or not the play would have received as negative a response if it had been presented in the region from where its material derived. Clearly, New York audiences and critics were not receptive to this example of a FTP regional play.

The new New York production board initiated in the spring of 1937 created a central casting agency for FTP and thereby took away a FTP producer's right to have his own acting company. The production board also created other guidelines which virtually eliminated autonomous theatre organizations, since all artistic personnel and production facilities would be centralized. The board would select new plays for units, and specialized theatres would no longer have separate companies and facilities. These new policies virtually disbanded the specialized theatres as autonomous organizations. Also during this period, and even earlier, more actors were allowed to leave because they found employment in the commercial theatre.

As early as December 1936, various problems threatening the smooth functioning of the Experimental emerged. The loss of actors who had found regular employment cut sharply into the work of the unit, making rehearsal and production dates uncertain. Thus, the productions of plays were delayed because of the resignations of leading members of their casts.[46] As a result of this and the policy of the new FTP production board stripping him of his autonomous control of the Experimental, and also probably because of his discontent over the reviews given Native Ground, Virgil Geddes severed his association with the theatre as Managing Producer as of the middle of May 1937. Rita Hassan, an administrative assistant, was appointed his successor.[47] After Hassan's appointment, various plans for future productions were made. However, they never materialized due to the unit's imminent termination.

During the period of Hassan's brief tenure, a production of Pierre Patalin, an anonymous fifteenth-century French farce dealing with the shrewd lawyer outdone and the swindler thwarted, was approved for

Caravan Theatre bookings. A production was scheduled with rehearsals to begin June 9. Dog Beneath the Skin, a satire with music by W.H. Auden and Christopher Isherwood, was scheduled for a fall opening. These plans were held in abeyance until the status of the unit was determined, based upon the FTP's new production board guidelines. When the Experimental unit ceased to exist as an autonomous producing unit in June 1937, plans to produce the two plays were abandoned.[48]

Prior to his resignation, Virgil Geddes submitted for consideration a set of plans for the reorganization of the unit. In his plans, priority was given to the task of finding a better, permanent place of operation. Geddes indicated that the disruption caused by not having a permanent, exclusive home at the Experimental Theatre on 63rd Street--there were constant "loan-outs" of the the theatre to other units--made it difficult to work consistently and with purpose. He suggested that a small theatre (300-500 seating capacity) be leased and indicated the following theatres as ideal: the President (Artef), Bayes Theatre, New Amsterdam Roof Theatre, Belmont Theatre, and Labor Stage. Geddes urged the formation of a permanent acting group and suggested that not less than 20 experienced actors be engaged. He also proposed the hiring of three permanent stage directors who could work creatively with playwrights and actors on a new script, nurturing it in a "studio theatre" setting until it was "ready" for public performance. However, he insisted that "studio" performances be given before a public audience to facilitate exposure of the work of actors and directors as well as to determine the play's viability for major production by the Experimental or other units. Regarding these plans, Geddes indicated that problems would result when the Play Policy Board began exercising its authority in selecting plays. Getting script approval was a long, drawn-out procedure under the Play Policy Board's jurisdiction and it slowed preparations for new productions. Geddes was also displeased with the "central casting" arrangement headed by Madolyn O'Shea. In short, with his executive control reduced, Geddes made a few feeble efforts to save the unit as he envisioned it. This was, of course, impossible, and therefore he submitted his resignation.[49]

The final production of the Experimental Theatre was the presentation of two one-act plays by Paul Green: "Hymn to the Rising Sun," depicting a tragic incident in a Georgia chain-gang camp, and "Unto Such Glory," a comedy satirizing itinerant religious "visionaries." The plays were presented at four matinee performances at the Ritz Theatre on May 6, 8, 13, and 15, 1937, given to aid the Experimental Planning Board in determining booking policy. They were later presented at the Adelphi beginning June 3, playing matinees on Thursdays, Fridays, and Saturdays until July 10.[50]

"Hymn to the Rising Sun" takes place in a prison camp very early in the morning, July 4th. While the convicts are chained to their bunks, Runt, a young Negro, is being punished in a sweatbox. Runt's cries disturb Bright Boy, a new convict who tries to help Runt. Bright Boy's pleadings cause a guard to beat Runt more intensely while delivering a long political discourse. Finally, Runt falls out of the box dead. The guard justifies his beating and demands that the prisoners sing "America." Only Bright Boy knows the song, and, despite the great pain inflicted upon Runt, leads the convicts in singing as they carry Runt off for burial in a railroad bank where they are working. Day breaks as the cook sings a few bars from "America."[51]

Critical response to the Green plays revealed that New York would take folk and regional material seriously if the quality of the writing warranted it. In contrast to comments made about <u>Native Ground</u>'s lack of authenticity as an honest, forceful regional play, critics made positive statements about Green's two one-acts. They were viewed as honest, direct, and passionate in theme and presentation.

In his review in the <u>World Telegram</u>, Douglas Gilbert praised Green's writing talent as "precise" and his "scorn direct and bitter." Gilbert contrasted Green with Geddes as a playwright by saying that Green "does not wander about in the arty befuddlement of his colleague, Virgil Geddes, but says his say, and strikes his curtain as an honest artist." However, Gilbert resented Green's "directness" in "Hymn to the Rising Sun": "His very bluntness makes for a tabloid obviousness that defeats his drama and his message. It is the fault, I think, of his anger. His 'Hymn to the Rising Sun' is compact as a missile; a deadly indictment of the chain gang and its brutality."[52]

Brooks Atkinson did not find the writing in "Unto Such Glory" particularly inventive but stated that Green wielded "the slapstick in the easy style of a folk-drama and makes a good prank of it all." Atkinson also stated that, "In 'Hymn to the Rising Sun' Mr. Green writes with the firmness of style and the passionate emotions of a master of the stage." Although the form was simple, Atkinson observed that it gave Green enough latitude to "express all of the scorn, irony and contempt a high-minded man instinctively has for ignobility and inhumanity."[53]

The stipulations made by the new production board in the spring of 1937 definitely curtailed the burgeoning growth of the various units under Philip Barber, especially the Popular Price Theatre, Manager's Try-Out, and Experimental Theatres. The short life of these groups functioning as autonomous units, culminating in the resignation of Virgil Geddes as Managing Producer of the Experimental Theatre, reveals the fragility and ephemeral nature of the FTP enterprise.[54] Seen in the work of the "big three," was all of the hope and high aspiration of artists collaboratively working toward the illusory goal of marrying high artistic intention to the exigencies of the market place--all done as an on-going but insecure process of a federally subsidized theatre. The many internal and external pressures plaguing FTP will be explored later. However, it was apparent that even after some glittering early successes, bureaucratic problems threatened the survival of some Federal Theatre units during the early, embryonic stages of FTP development.

Notes

[1]Virgil Geddes, "Data for Experiment: Notes on One of the WPA's Recently Proposed Trial Theatres," New York Times, 3 November 1935.

[2]Robert Garland, "Virgil Geddes Talks on Federal Theatre," World Telegram, 6 November 1935.

[3]Ibid.

[4]Ibid.

[5]Ibid.

[6]"Report on the Experimental Theatre," 4 April 1938, pp. 3-4. At George Mason University.

[7]Mordecai Gorelik, "On the Meaning of Experimental Theatre," report of an address made by Mordecai Gorelik at the first personnel meeting of Experimental Theatre, 3 January 1936, pp. 2 and 3. At George Mason University.

[8]Ibid., pp. 5 and 6.

[9]Synopsis at George Mason University.

[10]O'Connor and Brown, p. 9.

[11]New York Post, 5 March 1936.

[12]New York Sun, 5 March 1936.

[13]New York World Telegram, 3 March 1936.

[14]New York Morning Telegraph, 3 March 1936.

[15]Interview with Michael Blankfort conducted by Lorraine Brown, 22 July 1977. Tape at George Mason University.

[16]Synopsis at George Mason University.

[17]Interview with Michael Blankfort.

[18]Ibid.

[19]New York Times, 23 May 1936.

[20]New York Daily News, 23 May 1936.

[21]Promotion Notes, Production Notebook for Battle Hymn, n.d., p. 5. At George Mason University.

[22]New York Sun, 23 May 1936.

[23]Press Release, "Exclusive to Sunday Worker," Department of Information, FTP, 30 August 1936. At George Mason University.

[24]Louis Vittes, Playreaders Report, 10 July 1936. At George Mason University.

[25]Francis Bosworth, Playreaders Report, 14 April 1936. At George Mason University.

[26]Daily Worker, 21 September 1936.

[27]Ibid.

[28]Herald Tribune, 18 September 1936.

[29]Synopsis of Native Ground sent as a memorandum from Pierre Loving to Philip Barber, et al. Record Group 69, United States National Archives.

[30]Ibid., p. 2.

[31]Ibid.

[32]Ibid., p. 3.

[33]Francis Bosworth, Playreaders Report, 1 July 1936. At George Mason University.

[34]John Rimassa, Playreaders Report, 21 July 1936. At George Mason University.

[35]Nicholas Andromedas, Playreaders Report, 21 December 1936. At George Mason University.

[36]Fanny Malkin, Playreaders Report, 23 December 1936. At George Mason University.

[37]Charles Feinberg, Playreaders Report, 19 June 1936. At George Mason University.

[38]Variety, 3 February 1937.

[39]Monthly Progress Report for February and March 1937, Experimental Theatre Correspondence of the New York City Office, FTP. Record Group 69, United States National Archives.

[40]New York Herald Tribune, 24 March 1937.

[41]New York Times, 24 March 1937.

[42]New York Daily News, 24 March 1937.

[43]New York Herald Tribune, 13 April 1937.

[44]Press Release to Brooklyn Daily Eagle from FTP Department of Information. Record Group 69, United States National Archives.

[45]Ibid.

[46]Monthly Reports of Experimental Theatre, December 1936. At George Mason University.

[47]Monthly Reports of Experimental Theatre, May 1937. At George Mason University.

[48]Monthly Reports of Experimental Theatre, June/July 1937. FTP records of the Experimental Theatre. Record Group 69, United States National Archives.

[49]Virgil Geddes, "Reorganization and Plans for the Experimental Theatre Unit," n.d., n.p. FTP records of the Experimental Theatre. Record Group 69, United States National Archives.

[50]FTP records of Experimental Theatre. Record Group 69, United States National Archives.

[51]Synopsis at George Mason University.

[52]World Telegram, 7 May 1937.

[53]New York Times, 7 May 1937.

[54]Monthly Reports of Experimental Theatre, November 1936/June 1937. FTP records of Experimental Theatre. Record Group 69, United States National Archives.

## CHAPTER V

## INDEPENDENT PRODUCTIONS

The new production board's restructuring of activity in New York under Philip Barber's direction essentially stripped all specialized, independently run theatres of their autonomy. All new plays presented after the spring of 1937 were presented by FTP's production facilities rather than any particular FTP-sponsored theatre. These plays (which were also referred to as non-allocated productions) included, in chronological order: Professor Mamlock, No More Peace, On the Rocks, The Big Blow, and Life and Death of an American. Also considered non-allocated productions, but presented before the new production board began its operation, were It Can't Happen Here and Jefferson Davis. It Can't Happen Here was a special case because it involved simultaneous openings throughout the country. Jefferson Davis was the first FTP production presented on Broadway--before any of the units were completely established.[1]

The very first FTP production on Broadway, Jefferson Davis, an historical play about the President of the Confederacy, opened at the Biltmore on February 18, 1936. Presented while theatre units were being formed, the risky venture provoked much controversy and prompted Hallie Flanagan to say, "It speaks very well for the magnaminity of the public and critics that they forgave us this indiscretion."[2] The dramatization of the life of the President of the Confederacy, written by John McGee, FTP regional director in the Southeast, had its Broadway world premiere on the 75th anniversary of Davis's inauguration at Montgomery, Alabama, as Confederate President.

The United Daughters of the Confederacy sponsored the show They regretted the decision, feeling that the stirring up of old NorthSouth feelings of antagonism were not worth opening the play above the Mason-Dixon line, even though their original ultimate aim was to then tour it extensively in 44 cities in the South.[3]

Jefferson Davis traces the early signals of tension between the states before Lincoln's election. Davis is portrayed as a man who insists that it was not slavery as an issue that divided the country but the North's challenge to the South as a determiner of its own fate The second act depicts Davis's life through the stormy period of the Civil War, gently emphasizing his egotism and the political climate surrounding the Confederate government and how this affected the military campaign. The play ends with Davis's death, and with a eulogy given at the head of his coffin draped by a Confederate flag.[4]

Critics agreed with the United Daughters of the Confederacy that New York was not the place to open such a play. They also felt the play was grossly overwritten and definitely not up to Broadway standards. They dismissed the choice as an early FTP error.

The idea for the boldest venture attempted by the FTP, perhaps in the American theatre, originated with Francis Bosworth, Director of the Play Bureau, during an FTP summer conference at Vassar in 1936. Bosworth's brainstorm emerged as a strategy for getting Sinclair Lewis to offer FTP the rights to adapt and present his 1935 Nobel Prize winning novel about fascism coming to America, It Can't Happen Here, by promising 21 productions opening simultaneously in 18 cities. The drama which occurred during the adaptation's development, along with the behind-the-scenes hysteria, is one of the legendary FTP stories With intense effort and energy, Hallie Flanagan and her stalwart collaborators managed to open It Can't Happen Here on October 27, 1936, in New York at the Adelphi, along with a Yiddish version at the Biltmore and a Suitcase Theatre production at a Jewish center in Staten Island. The show opened simultaneously that night in Birmingham, Boston, Bridgeport, Chicago, Cleveland, Denver, Detroit, Indianapolis, Los Angeles (two), Miami, Newark, Omaha, San Francisco, Tacoma, Tampa (in Spanish), and Yonkers. More than 379,000 persons attended 584 performances of the play.[5] In New York City at the Adelphi, there were 95 performances with an attendance of 110,518; the Yiddish production played 86 performances to 25,160 playgoers; the Suitcase production gave 133 performances to an audience of 179,209, touring the boroughs and playing in repertory from the October opening until July 1937.[6]

This gargantuan undertaking was not one that elicited positive responses by all members of the press. From the moment the project was announced, it became controversial. As Flanagan recalled:

> Meanwhile the press was equally eloquent on the subject; there were stories and editorials for and against, from one end of the country to another. Some people thought the play was designed to re-elect Mr. Roosevelt; others thought it was planned in order to defeat him. Some thought it proved Federal Theatre was communistic; others that it was New Deal; others that it was subconsciously fascist. All apparently agreed that the date October 27 must have some mystic connection with the coming election.[7]

Despite this clamor, with resolute zeal, Flanagan launched the project, claiming, as she was quoted in the Herald Tribune:

We want to do <u>It Can't Happen Here</u> because it is a play by one of our most distinguished American writers. We want to do it because it is a play about American life today, based on a passionate belief in American democracy. The play says that when dictatorship comes to threaten such a democracy it comes in an apparently harmless guise, with parades and promises; but that when such dictatorship arrives, the promises are not kept, and the parade grounds become encampments.[8]

For his part, Sinclair Lewis stated, "I prefer to give it to FTP for two reasons: first, because of my tremendous enthusiasm for its work and, second, because I know I can depend on the FTP for a nonpartisan point of view."[9] Hollywood had already rejected the novel as a possible film production.

John C. Moffitt, a Hollywood scenarist, was engaged to collaborate with Lewis on the first draft. This version was the one finally presented at the Adelphi after numerous changes were made during the initial writing and rehearsal period. The Lewis-Moffitt collaboration was a tempest of temperamental fury, and Flanagan recalled how the collaboration continued at the Essex House in New York:

Written? Too mild a word. The play was produced by polygenesis It was partially created by Mr. Moffitt, who paced up and down in his apartment at the Essex House and threatened, if Mr. Lewis did not omit certain scenes and include others, various unusual reprisals; it was simultaneously springing almost invisibly from the brain of Sinclair Lewis, who, in another apartment at the Essex House, composed and acted every part differently every day. "Let's change the whole scene to an interior and have the Corpos beat Doremus almost to death--Bosworth, take the typewriter in the other room and pound out a rough draft, and Hallie and I will just sketch through the details." At this point a note would be slipped under the door saying that Mr. Moffitt would appreciate it if I would communicate certain things to Mr. Moffitt, and since by that time I was the only acceptable medium of communication between the embattled collaborators, I would on the way up to Mr. Moffitt with the message, communicate certain things to the almighty, the only being in whom I could safely confide.[10]

H.L. Fishel of the Play Bureau recalls how he and Francis Bosworth contributed to the Moffitt-Lewis collaboration at the Essex House:

Now to get the thing going too then we began to bring people like Converse Tyler and other playwrights, other writers, from our project, up there--and I do not mean to say that any of us had anything to do with the writing of that play, we did not. But we used to block out, just block out, what we thought might make a good scene. And it may not be related to the thing he was working on, but we were going through the book and blocking out suggestions, that's all. As he finished his day's work, at around three-four o'clock in the afternoon, we had people there to rush [them] to our project. And they would be translated then in Yiddish, and Spanish, and German and French.[11]

What finally emerged was what the FTP described as a social melodrama depicting the rise of fascism in America:

In this play the rise and course of a possible American dictatorship are traced through their effects on the lives of Doremus Jessup, a liberal editor of a Vermont newspaper, his family and associates, who are typical middle-class Americans. They have complacently watched the swift rise of power of Senator Berzelius Windrip and fail to detect in the latter's apparent plans for a socalled rational disciplining of American labor and unemployed, and American youth, a subtle trend toward fascism. With the support of Francis Tasbrough, Ft. Beulah's industrial magnate, and Pastor Paul Peter Prang, radio preacher, and his League of Forgotten Men, the maelstrom that is to whirl across America in a fury of blood and hate is well launched. With the first success of dictatorship in 1936, there is the immediate rise of an underground counterrevolutionary program carried on by the People's Party under the leadership of Walt Trowbridge. Doremus Jessup recoils from the inhuman brutalities of Windrip and his fascist Corpos and aligns himself with the People's Party. He is tortured and imprisoned, but later makes his escape to Montreal, where he plans to carry on with Walt Trowbridge. As the final curtain descends, we feel that the Windrip dictatorship is approaching coup de grace by a now aroused and thinking people. And we know that, in the words of one of the characters in the play, "The Doremus Jessups can never die," that their purged spirit is still true of the traditional COMMON MAN who is the mold and backbone of America.[12]

The New York production was by no means a smooth enterprise New York administrators Barber, Watson, and Goodman all felt that simultaneous openings were a bad idea, that they would be considered "hick town" try-outs. They urged that the opening be in New York first and then in the regions. Flanagan commented that this was one of several times when she was "furious with the provincialism of the New York project and its lack of any sense of the theatre we were trying to build."[13] According to Flanagan, new plays justified nationwide openings, and she held that It Can't Happen Here was appropriate because the FTP stressed contemporary American material and that It Can't Happen Here was "by a distinguished American with a burning belief in American democracy."[14]

Based upon Flanagan's strong conviction that Lewis's play fostered optimistic democratic ideals, E.E. McCleish in the Washington office worked out a promotion plan for It Can't Happen Here urging all units throughout the U.S. to:

Avoid all controversial issues--political angles of any degree--special appeals--racial or group appeals--or inferences in any of these directions, since Federal Theatre is interested only in presenting good theatre, neither adapting nor assuming any viewpoint beyond presenting a new and vital drama of our times, emerging from the social and economic forces of the day. . . . Also forbidden in most positive terms are any references to any foreign power, any policy of a foreign power, the personalities of any foreign power or government, any comparison between the United States and any specific foreign power or government; any comparison between the United States and any specific foreign power, system, personality, etc. Our business is with a play of our time and country by a great writer of our time and country, and our job is wholly a job of theatre.[15]

The New York production proceeded as Vincent Sherman, the director of the Adelphi presentation, collabored with Lewis, rewriting earlier versions while a staff of typists, working in day and night shifts, typed fresh versions and rushed them to the various parties involved. Lewis, during all of this, still insisted on interviewing all actors, hearing them read, and carefully, personally selecting each one in a manner typical of an "enflamed martinet." He became distracted by the details and, as the hysteria mounted, made one of his famous telephone calls to Flanagan on October 25, indicating that he had not slept all night:

. . .For the matter of that, as you know, I haven't slept for weeks.  Nobody can say I haven't given everything to the Federal Theatre. . . . Now it is all terrible--everybody has gone into a coma . . . and I want you to come to New York and postpone the play a week and get new people to do everything or do it yourself.[16]

Based upon Lewis's urgent plea, Flanagan asked Lewis, Sherman, and Crascraft to leave the theatre the day before the opening, and then:

We [technicians and stage personnel] locked the doors of the theatre and got to work. With the assistance of a few stage-hands, we set up, scene-by-scene, Mr. Crascraft's realistic sets, which somehow had been bungled in the execution. We started in to rearrange, re-paint, and re-dress the sets. Somehow we got into our warehouses and secured different furniture and draperies and lamps and pictures.[17]

The production at the Adelphi eventually opened, and to make the event as noteworthy as possible, during the intermission ushers with an air of gravity and secrecy sureptitiously gave members of the audience sheets of paper representing the "underground" newspaper supposedly published by liberals after the press was curtailed by the Windrip dictatorship. Originally the plan was to present in the "underground newspaper" the entire Windrip fascist program as it appeared in the Lewis novel. However, this strategy was abandoned because of the potential controversy the inflamatory anti-Semitic material could have provoked.[18]

It Can't Happen Here was FTP's first smash hit and its boldest and riskiest venture, stating very strongly its commitment to presenting serious, socially relevant plays. Because the play had been rejected as a film vehicle, FTP wanted to show that it could, in a limited way, compete with the film industry, and it garnered a great deal of publicity by doing what had never been done in the American theatre before--21 simultaneous openings in 18 cities throughout the country.

Critics and FTP playreaders agreed that the Lewis-Moffitt adaptation of the novel was not credible or sufficiently plausible because, unlike the novel, the stage version lacked violence and a sense of urgency. In his playreaders' report, H.L. Fishel indicated that the play's major weakness was that it tended to convey the impression that fascism was menacing to only one small town in Vermont. Fishel stressed that "offshoots of pioneers and puritans would not stand for a complete breakdown of law and order." He questioned the play's credibility: "Even totalitarian governments, no matter how much we dislike them, are not fools. . . . The whole play is badly thought out--badly planned and badly carried through."[19]

Controversy was generated from the moment the idea was conceived. Lewis was saying that fascism could come to America because the unwary average good citizen American would allow it through lack of vigilence and that only the liberal middle-class could prevent a fascist dictatorship from taking root in the United States. This message was strongly rejected by the leftist press, which held that the liberal approach would never save America from fascism.

The production at the Adelphi Theatre was not credible. Critics generally indicated that the play was never terrifying or alarming and failed to provoke anger. Reviewers criticized the melodramatic approach, which tended to burlesque the situations, making the characters seem like clowns or fools. A real sense of menace and the sinister was absent.

Richard Watts, Brooks Atkinson, and Joseph Wood Krutch were particularly unconvinced of the play's plausibility or terrifying menace. Regarding the Adelphi production, Brooks Atkinson in his review began by criticizing the book as "no great shakes . . . with many hackneyed fictional devices running through it." He emphasized that it was the "grim plausibility of the story and the red flame of the Lewis spirit [that] were the qualities that made it as electric as a piece of news." He continued to state that,

In the stage version the . . . story ought to incite alarm in the
audience by the swiftness and inevitability of the narrative. . .
But it hardly fulfills the opportunity Mr. Lewis has given to the
stage, for the characters are meagerly defined, the dialogue is
undistinguished, and many of the scenes dawdle on one foot.[20]

Richard Watts felt that "the play . . . does not make the attack on

fascism as bitter and angry as it should be. It Can't Happen Here should

both frighten you and make you mad, and we don't think that it achieves

either result as completely as it should." However, Watts did indicate that

a more strident tone may have been less convincing to those who were

complacent. Watts continued to say:

By keeping the manner, if not the details, of their indictment
calm and avoiding all extraneous issues, they [the authors] have
certainly made the matter of their attack clear-cut. Unless you
are a frank advocate of a Fascist regime hereabouts, there is no
reason why you should be any more annoyed at the viewpoint of
the play then you would if it indicted the man-eating shark. . . .
while the rest of the narrative is in deadly earnest, the account of
the two Corpo leaders is done in terms of sheer burlesque. The
two villains are merely clowns, without any possible suggestion
of the sinister about them.[21]

Writing in the Nation, Joseph Wood Krutch found the play

"reasonably well-acted but pedestrian and just so-so," obvious in its plot

development. He complained about the tendency to burlesque important

scenes and characters tending to underplay the menacing tone. Krutch

also stated that "with such elements of burlesque present, there is no

possibility that it shall [happen]. It is a solemn warning, or is it a reductio

ad absurdum whose title is to be taken literally? At the dramatic version,

one can't be sure."[22]

Rejecting the liberal approach as a defense against fascism, Charles Dexter, writing in the Daily Worker, offered the Communist Party line. He cited as a major weakness in the play Lewis's not confronting the issue of fascism directly as "a reign of terror established by capitalists in an effort to retain their declining power." Dexter criticized Lewis's belief in the credo that a "free, inquiring, critical spirit" is the heritage of every true American because "this individualistic doctrine fails to hold off the Fascist beasts," and that Lewis "offers no solution, no analytical understanding of the causes of Fascism, no defense against its onslaught." Dexter concluded:

> The dramatic version . . . should have been high melodrama, with the motives plainly underscored for all to see. . . . an answer to Fascism, the ringing appeal to a unity of all forces which is the only answer. It should have said, sharply, clearly, forcefully . . . "On to the People's Front! The enemy is known! Don't wait until you see the whites of his eyes! Let him have it with both barrels! If you treasure your democracy, be prepared to fight for it! Join hands and arms and living bodies in a front which will retreat not one inch in the Fascist war against liberty."[23]

Flanagan noted differences among the three New York productions. In the Yiddish version, the acting was more fluent and expressive, and the scenography more evocative. Other critics familiar with Yiddish concurred that the "fluent" acting helped strengthen the play's credibility. To attend the Yiddish version of It Can't Happen Here at the Biltmore, Flanagan had to hurriedly taxi over to the theatre to catch the second act and reported that it was,

> Amazing to come into a different theatre and see the same play in another language. Here the continental volubility and

126

gesticulation was in contrast to the quiet playing at the Adelphi. The Yiddish version included several scenes, notably the concentration camp scene, omitted at the Adelphi, and on the whole I thought it a better show.[24]

Flanagan also found the staging different in style and mood: "impressionistic fragments against space, securing through the designs . . . an effect of light and shade almost Rembrandt in quality."[25]

The audience success of It Can't Happen Here, although qualified by some critics, proved how dynamic FTP could be in working experimentally with all of the advantages placed at its disposal. The collaborative effort made among the writers and FTP executives in New York demonstrated how creative and flexible Federal Theatre could be in doctoring scripts and mounting productions according to the exigencies of time and place. The fact that the production was enormously exhausting and time-consuming for everyone involved forced FTP to abandon the idea of doing the same with the works of Shaw and O'Neill. When FTP obtained the rights to the O'Neill and Shaw plays, it was not with the intention of doing simultaneous openings of a single script.

The Experimental Theatre frequently loaned its space to other FTP units. This policy was an economic move to utilize maximally space already leased by the Project. When theatres such as the Experimental were dark and could be used by other performance groups, arrangements would be made to allow them to rehearse and perform on a "one show" basis. Under this arrangement, the FTP Jewish Theatre occupied the Experimental for its production of Professor Mamlock by Friedrich Wolf, translated by Anne Bromberger and directed by Harold Bolton. It opened April 14, 1937, and played 76 performances Professor Mamlock was seen by approximately 45,750 playgoers. This figure includes the audience attending the 31 spot-bookings on a circuit within the New York City metropolitan area between October 27December 22, 1937.[26]

The play reveals how Professor Mamlock, a highly regarded surgeon in Nazi Germany, faces the anti-Semitism of the new fascist regime. As a result of the chaotic events following Hitler's rise to power, Mamlock's son becomes a communist and is forced to leave the country; his daughter is beaten, insulted, and driven from her school Professor. Mamlock is dismissed from his position at the State Hospital when it begins "purging" Jews from its professional staff. The professor attempts to adjust to the terror facing him but is unable to negate his dedication to science and renounce his obligations as a professional. Unable to accept the oppression facing him and his colleagues, Professor Mamlock commits suicide.[27]

A curiously coincidental event occurred three days after the opening of the production; a real Professor Mamlok (spelled differently), an exiled German doctor and former head of the Department of Dentistry at the University of Berlin, arrived in America seekly asylum from Nazi persecution after being stripped of his professional practice and left destitute. The author, himself an exiled German doctor, denied any knowledge of the recently arrived Professor Mamlok and insisted that the play "was a fiction, though freely based on the experience of several German-Jewish scientists with whose lives he was familiar."[28] The "real" Professor Mamlok stated that the play was indeed based upon the events and circumstances of his life.[29]

Professor Mamlock had already been presented in Warsaw, Basle, Zurich, Moscow, Leningrad, Johanesburg, and Tokyo.[30] Wolf, the author, was familiar with persecution, having been arrested repeatedly in

Germany and condemned to death due to his political activities. He escaped Nazi terror by fleeing to the Soviet Union. In the U.S.S.R., he wrote Professor Mamlock, which was produced in Moscow for a two-year run. While in Moscow, he met another exile, Herbert Rappaport, formerly assistant to the Viennese director Pabst, who was convinced that Professor Mamlock would be most fully realized in a film.Rappaport wrote the scenario for a Russian film version produced by Lenfilm Studios in Leningrad. In its run at the Cameo Cinema in New York City in November 1938, the film adaptation of Professor Mamlock had the longest run on Broadway of any Russian-made film up to 1939.[31]

Although many critics viewed Professor Mamlock as a strong anti-Nazi play revealing the suffering and persecution of the Jews, some felt that the focus on the psychological torment of one family limited the play's scope to the telling of a single personal tragedy.Some Marxist critics expressed dislike for the interpretation that the Nazi persecution of the Jews was based on "race" and not on class. The Marxist press was pleased that FTP presented an anti-fascist play but rejected the emphasis on the psychological, urging a Marxist analysis which would reveal that anti-Semitism was a manifestation of the terminal phase of capitalism.

Brooks Atkinson was particularly displeased about the fact that Professor Mamlock was presented as a personal psychological study of the effect of tyranny on one man. He strongly felt that the story of the persecution of the Jews in Nazi Germany should have been raised to epic proportions. He conceded the difficulty of adequately portraying the horror and terror of Nazi tyranny on the stage, but eloquently pleaded for a drama which would deal with the theme in terms of its universal meanings regarding justice and catastrophic inhumanity to man. In his article "Culture Under the Nazis," Atkinson stated that the terroristic persecution of the Jews in Nazi Germany "cannot be effectively represented on the stage." He cited examples of plays which tried but failed to adequately depict Nazi persecution: Kultur, Birthright, and The Shattered Lamp--all produced in 1933 and 1934: "Although the subject was fresh then and also grisly and painful, and although public sensibilities were particularly tender, the craftmanship in these plays was sorely [sic] adequate to an incomprehensibly tragic theme." In reference to Professor Mamlock, he reflected that the "whole difficulty of plays about the Third Reich: the callous and aggressive persecution of the Jews may be too great a topic for ordinary make-believe craftmanship on the stage. . . . what we need to know is how this relapse into ignorance and barbarism came about." Atkinson further stated:

And this is a theme not for conventional playmakers, but for epic drama--the furies unleashed, man crying his knowledge and his will against the atavistic whirlwind. This is a theme that involves not merely human suffering but universal justice and needs exaltation to lift it above human agony into the agony of the spirit, where even those who are innocent and those who are safe share responsibility for the crimes of mankind.[32]

Critics praised the acting and directing as strong, forceful, and full of conviction. The acting was considered by several critics to be superior to the acting in other plays running in the Broadway area. They stressed that the level of force and conviction in the acting gave the play a distinction and power to convince as few FTP, or other commercial productions, were able to accomplish. Burns Mantle stated: "Only two of the Federal Theatre productions that I have seen have approached in artistic merit and general excellence of direction this sample of the Jewish project's competence. . . . The actors are definitely professional in training and in their handling of the play."[33]

Henry Senber in the Morning Telegraph agreed about the quality of the acting: "The Federal Theater actors match the author's sincerity with their performances. The commercial theater might be able to hire better known players, but any producer, government or private, would have to look a long way to find actors who could put more guts into their work." He indicated that the company rehearsed Professor Mamlock with tears in their eyes.[34]

These favorable comments about FTP acting are significant because they reveal one of the few instances when Federal Theatre acting was superior and an advantage to a FTP production in New York.

No More Peace, Ernst Toller's anti-war satirical fantasy, was first produced by the Roslyn, Long Island, unit on June 3, 1937, in a translation by Edward Crankshaw with lyrics by W.H. Auden.[35] It was later presented by the Roslyn unit at the Maxine Elliott, January 28, 1938:

The play opens on Mount Olympus where several of history's great are gathered, discussing their individual theories and philosophies concerning mankind. The conversation turns to war, and Napoleon makes a wager with St. Francis that he, Napoleon, can precipitate a war in any earthly country. St. Francis, ever the optimist, insists that man is becoming more wise and peace-loving and points to the placid people of Dunkelstein as an illustration. Napoleon selects this country for the scene of war. A radiogram is sent to the unfortunate nation informing it that it is on the verge of hostilities. The news comes while a peace celebration is in progress. The whole nation is offering a sacrifice on the altar of peace, but at once the situation is changed. The offerings are retrieved, and the whole attitude of the populace is reversed. They have a tough time digging up an adversary, but Cain, a neurotic ego-maniac, is set up as dictator, and he falls upon a traditional, hereditary enemy to make the conflict a success. There follows a succession of episodes depicting the horrors that follow when the war god is in the saddle. The ruin of the country is imminent when an Olympian angel tells a Dunkelstein official the secret of the cruel hoax in exchange for a pair of chic, Parisian wings. The dictator, however, refuses to cease his violent purges until he discovers that he has in his own veins the blood of the race that he has been persecuting.[36]

For FTP's production of No More Peace, a member of the Play Bureau not only read the play but went "into the field" to evaluate its production. Alfred Kuttner's remarks are revelatory because they indicated not only how he evaluated the play in reading it but also how his opinion of the play was reinforced after he saw it in performance. His comments vividly described the production as amateurish. He said about the Roslyn Unit's opening night: "On the whole this turned out to be an amiable production, though hardly of professional standard, in a plesantly situated theatre before a kindly disposed audience." Regarding the set, Kuttner observed:

> Olympus was represented by a little platform on one side of the stage about eight feet above us, with access through a hollow masthead. The stage itself served alternately as an open-air City Hall and an equally open-air prison cell, with practically no stage accessories. (Credits to The Experimental Theatre, Vassar College.)

He found the acting undistinguished, "with a negligible Napoleon, a picture book St. Francis and a Socrates achieving a somewhat hilarious effect. Cain, the hairdresser, did a fair take-off on Hitler." He concluded his report of the Roslyn production by saying that, even in the farcical approach given in the production, the play could not be taken seriously as an anti-war play: "Even more in the acting than in the reading, it impresses one as being the work either of a stage sophomore or as the posthumous work of a dramatist who was no longer in his full vigor."[37]

When No More Peace was then produced in New York at the Maxine Elliott, critics viewed the script as sophomoric and lacking vigor They saw the play as being "diffuse," "feeble," without "bite" and sense of outrage, and a pretentious, muddled, and somewhat unimaginative tract full of platitudes. The fantasy was a pessimistic plea for peace, placing the blame for war on man's nature rather than on society. Ultimately, the general opinion was that it was a hopelessly pseudo-intellectual bit of trivia. There is no available information to indicate whether the production at the Maxine Elliott was changed or altered in any significant way, particularly in the writing, based upon Kuttner's assessment of the Roslyn production.

By the time George Bernard Shaw's political comedy On The Rocks was presented by FTP at Daly's Theatre, the theatre was no longer referred to by its interim appellation of Experimental Theatre. The show opened on June 15, 1938, and closed December 3, 1938. It was the first time a Shaw play had been presented in the United States by any group other than the Theatre Guild since the Guild's founding in 1919. Shaw gave FTP the rights to produce On The Rocks with the provision that 55 cents be the top ticket price, and not the customary FTP top scale of $1.10. Desiring to allow a wide audience to attend the theatre and see his plays, Shaw had already established a precedent when On The Rocks was presented at the large Winter Garden Theatre in London for an eight-week run at significantly reduced ticket prices. This followed Shaw's complaint that the better seats in most West End theatres were too costly for the potential mass theatre audience.[38]

On The Rocks, translated by Florjan Sobieniowski, was premiered in Warsaw at the Polish Theatre on November 24, 1933, directed by Shaw's official Polish representative, Arnold Szyfman. The following evening, November 25, it opened at the Winter Garden directed by Lewis Casson. It was then produced in Berlin at the Berliner Volksbuhne in March 1934.[39]

Shaw began writing On The Rocks while on board a ship during a world tour in 1933. Upon his return, he told the press that the play was inspired by English politics and politicians, a "comedy of modern English politics and something of its tragedy, too."[40] The Theatre Guild, which had first refusal on all Shaw's plays, opted not to produce On The Rocks. Milton Shubert also eventually decided against it.[41]

The action of the play centers on the Prime Minister, Sir Arthur Chavender's, attempts to solve England's economic problems When the play begins, he is told by a woman doctor that he is suffering from mental fatigue and stagnation and should rest for a few weeks in Wales. He is advised to take with him to his retreat the works of Lenin, Marx, and Stalin. During his sojourn, he frenetically ponders the ideas of these political thinkers. Returning to London, Chavender is prepared to implement a radically new revolutionary program for social change: nationalization of lands, the taxing of unearned income, forced labor, the banning of strikes, an increased police force, and an enlarged Navy. In short, he emerges as a "liberal Fascist," completely disillusioned about the possibility of democracy ever working. The reforms are countered by Sir Dexter Rightside, who sends young patriots wearing colored shirts into the street to actively oppose the Prime Minister's plans. Sir Arthur finally gives up and resigns to let England go "on the rocks," and his "liberal Fascism" is defeated by Sir Dexter's "reactionary Fascism." However, a veteran labor leader, a kind of Fascist himself, has the last word: "I'm for any Napoleon or Mussolini, too, or Lenin or Chavender that has the stuff to take both the people and the spoilers by the scruff of their silly necks and just sling them into the way they should go."

There was much criticism of the play on all ends of the political spectrum. Shaw was called a Fascist by some, a Communist by others, and a doddering, muddled old man by many members of the press In reply, the playwright, attempting to justify the fogginess in the ideology, noted:

> I went around the world preaching that if Russia was thrust back from Communism into competitive capitalism, and China developed into a predatory capitalist state, either independently or as part of a Japanese Asiatic hegemony, all the Western states would have to quintuple their armies and lie awake at night in continual dread of hostile airplanes.[42]

Critical reaction to On The Rocks was far more favorable than to Toller's play. Reviewers indicated an appreciation for the fact that FTP now had the rights to do Shaw's plays, but also reflected upon the controversy. Because Shaw was not specific about his remedy, except for the call for a strong leader to take the situation in hand, On The Rocks was seen by many as a call for authoritarian rule, depending upon the viewer, rule of either the communist or fascist type.

Brooks Atkinson was favorably impressed with the prices and the production:

> It has been staged abroad though with no great success. Now the Federal Theatre, which has the invaluable asset of access to Mr Shaw's plays, has put it on crisply and wittily, with some

mighty good acting all the way through. As a lecture written out of sublime disillusionment by the foremost man of letters in the world today, it is worth an evening of concentrated listening. Or, to take an odious materialistic point of view, it is the best fiftyfive-cent buy in the show booths just now. If the tariff were $3.50, the acting would be no better and the handsprings of logic no more agile or caustic.[43]

Left-wing critics viewed On The Rocks as a fascist play and stated that a Marxist interpretation would be the only approach that would save the Shaw work from the infamous label of fascist orientation. The Daily Worker's John Cambridge regarded On The Rocks as a positive plea for Fascism, especially when seen without the "complementary and often contradictory preface," and a "disservice to democracy." Cambridge, expressing further displeasure with the ideology, stated: "Here, I would only repeat that if On The Rocks had followed a real Marxist line, a conflict would have logically followed, which must inevitably have increased immensely the dramatic force of the play."[44]

Brooks Atkinson offered a sharp rebuttal to the charge that Shaw was a fascist and saw the play as far more complex. Regarding the charge that Shaw had become a fascist, Atkinson stated:

Some people have got it into their heads that England's chief devil's disciple is advocating fascism in this play and, in a burst of virtuous pride, have indignantly cancelled their reservations Perhaps they are right, but Mr. Shaw is also advocating communism, in case that is any better, and almost anything else for a decent change. For, at the summit of his years, he is reading a topsyturvy lecture on perplexities of modern government.[45]

The FTP production of Shaw's On The Rocks was significant because Federal Theatre offered a play with a cerebral discourse on modern problems to a mass audience at popular prices. A play by a playwright of world renown was now available to audiences at the price of a movie admission. The endless Shaw discourses were problematic to some members of the audience. However, Atkinson defended Shaw's loquacity. In response to critical reaction characterizing the play as "talky," Atkinson concluded that: "Mr. Shaw's composure is always at one level of white intelligence. But the level is miraculously high The talk is sententious, wise and, in spite of its chatty style, profoundly informed."[46]

Critics were generally very positive about the high professional level of the production of On The Rocks. They made particular mention of the acting as strongly contributing to the show's success, and also to making the difficult play more accesible to mass audiences.Atkinson reported:

> Robert Ross, as director, and James Ullman, as producer, have had the good sense to stage it with a light touch and an impish imitation of dignity. They have made up Philip Bourneuf, as Prime Minister, to look like G.B.S. in his electric and Socialistic days --lean, saturnine, keen-minded and artful. This device, which was also useful in the Mercury revival of Heartbreak House, helps a theatregoer to know where he is during a tornado of syllogism and Socratic questions.[47]

For its final season, the FTP had one of its biggest coast-tocoast hits in Theodore Pratt's Big Blow, a melodrama of a hurricane devastating the Florida coast (as one had already done in 1936) and of Yankee farmers settling in Florida confronting Florida's "crackers." Lorraine Brown and John O'Connor, in their book, Free, Adult and Uncensored, described Big Blow as, "A good example of the standard fare of many FTP units. Big Blow satisfied Hallie Flanagan's guidelines that the FTP produce new plays with social themes and regional settings, but its real appeal was its lovely romance, violence and suspense."[48] It opened at the Maxine Elliott on October 1, 1938, and ran until April 1, 1939.

Based on Pratt's novel of the same title, the story relates the trials of a young Nebraskan farmer who, bringing his ailing mother to the warm Florida climate, meets with hostility and deviousness on the part of the "crackers," who want him to leave for reasons never fully clarified. The Nebraskan is befriended by a congenial young woman, a native of the area who was rescued from the clutches of the play's villain by a faithful black servant. The young hero from Nebraska hides the black man from the raging anger of the local populace, who are out to lynch him. Hateful passions are fanned at a Holy Roller meeting, but the storm comes, bringing a new outlook along with desolation. The play ends with the villain being killed by his own henchmen, who have had a change of heart.

Discussing his writing of the play, the author stated that, "It took me nearly two years of continual research--inland, as far from the winter tourist coasts as I could get, drinking bad whiskey with the crackers, farming with them, 'gabbing wad of snuff,' going to cockfights and Holy Roller meetings and living through two hurricanes--to get material for Big Blow."[49] Southerners felt the play reinforced northerner's "stereotypical" images of southerners and the South; therefore, the play was never produced in Florida or any other southern state.

Big Blow was an important New York FTP production for several reasons. It was a regional play for which the author spent a great deal of time researching a "native landscape." Because it was a big hit, it was given several productions throughout the country. However, ultimately it could not be presented in the region, because it was viewed by Floridians as portraying them in a very unflattering, stereotypical manner. The mildly stated theme had some social significance but was not the focal point, and, despite the script's weaknesses in dramaturgy, the play was successful because it had wide popular appeal. FTP made a concerted effort to borrow sound effects used in movies and other cinematic techniques to offer entertainment that could compete with motion pictures. Reflecting this, Variety reviewed the production favorably:

> Big Blow is by no means a perfect work, but it provides an engrossing evening in the theatre and should have a satisfactory run . . . Yet, despite its incompletely worked out pattern, its disjointed plot development and its inconclusive scenes, the drama is studded with arresting characters. And when that wind begins to howl through the wings and roar across the footlights, it's enough to make even a hardy spectator cling to his seat. Much of the impressiveness of the Big Blow is due to the storm sound effects recorded from the sound track of Samuel Goldwyn's picture, Hurricane.[50]

George Sklar's Life and Death of an American was one of the major productions still running when the Project closed on June 30, 1939.[51] The production was a great success and proved to all detractors that FTP was not only an agency for relief but an important theatre organization employing highly talented artists in experimental productions that the commercial theatre would never attempt.

Opening May 19 at the Maxine Elliott, Life and Death of an American depicts the life of an American "Everyman," Jerry Dorgan, the first American born in the twentieth century--twelve seconds after midnight, January 1, 1900. From a poor Irish family, Dorgan had to drop out of college to support his mother after his father's death. He becomes a flyer in World War I and, during the prosperous period of the 1920s, gets an aviation drafting job because of his diligence and native intelligence.

When the Depression follows, Jerry loses his job, becomes involved in the labor movement, and is killed during a demonstration. In the original version, Sklar wanted Jerry Dorgan to go back to his first love, stunt flying, getting killed in one of the tests.

Originally written for the Theatre Union in 1937, plans for producing the play by that organization collapsed when it folded. It was then acquired by the FTP. Sklar had spent five years writing the play and nine years formulating it in his mind while collaborating with Albert Maltz on Merry Go Round and Peace on Earth, and with Paul Peters on Stevedore and Parade. Staged in 50 scenes, Life and Death of an American spans a period of almost forty years. Originally titled John Doe, the play was presented at the Maxine Elliott on a raked stage going upward to a height of three-and-one-half feet. It employed jazz music, torch songs, dance routines, and the slangy language of the "common man." These features, plus the impressive set by Howard Bay, incidental music by Alex North and Earl Robinson, the costumes by Alexander Jones, and dance routines by Lily Mehleman, gave the show its enormous excitement. The cast of 70 was headed by Arthur Kennedy and Mary Rolfe along with John Pete, Helen C. Ambrose, and Eleanor Scherer.[52]

Hallie Flanagan quoted Erwin Piscator as saying that Life and Death of an American was the "most superb stage production" he had ever seen in America. Even though the play differed in its style and theme, it was frequently compared to Kaufman and Hart's American Way because both plays attempted to capture the atmosphere and life of America during the turn-of-the-century.

Talking about the production and why it was selected, George Sklar
stated that George Kondolf, the New York Regional Director, welcomed
the play:

> He was excited about it, and I was quite delighted to have it
> done on the Project because it would reach a bigger audience
> and, too, because it was a very demanding play technically. It
> had an enormous cast; it was a multi-media thing long before
> multi-media things were being done. I mean, not only songs, but
> dance and movement; it was a multi-scene production and had a
> fluidity that was almost cinematic. Broadway couldn't afford to
> do a play like that; it was an art thing. The one misgiving I had
> about the thing was that Kondolf and, I guess, the director,
> Charles K. Freeman, wanted me to re-write the ending.[53]

Life and Death of an American was one of the most experimental
productions produced by FTP and a clear example of how innovations in
scene design and stage-craft in the late 1930s influenced playwriting
Borrowing the episodic structure of the Living Newspapers, the play
exemplified the early use of the "open stage." The epic form and style of
the production reflected the influences of Brecht and Piscator.Howard Bay,
the show's designer, credits Russian stage design and the ideas of Lee
Simonson and Mordecai Gorelik as strongly influencing his work in Life
and Death of an American. Sklar's play was one of the best examples of
an ambitious experimental production that never could have been
produced on Broadway, if not by the Federal Theatre.[54]

Critics applauded the ambitious nature of the production, but
generally agreed that the way the dramatic form was employed worked
against the telling of the play's story. The brevity of the many short,
sketchy episodes created the impression that the play was merely an
outline or scenario. The bareness of its construction made it seem

"clinical," "documentary," segmented, and lacking in warmth. Reviewers found the story routine and unconvincing. While the staging was hailed as a brilliant achievement, the pervasive opinion about the characterizations was that they were undeveloped and too generalized and lacking in substance.

John Mason Brown agreed with some critics who felt the play was "bare" to the point of being little more than a scenario; however, he defended Sklar's approach by saying, "His approach to his material is blessedly as free of jingoism as it is of shrill propaganda, and his method is arresting." Brown also felt that the play was, "a sequel if not an antidote to the flag-waving of the <u>American Way</u>." Defending further Sklar's work, he continued:

> If the writing of his individual scenes is hurried and often stereotyped, if a strange chill lurks upon even some of his supposedly most poignant episodes, and if ultimately his play is victimized by the very bareness of its outline form, there can be no denying either that Mr. Sklar's drama holds the attention or that it has been brilliantly stage.[55]

Again, this was another example of unqualified praise given to the director, lighting, and set designer for exalting a problematic play.

John Anderson was not in agreement with Brown's assessment. He saw the play as a scenario and clinical history,

> in which details are often vivid and challenging, yet lack the warmth and compassion to make the case dramatically moving. It is convincing without being emotionally stirring, and towards the end especially, his carefully built-up character takes on the laboratory aspect of an economic guinea pig. This is due partly to the brevity of the many episodes, the inevitable swiftness of the scenes, in covering so many years, and the fact that in

compressing such a biography into play length Mr. Sklar has written merely a scenario.[58]

The docu-drama approach did not convince Richard Lockridge, who stated: "it remains scrappy and segmented, like a landscape seen through a picket fence. . . . It is documentary rather than dramatic It is a chart of a typical life, and bloodless like a chart."[57]

Concurring generally with other critics, Brooks Atkinson elaborated:

When it is pungently written and staged with a flare, the epic form can be overwhelmingly emotional as it is in the Kaufman and Hart The American Way. But Mr. Sklar's writing is bare, his characters are poorly defined and his story is routine. Although the Federal Theatre has contrived an interesting production in skeletonized style, Life and Death of an American seems to this theatregoer to be only Horatio Alger in reverse--completely wanting in distinction. That is the substance of the biography. Mr. Sklar's style is compounded of expressionism and Living Newspaper techniques with songs and dances of the machine-shop interpolated. . . . What it lacks is what John Steinbeck has put into his epochal novel, The Grapes of Wrath--a warm understanding of character, intimate knowledge of the material, muscular strength and fierce passion for justice. Those are dramatic qualities. Life and Death of an American is scarcely more than the outline of a play.[58]

The Daily Worker did not approve the characterization of the worker as "everyman." According to John Cambridge, the main weakness in the play was the treatment of character:

The faults of the play, it seems to me, arise from the author's concentration on form rather than on his central character. There is a perhaps inescapable lack of essential surprise at any point in the narrative, but such emotional impact as it has derives more from external accidents than the internal dynamics of character . . . Mr. Sklar may retort that his Jerry is in fact the recognizable likeness of many a worker. The business of the dramatist, however, must be to probe beneath the surface: not to photograph, but to paint a portrait. A revolutionary dramatist especially has a great responsibility. His characters must not be puppets, but he must give to each individual his fullest personal value.[59]

This was a departure from the usual doctrinaire analysis given by the Daily Worker. Jerry should have been an individual, not a collective persona.

There is nothing concrete to suggest that the independent productions were helped or hindered by the policy change made by the new production board's guidelines. The non-allocated productions were among the most noteworthy presented by FTP.[60] They were noteworthy because in each case the FTP was doing something particular to reveal its strengths as a producing organization. It Can't Happen Here made history as FTP's and America's boldest theatrical venture. On The Rocks initiated the presentation of Shaw plays to Broadway audiences at popular prices. Big Blow revealed FTP's capacity to compete with motion pictures. Life and Death of an American was one of Federal Theatre's best examples of how experimental, challenging, and original FTP could be in producing a new play that would never have been considered for production in the commercial theatre. FTP did not hold strongly to its intention of focusing on new American plays, with three out of the four plays presented in the category of independent productions being foreign. All of the plays presented as non-allocated productions were plays that probably would never have been produced commercially. None, however, are being produced today.

144

Notes

<sup>1</sup>Information indicating the way productions were grouped into various categories, i.e., independent productions, non-allocated productions, is provided by the FTP Research Center at George Mason University.

<sup>2</sup>Flanagan, Arena, p. 69.

<sup>3</sup>Ibid.

<sup>4</sup>Synopsis at George Mason University.

<sup>5</sup>Press Release from FTP Department of Information, 17 February 1937.

<sup>6</sup>Flanagan, Arena, p. 127.

<sup>7</sup>Ibid., p. 117.

<sup>8</sup>Quoted in the Herald Tribune, 28 October 1936, from an article written by Flanagan for Federal Theatre Magazine.

<sup>9</sup>Sinclair Lewis, quoted in Flanagan, Arena, pp. 120-121.

<sup>10</sup>Flanagan, Arena, p. 116.

<sup>11</sup>Interview with H.L. Fishel conducted by Lorraine Brown, 26 October 1976. Tape at George Mason University.

<sup>12</sup>Synopsis at George Mason University.

<sup>13</sup>Flanagan, Arena, p. 119.

<sup>14</sup>Ibid., p. 120.

<sup>15</sup>Ibid., p. 121.

[16]Telephone conversation, Hallie Flanagan and Sinclair Lewis, 10 October 1936, quoted in Flanagan, Arena, p. 122.

[17]Ibid., p. 123.

[18]New York World Telegram, 28 October 1936.

[19]H.L. Fishel, Playreaders' Report, n.d.   At George Mason University.

[20]New York Times, 28 October 1936.

[21]Herald Tribune, 28 October 1936.

[22]oseph Wood Krutch, "Drama," Nation, 7 November 1936, pp. 557-58.

[23]Charles E. Dexter, "Sinclair Lewis Delivers a Telling Blow to Fascism," Daily Worker, 29 October 1936.

[24]Flanagan, Arena, p. 123.

[25]Hallie Flanagan to All State and Local Administrators, 4 November 1936.  At George Mason University.

[26]Memorandum citing attendance figures and critical response for Professor Mamlock, n.d.  At George Mason University.

[27]Synopsis at George Mason University.

[28]Burns Mantle, New York Times, 25 April 1937.

[29]World Telegram, 16 April 1937.

[30]Brooklyn Citizen, 14 April 1937.

[31]New York Bronx News, 29 January 1939.

[32]New York Times, 9 May 1937.

[33]New York Daily News, 14 April 1937.

[34]Morning Telegraph, 15 April 1937.

[35]The Theatre of Four Seasons headed by Charles Hopkins in Roslyn, Long Island was the headquarters of the New York State Unit. The Roslyn Unit production of No More Peace is considered as a New York City production because the Roslyn production was actually a try-out of the play for the Maxine Elliott production.

[36]Synopsis at George Mason University.

[37]Production report for No More Peace, written by Alfred B. Kuttner, 4 June 1937. At George Mason University.

[38]Publicity memorandum of the Play Bureau, 16 June 1938, p. 1. At George Mason University.

[39]Ibid.

[40]Ibid., pp. 2-3.

[41]Buffalo Courier Express, 25 June 1938.

[42]George Bernard Shaw, preface to On The Rocks, quoted in Burns Mantle, Buffalo Courier Express, 25 June 1938.

[43]New York Times, 16 June 1938.

[44]Daily Worker, 26 June 1938. The preface to On The Rocks was lengthy, explanatory, and discursive.

[45]New York Times, 16 June 1938.

[46]Ibid.

[47]Ibid.

[48]O'Connor and Brown, p. 109.

[49]Ibid., p. 110.

[50]Variety, 5 October 1938.

[51]Buttitta and Witham, p. 226. To announce the closing of the show after its playing a little over a month, the play's director, Charles Freeman, told a shocked audience that FTP ceased to exist. "Quite simply, we have been eliminated."

[52]Press Release from FTP Department of Information, 15 May 1939. Record Group 69, United States National Archives.

[53]O'Connor and Brown, p. 203.

[54]Ibid., p. 204.

[55]New York Evening Post, 20 May 1939.

[56]New York Evening Journal, 20 May 1939.

[57]New York Sun, 20 May 1939.

[58]New York Times, 20 May 1939.

[59]Daily Worker, 22 May 1939.

[60]Non-allocated productions means the same as independent production, as defined by the FTP Research Center, George Mason University.

# CHAPTER VI
## SPECIALIZED THEATRES

Along with the Popular Price, the Managers' Try-Out, and the Experimental, there were various smaller specialized theatres initiated in New York City, which also became early FTP casualties. These units were the One-Act Experimental Theatre, the Poetic Theatre, the American Historical Theatre, the Irish Players, and the Variety unit. The lives of these smaller groups were cut short due to budget cutting and to the new production board's re-structuring, which took place during the early part of 1937. In some instances their termination was prompted by poor critical response to production efforts. The specialized units did only one production each.

The specialized units were set up to do new plays during the early part of FTP's career in New York. It is misleading to call them small because they were created to employ a large number of unemployed theatre workers, particularly actors, and in some cases, they hired over 100 workers in the various artistic and technical categories

Each specialized unit was initiated to offer performances in a particular type of theatrical activity. Although the artists were generally young and relatively inexperienced, they compensated for their lack of experience with a special enthusiasm for doing experimental and innovative work. Critics frequently expressed a certain condescension toward the work of these small units; they forgot that 90% of the actors had to be professional in order to work for FTP and referred to them at times as amateurs. It was almost as if the reservations some critics had about the legitimacy of FTP or its potential to do meaningful performances were maximized when reviewing the productions of the small units.

Generally, critics did not take the work seriously enough to comment very extensively on the playwriting. Instead, reviewers devoted space to the acting, the physical production, and direction.

The One-Act Experimental did an evening of one acts: Shaw's "The Great Catherine" and Emjo Basshe's new anti-war play, "The Snickering Horses." Moliere's Miser was also presented on that program. The Poetic Theatre opened and closed doing W.H. Auden's Dance of Death. The only production of the American Historical Theatre was The Ballad of Davy Crockett. The Studio Theatre presented The Cherokee Night and Tobias and the Angel. The Irish Players did Mr. Jiggins in Jigginstown and the Variety Unit performed Machine Age.

The One-Act Experimental's evening of one-acts was presented on May 13, 1936, at the Experimental (Daly) Theatre. New Theatre Magazine published a synopsis of "The Snickering Horses":

A satire against war (one act) using the montage technique. There is a monologue by the bartender which is the only portion suitable for our purpose. The Bartender was paid by Mr. Fullerton, owner of a meat packing corporation, to take his place in the trenches, with the assurance that if anything happened, he'd be taken care of for life. So when he comes home in a basket, he's reconstructed of aluminum, etc. and given a job in Fullerton's smart nightclub--"The Trench Rat." There's a celebration in the bar (forget what for). After a drinking bout the scene changes. The Bartender begins to relive the (telescoped) experience of trench warfare. The horror is symbolized by means of identifying the horses who pull the stuck artillery out of the mud, and are blown to bits,--with the soldiers --only the horses are smarter. They know enough to snicker at the hocus-pocus of "dying for God and Country." The soldiers, blown to chunks, are now on a par with the ice-packed five-star beef shipped East to feed the army, only the corpses are shipped West (also on ice) to be delivered to their respective families, at the back door, along with the milk and the morning paper. Lights, sound effects, etc. suggest trench fighting.[1]

Directed by Maurice Clark, the play in four short scenes shows the relationship between the man fighting at the front and the people who stay at home. The scene breakdown is given by Clark:

Scene 1

In which the soldier is asked to take the place of the Meat Packer, so that the Meat Packer can stay at home and fulfill his duty by supplying the Army. The soldier agrees

Scene 2

The soldier at the front with flashback interludes showing the various works being done "at Home."

1. FLASH-The chorus that sings cheerful songs. "Keep the Home Fires Burning," etc

2. FLASH-The appeal being made for funds, etc

3. FLASH-The Judge condemning Conscientious Objectors

Back to the front again and the disabling of the soldier

Scene 3 Armistice-The soldier comes back, the Meat Packer promises to help him and gets him artificial arms to take the place of those he has lost for him. . .

Scene 4 The soldier forms his own conclusions.[2]

Beginning his review by posing the question, "Are amateur actors people? And if so, must they eat?" Burns Mantle answered in the affirmative: "The young people of the municipal unit (One-Act Experimental) entered into the evening's activity with more enthusiasm than understanding, but also with the best intentions." However, he also indicated that they performed with facility: "There was considerable skill displayed in the projection of the anti-war item. Most of it was acted back of a mesh screen in which a series of titles was displayed carrying the action forward and indicating the location of scenes."[3] More than 100 performers, stage technicians, and other workers were employed for the production of the three plays. The Variety reviewer stated: "It is a chattery and undeveloped theme, juvenile in thought, and from an acting standpoint, amateurish."[4]

The Studio Theatre, located at the Provincetown Playhouse on McDougall Street, functioned, along with the Community Drama group, under the umbrella of the Teaching of Theatre Technique Unit. Madolyn O'Shea was its Managing Producer. The purpose and plan of the Teaching Unit was described in the program for The Cherokee Night:

PURPOSE: Since many of these directors are highly specialized in some particular branch of the theatre, they have not the complete equipment to take over full supervision of a community theatre. The purpose of the Studio Theatre is to equip these directors with training and techniques, supplementing their present knowledge, qualifying them as authoritative directors in the field of community drama, and preparing them for whatever positions private industry opens up in this field
PLAN OF OPERATION: A group of thirty-five directors is brought in from the community drama field to the Studio Theatre for training in the various branches of play production. In eight weeks this group makes the costumes, constructs the scenery and rehearses under the direction of the production staff. The play is then presented for two weeks. At the end of which time, these directors return to their community centers and a new group is brought in.[5]

Lynn Rigg's The Cherokee Night, which opened July 20, 1936, depicted the struggle of the American Indian, and particularly of one half-breed attempting to reconcile his heritage with the demands made upon him by modern civilization:

Episodes in the lives of several Cherokee Indians are depicted against a background of Claremore Mount in the Cherokee Nation. Bee, a whore, betrays a murderer, also a former friend. Viney, ashamed of her Indian blood, visits her married sister and is denounced. Hutch, Art, and Gar, three youngsters, find the spot where a negro was murdered and instinctively do a war dance. Gar runs away from school, finds himself a prisoner in the mountains near Claremore Mount where religious fanatics are holding services. He is offered his freedom, but prefers to stay and face the bullet he knows is coming rather than get it in the back. Hutch is living with an Osage girl. She has money. He has ease. His brother, college educated, visits him. Hutch disowns his brother. His brother advises him to go back to his farm and his horses. Chides him for taking money from an Osage, once the enemy of the Cherokee. At the finish, Spench, Gar's father, is hunted and shot by white men. Before he dies, he explains to a full-blooded Cherokee, Gray- Wolf, "I tried ever'-thing. Tried to farm. Too restless. Cattle herdin', ridin' fence. Sump'n always drove me on. The bosses! Burned down their barns, rustled their cattle, slept with their wives. Shot the bastard down--Sump'n inside--no rest, I don't know--Bad blood. Too much Indian, they tell me." Gray-Wolf replies, "Not enough Indian."[6]

The Cherokee Night had been first presented in 1932 by Jasper Deeter at the Hedgerow Theatre in Maylan Rose Valley, Pennsylvania, and since had become popular with little theatre groups around the country. The Studio Theatre production was its first in New York City.

The Cherokee Night was interesting because it was one of the few new FTP plays to use a non-linear narrative structure. Critics viewed it as a creative anomaly. Its episodic structure was described by the New York World Telegram as,

> an oddly constructed drama of supernatural mood and of an unchronological design. . . . Scurrying from time and place, he (Riggs) describes the thinning Cherokee blood and the passing of the Cherokee pride . . . into the corrupt influences of modern life. . . . Disjointedly, Mr. Riggs has recounted this tragedy of his people, transposing the scenes in a loose time sequence. . . And so poetic and stirring as it stands, it must lack a general appeal to many and interest the few who can admire creative unconventionality.

Despite this and the fact that the production was "Handicapped . . . by the pygmy breadth of the Provincetown Playhouse stage," the director, Anton Bundsman, is credited with creating a "remarkable effect," and the players "caught the spirit of the work and the futility of the theme."[7]

Writing in the Sunday Worker, Percy McAllister was concerned about the play's focus. Although he regarded Riggs as a talented playwright who "writes with sheer beauty of phrase and effect" and one whose characters "are round and easy to look upon," McAllister wished that the author "only knew in which direction humanity is moving." Despite Rigg's knowledge of the American plains and desert, the West and Southwest, and his sensitivity to the plight of the Indians, the reviewer wished that the playwright could "only strip away the confusion and see the truth." In effect, the truth, as McAllister saw it, was that:

> The Government seized the Indians' land and distributed it freely to sufferers from the great economic crisis of 1892. Since the days of the "land rush," these, in turn, have lost their all to

greed--land-hungry monopolies. Cherokees, Irish, German, Negroes alike have been victims, workers who might have lived side by side in peace and harmony, who might have created in the glorious South- west a civilization unique in history.

Finally McAllister implored Riggs, "Here is the story you will write if you look away from pity and beauty and poignancy and toward greed-- rapacious greed--power in the hands of the few."[8] Journalists of the left had a wide readership in New York during the thirties, so these statements were taken seriously by readers when they decided which shows to see.

The next production presented by the Studio Theatre was Tobias and the Angel, a fantasy by Scottish playwright James Bridie, that opened April 28, 1937. Bridie's Storm Over Patsy had been seen recently on Broadway. Tobias and the Angel is a dramatization of the Biblical characters found in the Apocryphal Book of Tobit. The story relates how the young and simple-minded Tobias embarks on the long, adventurous task of regaining the money that his blind father, Tobit, had loaned twenty years earlier to a friend in Northern Persia. The Archangel Raphael appears in an earthly form to guide and protect the young man on his journey. Together they endure many hardships, and Tobias is never aware of his companion's true identity. Eventually, thanks to old Raphael, Tobias returns safely home far richer than when he left. Finally Raphael reveals his identity, and his ultimate good deed is to bless Tobit's righteousness by restoring his sight.[9]

The work of the Studio Theatre was done in cramped space. Some critics were sympathetic to the problem; others, however, deprecated the group's efforts. To Burns Mantle, the twelve-foot-wide stage at the Provincetown was used to advantage, "achieving a frequest suggestion of beauty and pretty successfully minimizing the cramped and tortured type of small stage production."[10]

In reviewing Tobias and the Angel, one critic mentioned that, although the Studio Theatre was a director's workshop, the acting and directing were "pedestrian." Gould Cassal, writing in the Brooklyn Eagle, was not too favorably impressed:

> It is a simple, obvious story told with humor and occasional bits of adroit writing, but it never forces itself into effective drama or comedy. The imitations of Shavian epigrams never go beyond the familiar formula of "All men are so-and-so," "All women are so-and- so" and the like, and much of the humor is built on references to modern appliances. . . . [the actors] lack the experience necessary to project a semi-intellectual vehicle which demands suave playing.[11]

A common criticism leveled by reviewers at the work of the small theatres was that it, including the writing, was "arty" and pseudo-intellectual. Again, FTP actors were criticized for not being able to rise to the quality of the material in their performances.

Another short-lived venture, the Poetic Theatre, also had a tenuous existence. During the early months of 1936, Alfred Kreymborg set down plans for and defined the purpose of the Poetic Theatre:

> The formation of a permanent repertory company for the production of poetic dramas, classic and modern, whether in verse or prose, with special emphasis on the development of poetic drama by Americans. . . . The company will work toward the perfection of an American "style" in the theatre, a style expressive of our own lives and traditions, a style profound and real enough to affect a future, as well as the present, generation--a style, in short, which is poetic and not anemic, artistic and not "arty." . . . The word, poetic, is used in its broadest meanings. Where the people arrive at a point of common experience, as in the present era, the work of the poet-dramatist begins. He works in materials reflecting the race, and

shapes them into timeless forms. The prose writer who survives his time may also be called a poet-dramatist. It is the aim of the American poetic theatre to select plays which are timeless or have a timeless tendency.[12]

In a letter to Hallie Flanagan, Kreymborg stated his goals for the Poetic Theatre:

> Our further plans include Flecker's Hassan; my own There's A Moon Tonight, or four related one-acters with an economic background; An American Festival, a lusty review made up of skits, monologues, mass recitals, music and ballet; and a new play, possibly, by Cummings, and one by MacLeish. There is also The Dog Beneath The Skin. And one of the Aristophanic anti-war plays in modern dress. And I still cling to Anderson's Winesburg. We have also been offered a new version of Philip Barry's White Wings, with music by Douglas Moore of Columbia. And Lester Lang has suggested that I get in touch with Ida Hoyt Chamberlain with a view of putting on a Chinese classic. If I don't stop here, the list will go on and on. The main point is, we want to work, continuously and joyously. My group has forgotten all about the dole they graduated from. Handicaps or no handicaps, they want to move forward.

As a "P.S." he wrote, "I'm even dreaming of putting on some short American operas. Who's loony now?"[13]

The first and only play actually presented by the Poetic Theatre was W.H. Auden's poetic drama, The Dance of Death, which opened at the Adelphi, May 19, 1936. It was directed by Emile Beliveau with music by Clair Leonard. The review in the New York Times gave a clear description of the theme and dramatic action, characterizing the production as a joining of music, dance, and acting in a "theatrical wedlock":

> Death is a dancer, and the class is the middle class in flight, as the play begins, from reality and itself. The musical comedy-

ballet which follows sends the bourgeoisie from one aspect of decadence to another, from simple-minded love of nature to sentimentality, to Fascist regimentation and, finally, into a wild night club fling in which they collapse under the freight of their own stupidity. Comes the shadow of Karl Marx, huge behind a backdrop, to pronounce a dictum on the dying dancer: "The instruments of production have been too much for him. He is liquidated."[14]

The segments in Act One are titled:

1. Overture  2. Prologue  3. Come out in the Sun  4. The Cunarder Waltz  5. The Sun God Dance  6. The Soldiers of the King of Kings 7. The Demogogue Dance  8. The Ship of State  9. The Doctor 10. The Country Colony.  ACT TWO contains: 1. Prelude 2. The Flight into the Unknown  3. Alma Mater Night Club  4. The Will of History  5. The Gothic Rhumba  6. The Wedding March 7. The Dead March.[15]

Dance of Death, about the death of capitalism, seems not to have been taken too seriously by any of the critics except Charles Dexter. Most reviewers did not feel that the life of the bourgeosie would end imminently. In fact, most of the comments were about how entertaining the show was. The Wall Street Journal assured its readers that there was nothing to worry about and then proceeded to describe the stage action in such a way that it revealed why the whole event seemed more like a satire of itself than a serious philosophical statement. It explained that there was nothing macabre about the play, but that rather it was "raucous and roguishly rowdy." The dancing was described as "derived from Bernarr McFadden's antics." The speech was mocked, "There is a speaker who proclaims with a broad A the predicament of the working clawsses [sic]; the lines are unintelligible and in some instances unintelligent." The reviewer hastened to warn the readers that "savage satire" was confused with slapstick in the production. The acting was characterized as,

> The players flutter up and down the aisles. After every solemn bit . . . seem not just sure of their purpose (interpretation); stooges walk around out and hurl directions and advice. All that was lacking was the four Marx Brothers. . . . The cast indulges in a mild orgy amid much raving of empty glasses, and a lot of sing-song about modern decadence, frivolity and the like, all set to a blues melody while the symbolic dancer writhes on the floor in his death throes; then come the Revolutionary--and the dying and dead drag themselves away. . . . there must be some deep, mystic symbolism in the Dancer's frenzy against raincoats, but the meaning of it is far from clear.

He found the characters amusing: "Itsy, Bitsy, Mistress Longley, Mistress Swoonem, Master Gracious, Master Blondy, a decadent Duchess, a gigolo and a Motherly Soul, to say nothing of an erotician."[16]

John Mason Brown felt that the poetry failed to live up to Kreymborg's lofty intentions for his unit:

> Mr. Auden proves a very incompetent undertaker in arranging the burial of the bourgeoise class. His scheme is serviceable enough as a whole. It is moonstruck enough to satisfy even the most arty of the Sunday night dance-recital clan. In its broader outlines it is frequently as imaginative as it is bizarre. But it turns out to be a dance allegory that trips up over the details of its poetry. It is in his single verses that Mr. Auden fails himself and his audience. At times they seem to be poor copies of the ingenuousness which went into the writing of the Lutterworth Christmas play. At times they are sourly Gilbertian in their influence. At other times they sound as if they must have been found in Mr. Coward's scrap basket. But at most times, when they are audible above the group mumblings of the chorus, they are as ineffective as:

"He's Marvelous
He's Greek
When I see him
My legs go weak
He walks with such grace
Just like a cat
Where's my kodak
I must snap him just like that"[17]

Charles Dexter, the only critic who took the message seriously, was pleased that the play presented Fascism as an expression of the Capitalist system:

This then is Mr. Auden's historical record of what is indubitably true, the passing of a class. But he fails to point out that death is not a solution, that the petty bourgeosie dies in the decadence of its own system but finds renewed life in the bosom of the working class. . . . If it is optimistic, word could have been broadcast at the conclusion of The Dance of Death, perhaps even the old-school producer might have understood. Even so the shadow of revolution hovers over the spectacle; and it is to Mr. Auden's credit that he has characterized Fascism as the expression of the Capitalist system, a will which must inevitably blend before the force of historical events.[18]

Kreymborg did not fulfill the intentions for his unit. For the production of Dance of Death, neither the poet-dramatist, nor the style of the production was American. In all of the laughing about the production, with the Wall Street Journal being the least threatened by capitalism's death, the lofty purposes of the unit, and its only production were generally ridiculed. What is not clear from all of the information available is how seriously the unit intended to convey its message. Reactions given by various reviewers tend to imply that the whole venture may have been a manifestation of intentional camp.

The Irish Players, a part of the FTP Manhattan-Bronx Unit, announced on the program for its presentation of Mr. Jiggins of Jigginstown its policy "to bring you (the audience) contemporary and representative plays and performers." Regarding its selection of Mr. Jiggins of Jigginstown, the reason offered was that the play was a "light comedy . . . representative of changing Ireland and is built around the Irish landowners. Lady Langord, its author, is a well known contributor to Irish drama." The fact-based play was first produced at the Dublin Gate Theatre, March 25, 1933, and was then presented in Cork, Trales, and Birr. This production was its first in America.[19]

The storyline is as follows:

Mr. Jiggins is an old man and his relatives gather to see what they can do toward influencing his will. An Anglicized cousin and her two children offend his Irish sensibilities as well as his humane qualities by their callous social and political opportunism, and his young Irish cousin seems well assured of the heritage. However, his mild infatuation for the daughter of the Anglicized cousin complicates matters and leads him into indiscretions which show Mr. Jiggins his true nature. After using the young man's avarice as a means of getting the other away, Mr. Jiggins asserts his disgust and, calling his solicitor, wills his entire estate to charity.[20]

Not a play of great substance or "social significance," nor one that fulfills the theatre's purposes, its opening December 17, 1936, at the Labor Stage (formerly the Princess Theatre) was probably best characterized by the New York World Telegram:

The newly renovated, impressively simple Labor Stage . . . opened with a play last night which scarcely lives up to the promise suggested in the theater's name or its ideals. It was a little something the WPA Federal Theatre sponsored, possibly in the hopes of shuffling it through the holiday season. . . . the batting and trapping is entangled in philosophical dissertations several of them not without typical Irish earthiness and charm, but for the most part plodding. . . . For the audience seemed to have little patience for this dull, slow moving and actionless importation.[21]

The Variety Theatre, set up to utilize the talents of vaudevillians, presented a new musical comedy, Machine Age which "In two acts and twenty-four scenes . . . give us a fantastic commentary on the amusement industry in particular and the foibles of big business, labor, the courts, the press, and hill-billies."[22] It was presented at the Majestic Theatre in Brooklyn, from April 30 to May 29, 1937. William Sully wrote the book and lyrics, and Bert Reed provided the music. Machine Age was described by the Times Union as only "a number of venerable vaudeville acts frightened together by the ghost of a story."[23]

In Machine Age and Sing for Your Supper, Federal Theatre created musicals about vaudevillians or other unemployed actors, singers, and dancers put to work. This was also done, as we will see, in musicals in Chicago, Los Angeles, San Francisco, and Portland.

Historical plays were given emphasis during the early days of FTP. The American Historical Theatre, formed in 1935, presented its first production, The Ballad of Davy Crockett by H.R. Hays, in May 1936. Variety related the story as follows:

Taking one of the Davy Crockett ballads as a base, Hays's play fits each of the six scenes against the background of a corresponding verse in the ballad. Before the scene is presented, a pair of oldsters, with fiddle and concertina, emerge in a box close to the stage and rip off the proper ballad verse in hillbilly vein. Burlesque keynote is struck right away, and when the curtain goes up, the illusion persists that the actors are ladling out old-time melodrama straight as a die. Crockett is successively depicted as running away from home, holding conversation in the forest with animals, running for Congress on a ticket against land sharks, squabbling with President Jackson, and finally dying in the Alamo in an attempt to swipe Texas from the Mexicans. Conversing with animals and dying in the Alamo within an hour of each other is a tough acting assignment, and it's no fault of Hiram Hoover that he muffs it.[24]

The Ballad of Davy Crockett was not well received by critics. Variety described the production: "This is the type of play which leads a fair company into immediate hot water, and any lesser troupe into unconscious burlesque." The review explained that the sixty WPA players were "resigned to the burlesque keynote from the very start" and thought that the production defined Davy Crockett "about as well as the Hyksos dynasty of Old Egypt. . . . Nothing here to interest Broadway even remotely, though for the pictures, the Crockett theme might be a timely idea with the Texas Centennial on tap."[25]

John Gassner, in New Theatre, observed that Davy Crockett, "represents the pioneer element that was responsible for the successive waves of democratic protest without which the encroachments of finance and industrialism would have remained unchallenged." He stressed that Crockett's tragedy was that, as a result of his efforts to open up the West, the speculators became richer as land and liberty decreased for him and other pioneers. The play was seen as depicting the "defeat of pioneer America" and revealing that, "When the free land was gobbled up by the speculators something noble and poetic was lost from American life."

Hays's work was a "genuine attempt to weld folk-poetry and historical criticism."[26]

Here were two fundamentally different ways of looking at the content and form of a play. Variety's focus was on how commercial the play was; John Gassner's attention centered on how critical was the social analysis. FTP had to always try to satisfy different segments of its critical audience.

Opinions expressed in the Daily Worker, New Theatre, New Masses, and other left-oriented periodicals were significant because Federal Theatre was attracting a new, widely diversified, popular audience. Among the members of this new audience were left-leaning intellectuals, and a very large working class. Because FTP was not allowed to advertise, it had to rely on opinions reflected in the press, and word-of-mouth praise to publicize shows. Critics reviewing for the Worker and other Marxist papers and journals were addressing themselves to a very large readership in New York. Although they were technically not mainstream critics, their views held great sway over FTP's potential audience.

Variety revealed to Federal Theatre's management how its efforts were being responded to by proponents of commercial theatre. Eventually, the contrasting opinions expressed in the left periodicals, and the trade papers like Variety, came to haunt WPA theatre when it was being investigated by the Dies Committee for Un-American Activities.

One interesting venture of the FTP was the Community Drama unit which planned to use "social dramas" to reform "problem" neighborhoods. The unit's first play, Gravesend, depicted the social characteristics of the Gravesend section of Brooklyn. As reported in a newspaper article dated

April 29, 1937, the drama was to be presented in four elementary schools: P.S. 95, 212, 213, and 248. The children in the schools, as well as the principals and teachers, were to perform. The program was a pilot to determine whether school problems could be solved with the full cooperation of all members of the community.[27]

Three FTP playwrights were assigned to the project by the Play Bureau: Irving Kapner, Joseph Liss, and Rose Siegel. They explained that the Gravesend district resembled a Tobacco Road in "squalor and isolation." The area was populated by 30,000 inhabitants, 85 percent of whom were Italians who had moved to Gravesend from Manhattan's East Side. The other inhabitants were mostly the original settlers, the Scotch-Irish lobster fishermen whose livelihood was ruined by the pollution in Gravesend Bay. It was an area characterized as one in which:

Many still live in old wooden shacks, in which, up to 1925, they were squatters. More than 50 per cent of the families are on home relief. Some of the streets are muddy roads, and lighting is so poor parents fear to allow their daughters outdoors at night. Nearby is the Rubel plant that was robbed of $427,000 not long ago. There is a number of cellar clubs and a high rate of delinquency.[28]

The project was intended to instruct Gravesend residents. Reactions would be solicited from audiences after each performance. Plans to extend the activity to other communities were indicated in the article, but additional information about the unit's development is not available.

Despite the short life of the small specialized theatres, one sees, in their work and in their visions, the kind of energy and vitality generated by the FTP attempting to realize high aspirations. In reviewing the work of the New York units in fostering the presentation of new plays--even while considering once more the FTP's brief tenure-- one can ascertain the kind of grand scale, artistically challenging productions which could be ventured under the sponsorship of a federally subsidized theatre. The achievements of the New York City Federal Theatre Project left a significant impression in the annals of American theatrical history.

Notes

[1]New Theatre Magazine, 12 December 1934.

[2]Scene breakdown for "Snickering Horses," One-Act Experimental file. At George Mason University.

[3]New York Daily News, 14 May 1936.

[4]Variety, 20 May 1936.

[5]Program for The Cherokee Night. At George Mason University.

[6]Synopsis at George Mason University.

[7]New York World Telegram, 21 July 1936.

[8]Sunday Worker, 26 July 1936.

[9]Synopsis at George Mason University.

[10]Daily News, 29 April 1937.

[11]Brooklyn Eagle, 29 April 1937.

[12]Plans for the Poetic Theatre prepared by Alfred Kreymborg, n.d., n.p. At Billy Rose Collection.

[13]Alfred Kreymborg to Hallie Flanagan, 16 February 1936. At Billy Rose Collection.

[14]New York Times, 20 May 1936.

[15]Program for Dance of Death. At George Mason University.

[16]Wall Street Journal, 22 May 1936.

[17]New York Evening Post, 21 May 1936.

[18]Daily Worker, 24 May 1936.

[19]Program for Mr. Jiggins of Jigginstown. At George Mason University.

[20]Synopsis at George Mason University.

[21]New York World Telegram, 18 December 1936.

[22]Brooklyn Citizen, 1 May 1937.

[23]Times Union [Brooklyn], 1 May 1937.

[24]Variety, 27 May 1936.

[25]Ibid.

[26]New Theatre, July 1936, pp. 6, 27.

[27]Newspaper article dated 29 April 1937, source unknown. Located at the Billy Rose Collection.

[28]Ibid.

PART II

REGIONAL UNITS


A theatre speaking for the Eastern cosmopolis, for the West, the Midwest, and the South, . . . [is] increasingly necessary not only for the few who can afford it but for the many who cannot. Such a theatre can interpret region to region, emphasizing the united aspect of the states, and illuminate the United States for the other Americas. Such a theatre can oppose destructive forces without and within, a positive, creative force, a formidible upthrust of power against the death force of ignorance, greed, fear, and prejudice. Such a theatre is a life force, creating for our citizens a medium for freedom such as no other form of government can assure and offering people access to the arts, and tools of civilization which they themselves are helping to make. Such a theatre is at once an illustration and a bulwark of the democratic form of government.

Hallie Flanagan

# CHAPTER VII
## THE EAST
(Connecticut, Maine, Massachusetts, New Hampshire,
New Jersey, New York, Pennsylvania, Rhode Island, Vermont)[1]

Boston was the centripetal force in the Eastern Region. Plays were given try-outs in Salem and then transferred there. Hallie Flanagan characterized Boston as having a project that more than any other made FTP a successful venture under very difficult circumstances. The new plays produced in that city ended up being triumphs because of judicious selection and careful negotiation. FTP had a rough beginning in Boston; however, since the local critics were so loyal and supportive to FTP from the very start, the city famous for banning plays ended up receiving much acclaim for its work. Nonetheless, Flanagan was not always entirely enthusiastic about her colleagues.

Because of Boston's tradition of censoring plays, FTP tread lightly in that city to avoid controversy--anything reflecting economic conditions, politics, or the contemporary social scene in a way that would not be "traditional." This is perhaps why Boston favored the production of the classics, particularly when they were staged effectively in a competent, professional manner. However, revivals and recent Broadway successes and even the classics were criticized.

Hiram Motherwell was the Eastern Regional Director from October 1935 to April 1936, and it was during his tenure that most of the Eastern projects were established. However, even during the early planning period, censorship threatened his aspirations. Massachusetts FTP officials and Hallie Flanagan had a "banned in Boston" kind of censorship problem when Maxwell Anderson's Valley Forge (a revival of a recent Theatre Guild hit presented in February 1936) was criticized by a selectman from Plymouth who objected to the play for very obscure reasons. Later it was established that this selectman owned two movie houses in Plymouth and did not welcome competition. Flanagan countered the call for censorship by stating that the play was by a recognized American dramatist and that its production by the Theatre Guild had won critical acclaim. She also emphasized that Valley Forge was a highly-lauded runner-up for a Pulitzer Prize and dealt with an aspect of American history very relevant to the East. Despite these protestations made to the Massachusetts state administrator, Paul Edwards, the play was banned.

Because of this early confrontation, Edwards made a policy statement which set the tone for future FTP endeavors, commenting in the Boston Globe, "The people of Massachusetts are going to have the type of plays they want--not the type of plays a small group wishes to promote. If there is any scandal on the Federal Theatre Project, I intend to get to the bottom of it and clean it up."[2] The next day he stated that a Board of Censorship would be appointed "to prevent the production of such plays as Valley Forge." He included Winterset and Twelfth Night in his criticism in a veiled excuse for not producing those shows.

However, Edwards later realized in August 1936 that strict guidelines and censorship would never allow his state, and specifically Boston, to do challenging new productions that could be as illustrious and publicized as those done in New York. He was encouraged to soften his position, and consequently, did not establish a Board of Censorship. However, the Boston Project still felt the sting of the events surrounding the whole affair. Later, when recalling the incidents involving Edwards and his guidelines, Flanagan reflected that Edwards's initial position was similar to the position taken by many FTP regional directors who wanted the notoriety and glamour gained by the New York City units in doing risky plays, but were unwilling to take chances that could provoke local criticism.[3]

Despite initial conflicts regarding censorship, Flanagan hoped that Boston could develop its own unique approach and work on projects such as a chronicle history of the Constitution or the Boston Tea Party. However, these suggestions were not acted upon with much initiative. This, among other factors, prompted Hiram Motherwell to leave his position as Eastern Regional Director to assume the position of head of the national Play Policy Board. Flanagan, disheartened by Boston's poor initiative, suggested discontinuing the allocation of funds to that Project. It was scheduled to close in June 1936. However, further administrative changes were suggested and implemented. Consequently, the Project continued and the entire character of the Boston Project changed.

George Gerwing, an experienced FTP man, a former Assistant Director in California, replaced Motherwell as Eastern Regional Director. The appointment created a new impetus. Gerwing fostered the production of new plays, and the Eastern branch of the National Service Bureau increased its dedication to developing projects that were vitally and uniquely Eastern.[4]

The first new play presented in Boston was <u>Lucy Stone</u> by Maude Wood Park, first National President of the League of Women Voters. The play ran May 9-20, 1936. The Boston University Women's Council sponsored the opening which was attended by Park and Alice Stone Blackwell, Lucy Stone's daughter. The play, dealing with the life of the

Boston suffragist, was, according to Hallie Flanagan, limited in its general appeal due to its local historical interest. Reviewers agreed that the play was narrow in its appeal, and were generally not warmly receptive to the production.[5]

The second production of a new play in Massachusetts was American Wing by Talbot Jennings. It was presented in Salem, March 1419, 1938. The official play list of the Bureau of Research and Publication describes the play as about "contemporary social problems with a New England setting." In it, one "is shown how power and money in a 300-year-old American family has been used to loot America of its natural resources for the specific benefit of the family."[6]

The play tells how Gilbert Brown, "descendant of a long line of American statesmen and capitalists, wishes to use his family prestige to help put over an unsavory political deal." To accomplish this, he lures Morton, a young writer, to chronicle the family history using family documents and records. In working on the book, Morton discovers that the Browns had stolen public land. Gilbert Brown forces the writer to suppress the truth. However, Morton, during the writing of the book, has fallen in love with Brown's wife, who urges Morton to expose the facts. The book is written that bares the truth, but it cannot be published uncensored. Meanwhile, the 1929 Wall Street Crash destroys the Brown fortune, causing Gilbert's nephew to commit suicide. Finally, with his life devastated, Brown agrees to have an uncensored version of the family history published.[7]

Converse Tyler recommended the play to Francis Bosworth, Supervisor of the Play Bureau, as "a play that fulfills more than adequately all of the requirements for an intelligent, effective drama of the American scene. . . . The author clearly shows a liberal point of view but keeps obvious propaganda at arm's length." Tyler continued to praise the play as one developed with "delicacy and restraint . . . but [still exposing] those who have used great names and superior advantage to rob America of her resources." Tyler indicated that its contrived, obvious ending was "logical."[8]

The official FTP play list recommended the play without reservations, indicating, "The author has a true sense of the theatre and literature. He handles the situations he has created extremely well. His exposition of the social evil of big money in a few hands is true and written about convincingly."[9] Despite the play list's official endorsements, playreader Judson O'Donnell disagreed. He found the theme significant but the writing incompetent, and that the characters were unbelievable and contrived by the author to promote his viewpoint. Commenting further, O'Donnell found the exposition "very bad" and "hopelessly clumsy," the pace "sluggish," and the dialogue "rambling and literary." He also indicated that during emotional climaxes the author descended into "talkiness."[10] Fleet Munson reported that it was "collegiate" and "darned smooth," and only recommended it for summer theatre and Western stock.[11]

The decision to produce American Wing reflected FTP criteria for play selection. The play was regional in the sense that it dealt with the story of an old New England family and, most particularly, a family of "old money." Tyler's endorsement stressed "liberalism" rather than bold "propaganda" that would cause the kind of controversies the WPA officials were trying to avoid. It was a "social play," redeemed from its dramaturgical weaknesses by a "delicacy" and "restraint"--meaning the message was employed gently. These were the priorities that overshadowed any inherent shortcomings in the dramaturgy.

FTP did not have specific criteria for play selection, only very general guidelines. Younger, less influential readers usually pointed out weaknesses in the writing in their reports. However, their comments frequently showed lack of experience or knowledge and the reader's social, political, and literary biases. It must be remembered that the playreaders were usually aspiring writers. They were not always too eager to promote the writing of their peers, who would be nurtured by being given a Federal Theatre production. Sometimes the responses of critics were less politically biased, and more supportive or partisan to FTP. The readers' biased opinions frequently hindered their task of approving plays appropriate for Federal Theatre.

The most noteworthy production done in the Eastern region was Created Equal, written and directed by John Hunter Booth, presented first in Salem, May 24-28, 1938, then at the Copley Theatre in Boston, June 27-30, 1938. The theme of the play, as stated by playreader Henry Bennett, was "The struggle for true liberty throughout the course of American history."[12] Created Equal was a documentary that borrowed techniques of the Living Newspapers to depict (in two acts and 27 scenes) episodes in American history from the signing of the Declaration of Independence up to the 1930s. Eighty performers were in this pageant-like cavalcade of key moments: Declaration of Independence, Revolutionary War, the writing of the Constitution, the Dred Scot Decision, the Civil War, the era of the "industrial overlords," the Great War, the Crash of 1929, the Bonus Marches on Washington, and Roosevelt's 1932 election. The spectacle ended with the message that the United States was still in the process of achieving the ideals and aims for which it fought in 1776. The "Dedicatory" in the play's program stated:

To those keen students of American history, who re-live in their thoughts the trials and vicissitudes of their forefathers--to the boys and girls whose minds are now impressed with the deeds of our most illustrious great--to the patriotic Americans whose most glorious inheritance is the noble thought and daily prayer that America will always be supreme--to that solid great majority of our citizens from whom emanates the continual flow of ideals that still allows for a spirit of fair play--and lastly in respectful reverence to those most worthy souls and spirits, whose very deeds and acts we are dramatizing tonight.[13]

Converse Tyler found it a script which offered much to recommend it and at the same time one to lament. He faulted the choice of material and emphasis, and cited the error of attempting to include so much vital, factual material and at the same time the personal story of one family-- complete with the love scenes and other stage conventions of domestic drama. This approach abbreviated the amount of documentary material and diffused the play's intensity and dramatic impact. Tyler also criticized the imbalance resulting from 75 percent of the action taking place before the Civil War. This resulted in later events being "fore shortened" and "condensed to such an extent that they become vague."[14]

Playreader Henry Bennett agreed with Tyler: "He [Booth] had done his work with a great deal of enthusiasm, but his play is completely devoid of the incisiveness and the various attention getting devices that made the Living Newspaper so memorable." Bennett stated that "one of the chief motifs of the Living Newspaper productions was that each of their scenes went toward building up some special argument and point of view, driving home point after point with great assurance and dramatic ingenuity." He stressed that Created Equal lacked a true focus and that there were too many marginally linked scenes not related organically enough, causing confusion, and therefore: "As it stands now, the work suggests an ambitious high school pageant, and it might with some re-writing for clarity, and much condensation, be used for some such purpose."[15]

Both Tyler and Bennett gave the play an over-all evaluation of "rejected with reservation." The reasons for the decision to produce the play, despite two rejections, including one by Converse Tyler, who was now the head of the Playreading Department, were not apparent.

Created Equal seems to represent Boston's attempt to produce a play worthy of the attention given New York productions, even borrowing the episodic structure of the Living Newspapers to reflect American history and the social and economic problems of the present. The Boston Globe complimented Federal Theatre for its ingenuity in mounting a show without lavish sets, and staging it with the plasticity that made the New York Living Newspaper productions noteworthy: "The production moves against a plain back-drop and across a low platform, depending upon lighting, costumes and the grouping of the players [to make up for] the absence of scenery." The reviewer complimented everyone involved with the production as handling "a most difficult drama with competence and dignity."[16] Boston critics appreciated the way their city went all out for doing a "New York" type spectacle that used personnel from the Negro, Italian, and Vaudeville units.

Some critics disagreed sharply with the assessment of Created Equal given by playreaders. Variety did not agree with Henry Bennett that the show was only a high school pageant. Its reviewer praised its great educational value, being "the stuff that makes history for those un-moved by textbooks." Billboard applauded the production as a "tremendous piece of legitimate propaganda, enacted with subtlety and casting no reflections on any constituted authority."[17] This observation contradicted the opinion held by Bennett that Created Equal lacked force and potency.

The "subtle propaganda" was very much noticed in the review of Created Equal appearing in the Boston Herald. The Herald reviewer saw the play as one that "divides the citizenry of the past and present into two classes, the rich and poor, . . . one who owns property is to be regarded with suspicion." The reviewer indicated that the narrative was very effectively presented and relevant to the world of the thirties. The American Revolution was seen as highly unpopular among Tories, soldiers returning from the Revolutionary War could not find jobs, and the Constitution of the United States was viewed as a "series of compromises, necessary and otherwise." Agreeing with Tyler's view that the dramatic action was not structured and proportioned appropriately, the Herald reviewer saw Created Equal dealing disjointedly and in a biased manner with all of the problems concerning Americans during the Depression and other key moments in American history:

> The issue of prohibition is side-stepped, that of slavery intensively discussed, Wall Street assumes its not unexpected role of all powerful evil genius, the federalist principles for which Alexander Hamilton stood are condemned and the states' rights program upon which Jefferson took his stand is not overlooked, yet encroachments of federalism today are not mentioned.

Critics were more inclined sometimes to accept a script's viability, even when it was "politically" partisan, than were FTP playreaders. Reviewers such as the one for the Herald excused much more than the readers did, in their evaluation of FTP plays and complimented everyone involved with the production as handling "a most difficult form of drama with competence and dignity."[18]

Although Boston critics were supportive of FTP efforts generally, the Boston Herald frequently commented on "latent," "leftleaning" messages in Federal Theatre productions. The rival Boston Post was generally open to FTP--with regard to its messages and particularly with regard to the way its productions were mounted.

The next play, A Moral Entertainment by Richard Maibaum, was described by FTP as a comedy about life in old Massachusetts taking place in 1692. First presented by the Roslyn, New York, unit April 3-June 11, 1938, it later opened in Boston at the Copley Theatre on December 27, 1938, and ran through July 7, 1939. The play "tells the amusing story of what happens to a solemn Bible-reading community when a gay troupe of actors descends upon it." The comedy relates with a "sly and warm humor" the tale of how strolling actors arrive in Maundy, Massachusetts, to give a performance. Maundy, governed by the "sanctimonious" and self-righteous Reverend Parson Pillputt, considers the theatre a work of Satan. The Reverend shows his contempt by having the barn where the performance is given raided just as the show begins. The actors are carried off to jail. However, the Parson's actions are betrayed by his nephew, Deodate Wayne, who has become infatuated with the leading lady, and by the townfolk, who secretly sympathize with the mummers. Townspeople smuggle beef and rum to the jailed actors, whose incarceration becomes for them a delight. When the actors are brought to trial, they are threatened with extreme punishment unless they promise to reform and marry into the colony, an option offered because the town lacks husbands for the many unmarried women. Most of the troupe agree to accept the option; however, Tony, the producer, and Ned, the comedian, reject the offer. They are summarily thrown in the stocks. Deodate manages to rescue Ned and Tony while arranging for the leading lady to escape from jail so that he (Deodate) can elope with her.[19]

A Moral Entertainment exemplified the most "regional" play done in Boston, a play satirizing New England puritanism. The Forward to the script explained that in 1692 acting troupes, in order to avoid restrictions and punishment for performing plays, had to call their shows "Moral Entertainments." Converse Tyler endorsed the play because he said it was "an exceptionally droll piece of work" which succeeded because, "All . . . is accomplished in as humorous and effective a play as I have come across in a long time. The characterizations of both Puritans and players are legitimately funny without stooping to rowdy burlesque."[20] He strongly recommended the play for production.

After it opened, Elinor Hughes, writing in the Boston Herald, disagreed sharply with Tyler that the play was benign and humorous. Taking the traditions of her region seriously, Hughes suspected, as frequently was the case with critics commenting on FTP productions, that the FTP was attempting to present a "covert serious" treatment of a problem in the trappings of comedy and satire. She did not find it funny, writing that the play "suffers from a heavy-handedness, not only of acting but of writing, and the final act becomes downright grim." She further reflected that such topics as the "New England idea of slitting tongues, cutting off ears and putting people in stocks, not to mention hanging and burying for witchcraft are not the subjects for humor." Hughes questioned the author's intention: "Was it really farce or a covert, serious treatment of puritanism. The result was confusion in the writing and overall mood."[21]

The Boston Globe was generally more disposed to social commentary, and its critic thought the satire should have been stronger. The Globe reviewer saw the play as failing to fulfill its purpose, which was to "hold up to ridicule the bigotry and hypocrisy of Puritan New England." To maximize the script's effectiveness, the reviewer recommended that it be given "more pruning and better pacing" so that it could succeed as a "clever satire." To save the play from becoming a "moral lecture," a play doctor was recommended.[22]

The reviewer for the Boston Record totally differed with the Globe review and stated that the play "is not so forbiddingly puritanical as the title would lead you to expect." On the contrary, the Record reviewer found the play to be a "comedy of the gayest type" and suggested that if the play had a moral, it was that a "Spartan-like legal code freezes out the best part of men's natures." Ridicule is used to bring "full salvo upon the target of self-righteous hypocrisy." The review concluded that the production was so capably written and directed that the message "it bares comes home in full strength and without rancor."[23] The Boston American indicated that the opening night audience should have liked the play, but "the author could well afford to strengthen his plot, as it has a tendency to get out of hand. And there are times when it seems he is . . . on the point of saying something significant and pertinent to us, but he never does."[24]

The Globe and Boston American comments seem to indicate that in a set of priorities, frequently "regional emphasis" would take precedence over excellence in writing. The Globe reviewer recommended a play doctor. This recommendation is seen not only in the reaction of critics but also in playreaders' reports suggesting rewrites before making a positive recommendation. This reflects a FTP tendency to work swiftly within a critical time-frame in order to show government officials that the Federal Theatre was doing its job--albeit imperfectly. Government officials expected quick and frequent openings.

The Boston Project, through judicious selection and support given by the Boston press, provided the Federal Theatre with some of its most noteworthy achievements. Despite the early problems with censorship, and a lack of dynamism in leadership, the Boston Project inspired the entire Eastern region to take advantage of the opportunities Federal Theatre was providing. Boston wanted the publicity given New York for its daring in producing new plays, and also made a concerted effort to reflect its regional "material" and history. Boston critics and audiences were frequently more receptive to FTP plays than were FTP readers, a trend that developed as Boston continued its attempts to do new plays.

Feet on the Ground, presented in Reading, Pennsylvania, was written by an FTP employee for the unit with which he was afffiliated. H.A. Archibald was Director of the Reading unit when the regional comedy was given several "trial" performances to help him determine the play's viability and to enable him to do the necessary rewriting to prepare the script for its "premiere" performances in Reading, June 22-December 23, 1936.[25] Hallie Flanagan was pleased with the play and strongly endorsed it:

> This was the one original project in Pennsylvania, a play about the Dunkards . . . Everyone thought such a production a crazy idea; the Dunkards were "plain"; they didn't hold with playgoing; and anyway, who wanted to see a play about plain

people. As it turned out, everyone in the countryside wanted to
see it, for this story of uneventful lives in a Dutch community
had a quality of a penetration into character and motive, an
authoritative handling of the material.[26]

Flanagan further stated that the performances were successful and
convincing to audiences because Archibald had a deep understanding of
the Dunkards and of the performing abilities of his unit. After
performances in Reading, Feet on the Ground toured towns and villages
five times a week, at times offering three performances a day.[27]

Feet on the Ground tells the story of how a "jaded," "jazzy," city girl
marries a Dunkard farmer, rebels against her new life, is then reconciled
to it after a personal transformation. It tells how Tessie Barton, "a [New
York] night club girl," cannot make up her mind to become the mistress of a
racketeer who pursues her. He has money and can give her the sort of
wealth that her crowd has found the "greatest thing in the world." Tessie
leaves New York to visit her sister in Reading, where she soon takes a job
working in a dime store. Tessie meets a Dunkard farmer with whom she
eventually has an affair. She marries the farmer, much to the disbelief of
her New York friends. Her new husband, David, wants Tessie to adopt the
ways and customs of the Dunkard sect. However, Tessie refuses to "go
plain" and wear the required apparel and eventually also refuses David
his conjugal rights, since he does not provide the life-style she desires.
David possesses a formula for a homemade blasting powder sought by the
War Department. Being a pacifist, he refuses to sell the formula.
However, Tessie finds a way to sell the powder. When it is tested in a
barnfield, David's team of horses is frightened and runs away. David is
injured, and Tessie, afraid that he is killed, leaves the Dunkard area.
Tessie yearns for, but is ashamed to return to, the "sticks." Finally, David's

grandfather, who understands both Tessie and David's world, brings Tessie back to Reading, where she lives happily with David and, without hesitation, goes "plain."[28]

Hiram Motherwell, commenting on the play as reader and as Eastern Regional Director, reflected: "The strength of this play is the extremely rich and lovely speech of the Dunkards." He found the characterizations authentic, as if created by a writer fully aware of his people "to the last detail." However, Motherwell found the plot clumsy and full of situations that were developed without any preparation. He further stated that, despite the fact that "everything was wrong with the structure," the play was "fascinating nonetheless."[29]

Converse Tyler, in his playreader's report, stated that the outstanding quality of the play was its "complete simplicity." He recommended Feet on the Ground for production because the play's middle section is "warm with a certain type of American folk-life." He suggested that the play would appeal to those familiar with the Dunkard Sect but not to a general audience because "it does not measure up even to a modest standard as a play."[30] This reflected the way that the Playreading Department Supervisor would only recommend a play based on its regional appeal to a limited audience despite its weaknesses in writing.

When Feet on the Ground was presented in the Reading area, the local press applauded the author and FTP for presenting a play which authentically depicted the lives and aspirations of the "native" population. The Reading Times made particular mention of how well the play reflected the daily lives of the Dunkards and the values guiding their lives: "Archibald proves his knowledge of the people. The Dunkards in Feet on the Ground are gentle and kindly, taking enjoyment from their work, showing justice in their dealings with their fellow men, feeling religion deeply."[31]

Feet on the Ground was a successful production for several reasons. Foremost was the deep and sincere feeling for "native material" expressed in the writing and directing by an FTP official very familiar with his people and local territory. Critical response also suggested that Feet on the Ground reflected the lives and spirit of the Dunkards accurately and positively. The play succeeded in convincing its audience of its authenticity and legitimacy despite Flanagan's preconceived opinions of the audience's negative notions about "playgoing." Here FTP not only reflected "native" material in one of its productions, but also acted as a catalyst in helping a regional population overcome its prejudices about theatre and playgoing to then actively support a play written by one of its own.

Connecticut's only contribution to the writing and producing of new plays was Talbot Jenning's No More Frontiers. It played in Bridgeport, April 13-20, 1937. The readers' reports of this play are no longer in existence.

Although the Eastern region did not produce many new plays, every one was in some way regional--either in terms of history, mores, or sociology. Feet on the Ground was a play that reflected FTP's aspirations for regional plays because it was written by a FTP official for and about his native region. Boston was slow to respond to the opportunities offered by FTP, but when it finally did, it managed to produce plays which pleased audiences, critics, and WPA officials in good measure. Boston managed to make its points, without creating a lot of controversy, which is exactly what it set out to do. The Eastern Region answered Hallie Flanagan's call for regional plays in a conscientious, sober, and serious manner. Boston lifted its bans and joined the bandwagon.

Notes

[1]States where Federal Theatre had units within each region will be listed under chapter headings. However, only states which did new plays will be discussed. This will also follow for Chapters VIII, IX, and X.

[2]Quoted in Flanagan, Arena, pp. 224-225.

[3]Ibid., pp. 225-228.

[4]Ibid., pp. 226-227.

[5]Ibid., p. 230.

[6]Play list, Bureau of Research and Publication, Federal Theatre Project, 12 December 1935. At George Mason University.

[7]Synopsis at George Mason University.

[8]Converse Tyler, Memorandum to Francis Bosworth, Play Bureau Supervisor, 28 July 1936, at George Mason University.

[9]Play list.

[10]Judson O'Donnell, Playreaders Report, n.d. At George Mason University.

[11]Fleet Munson, Playreaders Report, n.d. At George Mason University.

[12]Henry Bennett, Playreaders Report, 31 October 1937. At George Mason University.

[13]Program for Created Equal. At George Mason University.

[14]Converse Tyler, Playreaders report, 14 January 1938. At George Mason University.

[15]Bennett, Playreaders report.

[16]Boston Globe, 11 June 1938.

[17]Quoted in Flanagan, Arena, p. 228.

[18]Boston Herald, 14 June 1938.

[19]Synopsis at George Mason University.

[20]Converse Tyler, Playreaders report, 10 January 1938. At George Mason University.

[21]Boston Herald, 28 December 1938.

[22]Boston Globe, 28 December 1938.

[23]Boston Record, 29 December 1938.

[24]Boston American, 28 December 1938.

[25]Hiram Motherwell, Playreaders report, 30 November 1936. At George Mason University.

[26]Flanagan, Arena, p. 248.

[27]Ibid.

[28]John Rimassa, Playreaders report and synopsis, 27 February 1937. At George Mason University.

[29]Motherwell, Playreaders report.

[30]Converse Tyler, Playreaders report, 1 November 1937. At George Mason University.

[31]Reading Times, n.d., cited in Flanagan, Arena, p. 248.

# CHAPTER VIII
# THE SOUTH

(Florida, Georgia, Louisiana, North Carolina, Oklahoma)

The South presented the most fertile territory for the FTP when it began to establish performing units there. As Hallie Flanagan observed, the South had "rich dramatic material in the variety of peoples, the historical developments, the contrasts between a rural civilization and a growing industrialization."[1] The dramatic material Flanagan described had virtually been untapped by playwrights. There was a dormant audience because for a long time theatrical activity in the South was limited to stock company performances and "third rate road shows."[2] A further detriment to the growth of theatrical activity was the South's fear of "any new type of play."[3]

Writers wrote about the South in extremes. The Birmingham Age Herald's John Graves stated to a meeting of FTP directors, "Writing about the South usually falls into one of two categories, moonlight and magnolias, or Tobacco Road. In between these extremes, both true of certain phases of the South, are many other problems worth dramatic treatment."[4]

The Florida Project was the most active in fostering the presentation of new plays. Dorothea Lynch, Florida State Director, announced in September 1936 that the Play Bureau, located in Jacksonville, would be seeking original plays by Florida writers. Lynch stressed that "We are particularly desirous of seeking original manuscripts covering some native side of Florida or Florida life, whether historical articles or of a technical nature." She emphasized that opportunities would be open to everyone, not just FTP employees.[5]

During the establishment of the Florida units, a constant ongoing conflict existed between Lynch and Flanagan regarding play selection. Flanagan prompted the conflict with her insistence that Florida do new "relevant" plays instead of the typical stock plays favored by many directors of local units. Flanagan asserted her authority through the Play Policy Board, which published a list of "approved plays" and made final decisions to accept or reject plays not on the list. Lynch objected to this control, stressing that special circumstances in Florida required more flexibility. She cited three reasons why Florida was a special case regarding play selection: the three producing centers--Miami, Tampa, and Jacksonville--were autonomously, individually run with highly diverse populations; the climate and tourism created other problems. Lynch claimed that the two diverse populations to consider in Florida--residents and Northern visitors-had very different tastes. Resident Floridians went for romantic and modern comedies while the Northerners generally preferred only modern comedies, not the sophisticated classics or new plays Flanagan suggested. The conflict continued to rage, and Lynch resisted Flanagan's "suggestions," indicating that she knew very well the taste of her state's resident and tourist population, and that their taste would have to be elevated gradually. Flanagan eventually conceded.[6]

Because Lynch played it safe in her selection, only one criticism of her play choices was voiced. A Tampa attorney, L.A. Graham found If Ye Break the Faith, an anti-war play, unpatriotic: "a satire upon those who lost their lives or fought the World War."[7]

The Miami unit best answered Lynch's call for new plays, producing five by Southerners: Rhapsody in Two Flats, Gallows Gate, Altars of Steel, If Ye Break the Faith, and Whom Dreams Possess.

Rhapsody in Two Flats was written by Miamian Edgar Hayes, a former actor who wrote a column for the Miami Herald called "Show Folks." A light comedy, the play was presented March 4-13, 1937. Playreaders' reports and reviews are unavailable for this production.

The second production, Gallows Gate by Marjory Stoneman Douglas, had won a prize in the St. Louis Little Theatre contest. It was presented June 14-19, 1937. Playreader Samuel Steinhardt described it as an American frontier tragedy. The plot revolves around the struggle for survival of the McDevitts, who lose their orange grove in central Florida. Mr. McDevitt thwarts Mrs. McDevitt's plans to build a new life by deserting the family in search of "easy money." Mrs. McDevitt moves to the Everglades to accept free land offered by the government to new settlers. Twenty years later, the McDevitt's son, George, meets a stranger who promises to make the young man rich. George and his brother, Joe, go along with the scheme and rob a bank. When the brothers are apprehended, Joe kills a sheriff during the melee. The stranger turns out to be Mr. McDevitt, the boys' father, who then tries to save Joe from the gallows but is stopped by Mrs. McDevitt, who threatens to shoot him, claiming "Joe's soul must be purged." Joe is hanged, and his mother is then "free" of her psychological torment.[8] Steinhardt reported that Gallows Gate was written with "distinction and dignity and has many fine dramatic situations." He also found the locale "interesting" and the dialogue "superior."[9]

194

However, commenting on the play, reader William Beyer said that it
was a,

> three act Grand Guignol horror piece of the dated Willard
> Mack, Sam Shipman calibre. . . . Once the play gets started, the
> characters resolve themselves into melodramatic types. . . .
> However, be that as it may, if played as a straight melodrama to
> unsophisticated hinterland audiences, there is the run-of-the-
> mill emotional impact in all horror pieces when horror is
> effectively piled on horror. That, this opus certainly achieves.

He recommended it for a stock company requiring a "genuine horror
piece," and for Southern units because there were many small parts for
"Negroes." He concluded, however, "Personally, I don't see what it is to be
gained by giving FTP audiences new pieces of this dated quality and
content."[10]  Ann Grosvenor Ayres, in her reader's report, advised the
author to choose a more "palatable" subject if she wished to continue
writing for the theatre: "Why produce plays that will send audiences from
the theatre enveloped in thick gloom."[11]

The setting for Gallows Gate was regional, the Florida Everglades,
and the theme not militantly social--a perfect combination for an FTP play.
Beyer's comments about the play reflected a tendency among the young
FTP playreaders to constantly compare the plays they were considering to
those already successfully produced professionally in terms of types of
plays, genres, styles, and authors. Aspiring writers seeking Federal
Theatre productions did what new writers frequently do--employ
derivative material, both in content and form. Beyer's observations were
of the useful type in the sense that they attempt to be somewhat precise
about the dramaturgical features of the script, potential audience, and as a
reminder that FTP was trying to give opportunities to "Negro"

performers. On the other hand, Ayres's views reflected a trend among certain playreaders to make general, subjective comments not very instructive to the selection committee.

Reviewing Gallows Gate for the Miami Life, Michael Damron expressed strong enthusiasm for the play and the production it was given. He stated that the Miami Federal Players "have rung a bell with their current play" and that it is "possibly the most nearly flawless of their many excellent performances." In high praise, Damron gave most credit to the play: "The simple fact remains they were fortunate, extremely so, in the vehicle itself." According to Damron, the play should have been able to bring Mrs Douglas into the "forefront of contemporary American playwrights." He continued to laud the play by saying,

> Her drama is real and therefore gripping; her character analysis is true and her types not over-drawn. The audiences consciously accepts them and becomes part and parcel of them while the action lasts. . . . We look forward to a brilliant future for this gifted author.[12]

Douglas's brilliant future apparently was never realized. There is no evidence that she ever wrote, or had one of her plays produced anywhere, ever again.

The Miami Life review exemplified the unrestrained enthusiasm shown by local critics, who were sometimes strongly supportive in their extravagant, over-blown statements. However, Damron's giving most credit to the play as a "flawless" vehicle creating the production's success was not typical. More frequently, the productions were given more credit than the plays themselves.

196

Following Graves's advice on "moonlight and magnolias" and Tobacco Road, the Miami unit produced Altars of Steel after its very successful presentation in Atlanta, April 1-8, 1937. The play was a portrayal of labor strife in the steel mills. The decision to do the play was lauded by the Miami Daily News claiming that the Miami Federal Theatre came of age with this production:

> All of that organization's poor play selection, bad acting and obvious mediocrity in the past is forgotten and forgiven by the public because of the effort, physical and creative, shown in the new play . . . quite probably the first modern controversial play presented in Miami.[13]

Altars of Steel by Thomas Hall-Rogers, combining the pungent commentary of social drama with melodrama, is set in a large, independent Southern steel mill. The three main characters confront each other about labor-management problems, private and absentee ownership. John Worth, the "liberalist" original owner of Southern Steel and Iron, seeks to run the mill as if it were a large family. He retains an over supply of workers, but is unable to pay bonuses as he attempts to maintain for the workers their pre-Depression salaries. Draper, a radical Communist, arrives at the mill as he tours the South organizing unions. His effort to organize Worth's loyal workers antagonizes them.

Things change when "rugged individualist" Carl Jung comes to town to gain control as a new manager of SS&I. Jung wants to produce at all costs and tyranically re-structures the company. Worth is retained as a nominal president as Jung consolidates his power by replacing workers with machines, reducing the number of safety experts, and eliminating the pension system. As Jung gains more power, Worth refuses to defer to him.

When Jung orders the firing of a defective furnace, Worth resigns with two superintendents to avoid responsibility for the risky venture. Despite Worth's protestations, the hearth is fired and explodes, killing 19 men. This provokes a workers' revolt which attempts an attack on Jung, who in his fear asks Worth to intercede on his behalf. Worth offers to help Jung only if he accepts full responsibility for the accident. Worth is then shot by Draper, who is killed by company guards. As a result of these events, the Jung admission is not declared. Following this, the last brief scene in the play is portrayed on a dimly lit stage while a voice over comments that the jury deliberating the cause of the explosion returns a verdict "absolving any individual from criminal guilt . . . There is no evidence to prove definitely who gave the order to fire the furnace. . . . [the verdict is] NOT GUILTY."[14]

The version of Altars of Steel presented in the Miami production differed in many ways from the original in Atlanta. The original ending had Worth regaining control of the company and also the respect of Draper and the workers. It also showed Jung signing an admission of guilt. In the Miami production, the ending was re-written to raise questions and cause controversy.

The play was a huge success. A large appreciative audience argued about the play's purpose and meaning. As Hallie Flanagan indicated, letters were written to the press expressing strong feelings such as "Dangerous propaganda" or "Dangerous! Bah. If this is propaganda, it is anti-communistic. Those who like their plays limited to lilacs, lavender and old lace, moonlight and roses, pale perfumes or circus lemonade--stay away!"[15]

Controversy was stirred up in the press. Flanagan reported that the Atlanta Georgian found it as "dangerous as Uncle Tom's Cabin." Tarleton Collier, writing for the paper, had said:

> It was a document as fundamental in its facts and just about as communistic as health talk. The exposition of Altars of Steel is the thing that everybody by this time ought to know, that the enlightened industrialist has known for a long time . . . anybody who doesn't still believe that pennies and babies come from heaven is aware that this region with its great natural wealth and its lack of financial resources has been exploited for three score years and ten.[16]

Much of the discussion about Altars of Steel centered on whether the production's success was due to the theme and script, or its set and staging. The Miami and Atlanta set was created by Josef Lentz who, in Atlanta (with a director imported from New York, H. Gordon Graham), promised a set "all in terms of construction--everything--even the curtains will be massive steel doors." They vowed to limit production costs to $500. Lentz designed a cyclorama which extended from the floor upward 85 feet to the grid. He even sewed the material as stage hands assisted in the assembly: "The 'gear effect' and parts seen in profile were drawn, cut and painted on stage from corrugated paper." The set had extraordinary visual power, "a fourstory-high cog wheel topped by administrative offices and flanked by gates going into administration and into labor." In the Atlanta production, Graham orchestrated the actors' movement to represent the rotational movement of machines. Lentz used a recording of actual steel mill sounds for "the sound of trucks."[17]

The Miami Daily News defended Altars of Steel as melodrama:

Actually, the battle of capitalism vs. socialism is drawn with such obviousness in dialogue and character that its own evangelistic fury kills its chance at credibility or realism. At the same time by its out-and-out theatrical quality, its obviousness, it becomes good old basic melodrama that keeps the audience both interested and aroused.

The reviewer wrote that the direction and production was so excellent that the audience was automatically swept up into the intensity of the action: "Just as an old-fashioned audience once hissed the villain when he attacked the heroine, so does the modern audience hiss the capitalist when he rapes the workers of their rights, and the question of any system against another is lost in the emotional drama."[18]

One of the ironies of FTP history was the production of Altars of Steel in Atlanta and Miami. Going from Dorothea Lynch's position favoring conservative, safe, traditional, stock plays to the decision to produce this drama of labor strife was a great leap forward. This move reflected how local WPA officials gradually wanted to join the wave of fame and notoriety gained by New York in presenting highly publicized "socially relevant" plays. The above comments made by the Miami Daily News endorsing the choice to produce "the first modern controversial play presented in Miami" helped gain the momentum. The South could see itself reversing the stereotype of being a conservative place where new plays were not welcome, to doing one of the most compelling and noteworthy plays produced by FTP in the entire nation. However, it should be indicated that the play is strongly "reformist." Since the communist, Draper, is not exactly the "good guy," the play ends up not "rocking the boat," and as the Miami Daily News indicated, the battle of capitalism versus socialism is so obvious that the play descends into a vibrant melodrama where the issues are lost in the "emotional drama." The play was seen as good melodrama, and then basically as anti-communist. When this was fully realized, the cries of danger were muted. This was a very successful production reflecting the lives and social, economic conditions in a particular region. It was not the type of play the Communist Party press in New York would have liked.

The next Miami production, If Ye Break Faith, by Maria M. Coxe, was presented June 20 through July 2, 1938. It was described by FTP as an anti-war fantasy. Six dead unknown soldiers symbolizing the heroism of all the dead soldiers of America, England, France, Italy, Austria, and Germany are sent back to the world by the Recorder of the Unknown Dead. Their mission is to tell the world about the horrors of war and to extol peace and harmony. The soldiers must succeed or else be doomed to endless suffering in the "void." The spirits of the men wander the earth, vainly praising the virtues of peace. They find that the growing insanity of war has infected everyone. In fact, they find that the world has memorialized them with war monuments. Defeated in their aims, the spirits of the unknown soldiers return to the Recorder, indicating that the world is preparing for still another war and that their deaths were "empty gestures and their heroism a sham."[19]

Louis Solomon's playreader's report rejected the script because it was "Not an unfamiliar theme by now. But worse, there isn't sufficient story, or suspense, and the necessary integration of material to make an absorbing whole. Honest, high minded, it has its good points, but not enough for a successful script."[20] Fleet Munson was even more negative in his report: "Even for a script emanating from the Fishbein office [Frieda Fishbein, the literary agent], this is terrible. A long harangue about the evils of war--not a play but a badly arranged series of scenes without cohesion. . . . Definitely lousy."[21] Edmund Fuller also rejected it vehemently by saying, "Until she can find a more substantial, impressive and adequate vehicle for her anti-war sentiments, she should possess her soul in patience. . . . This is the kind of treatment which makes the anti-war theme seem irritating to the most sympathetic."[22]

Alexander Cutner's report called it "An impassioned diatribe against war; this play assumes the tone and color of propaganda, timely but dangerous in extreme." Cutner recommended it for "radical groups, Theatre Union, Little Theatre, Provincetown Players, working class audiences, especially New York, and radical college students."[23] Acknowledging If Ye Break Faith as a spiritual legacy from plays like Miracle at Verdun and Bury the Dead, Converse Tyler wrote that Coxe's script "atones for any similarity" by giving the theme "great tenderness and a very moving and effective setting."[24] His report endorsed the script, as did Francis Bosworth's report stating, "This is a very moving play and certainly the best anti-war play that has been submitted to us."[25]

Eddie Cohen in the Miami Daily News wrote, "Miss Coxe has written her play with dignity and force . . . If Ye Break Faith, through exciting drama, expert direction, sensitive acting, and a striking set is a powerful denunciation of war that is both polemic and entertaining."[26]

Writing about If Ye Break Faith and Blockade, a film about the Spanish Civil War then appearing at a Miami cinema, a commentator in the Miami Daily News expressed concern that audiences viewing the two productions might become too partisan: "In regard to both productions, but particularly Blockade, there will be charges of bias and propaganda. . . . The federal play has perhaps, a faint anti-Nazi bias. The Spanish epic leans by implication pretty far onto the Loyalist side." However, the writer stated, "If one can absorb the scenes as an observer of warfare rather than as a partisan of one presently fighting faction, he will gain much from experience and nothing will be lost to American neutrality."[27]

Readers' comments for If Ye Break Faith reflected not only weary reactions to the overworking of anti-war themes, but also the rejection of pacifist, anti-war, peace plays on principle by certain "progressive" Popular Front observers of the events before World War II. Plays were called "defeatist" if they did not strongly endorse a defense against fascism. Cutner's remarks are extremely ironic in retrospect: an anti-war play was considered "dangerous" and as propagandizing a cause because it did not urge a call to arms against the menace of fascist tyranny. A further irony is that this play was recommended for production by radical groups, including the Theatre Union, but given its premiere in the conservative "neutral" South. Such were the many intricate workings of the FTP when seen from the inside. Again, Converse Tyler's judgment prevailed--he chose a neutral, pacifist play reminiscent of two other successful anti-war plays. The mood of a neutral administration pervaded the WPA admonition during the preparation for the production of Ethiopia, which the Living Newspaper cancelled in New York because of its unflattering view of Mussolini. Neutralist guidelines were given during the preparations for the production of It Can't Happen Here--that specifically identifying representations of current, or potential, fascist dictatorships was to be avoided. Therefore, also the suggestion that those dictatorships would cause war was also to be avoided.

The decision to do If Ye Break Faith represents vividly the three modes of thinking about FTP plays. Young playreaders were prompted by ideological considerations to dismiss a play later considered "tender" and "moving" by Playreading Department heads, who endorsed the "modish" play that was accepted by critics, who found it both "polemic" and "entertaining." Clearly, here the official view prevailed. One more irony in this is the view reflected in the Miami Daily News attacking "anti-Nazi biases." Plays that were too anti-Nazi were, depending upon the viewer, as unacceptable as plays that were too anti-war.

Originally presented in Atlanta, January 31-February 5, 1938, and then in Jacksonville, Man in the Tree by John Woodworth was later produced at the Miami Federal Theatre May 16, 1938. This was an example of a FTP project (written by Woodworth for the Oklahoma project), intended as a "fantastic comedy . . . [and an] answer to all those Southern and Southwestern units . . . looking for intelligent and amusing scripts of regional interest."[28] The play is based upon Washington Irving's account of his trip through the great Southwest in 1837, and tells its story "with flourishes of Rip Van Winkle and Berkeley Square." The story is as follows: The young Count Pourtales, who accompanies Irving on his trip, has learned many Indian legends, so that when he is lost, he invokes the God of lightning, Wah-Kon-Tah, to help him return to his party. Wah-Kon-Tah is able, according to legend, to give power to anyone finding his mocassins and wearing them to "ride the lightning to unknown destinations." Finding the God's mocassins, the Count puts them on and then finds refuge in a big tree. The next morning he awakens on top of an oil derrick on the campus of Washington Irving High School in Oklahoma City. The town is preparing to dedicate a monument on the very spot where Irving spent the night a hundred years earlier. The ceremony is prepared by the Daughters of the American Revolution. The Count feels betrayed by Wah-Kon-Tah, but falls in love with Wauhilla, an Indian maiden. He cannot convince the maiden that all is not a hoax and that he is the celebrated young Pourtales. He once again puts on the mocassins hoping to return to his proper time and place.[29]

Converse Tyler found the script a humorous satire on modern civilization and recommended it as having great regional interest.[30] Reader J. Edward Silver commented that it was essentially a children's play: "This one has some nicely imaginative scenes and a whimsical, though scarcely original, idea behind it. However, the Oklahoma City oil-well situation, I'm afraid, makes it almost strictly a local joke."[31]

The Miami Herald was not very impressed: "It may be that the Count, the man in the tree, was meant to personify an idealist, believed by the materialist to be insane." The reviewer thought that the point became muddled as the Count became increasingly more confused with oil drilling and things of the modern age: "He couldn't understand whether the oil business was drill, droll, droal or what. He was up in the tree and so was the audience."[32]

The Miami Daily News was less kind in saying that Woodworth wrote a bad play "rather well," but that it would have been more effective had he distributed it in pamphlet form with a foreword of instructions, "clarifying the hodgepodge of allegories and symbolisms that permeate the piece." The reviewer said he was thankful for the blackouts used for scene shifts because that allowed the audience to "escape from as tedious an evening in the theater we've ever spent." He further criticized the "clumsy," "amazing" characterizations and the "ludicrous offstage sound effects such as tinny thunder, 'human' wolf yelps, cap pistol guns and off key singing." Commenting on the theme, the reviewer stated: "Today, capital climbs into a tree to escape from labor. We like this bit of symbolism best of all. Had we stayed to see the end of the play, we might have selected a more exciting theatre."[33]

Man in the Tree was written for a specific project but produced elsewhere, in the South, not in the region where its "native landscape" is reflected. Considering this, Silver's reader's report is ironic in that he calls the "Oklahoma City oil well situation . . . a local joke." It was evidently produced anyway due to Converse Tyler's assessment that it was a humorous satire on modern civilization. Again, the comments indicating flourishes of Rip Van Winkle and Berkeley Square seem to be an attempt to give a FTP play a credibility and viability it would need if it were to be judged only on its own merits. Not only was originality not abundant in Federal Theatre plays, the lack of it was not particularly problematic. It did not seem to be a characteristic highly sought in play procurement.

The next new play offered by the Miami unit was Whom Dreams Possess, by Barbara Ring and Rudolph Elie, from April 13-27, 1939. The play's opening was scheduled to coincide with Pan-American Week. The play is based upon the life of South American liberator Simon Bolivar and his struggle to rid Los Angeles of the Spanish. The authors studied and researched their topic for years prior to writing the script. Dr. Ring was then considered one of America's leading authorities on Latin American history. She had written several plays as a result of her travels and research in Latin America. Her non-FTP plays, rehearsed and presented in Miami in observation of Pan American Week celebrations, include O'Higgins of Chile, Colombian Caravan, The Six Americans, Simon Bolivar, Liberator, Cuba Libre, and The Return of White Gods.[34]

One reviewer commented on the opening night:

There is a series of episodes covering a period of years, but the events are so skillfully merged that cohesion is maintained. It is the consistent battle of Bolivar against Spain, against his own betrayers, against the mob; a battle for freedom. All of the elements of the successful play are woven into the story--drama and melodrama, comedy and tragedy, violence, romance, action, effective scenery and costumes.[35]

The only new play to be given its first production in Jacksonville, based upon Robert Nathan's novel, and adapted by Lulie Hard McKinley, One More Spring was presented May 13-June 1, 1937. One More Spring was originally written and produced as an American feature film in 1935. The play relates how a small shop owner, a violinist, a prostitute, a street cleaner, and a banker, after losing their jobs and becoming destitute, take over an old shack in a park for the purpose of making it their shelter. They survive by stealing, begging, and telling each other their sad stories, passing the winter in the shack, waiting for another spring, and the opportunity to start a new life. Spring arrives and that opportunity is given to them.[36]

Reader Morris Levine found that the play lacked purpose: "Mr. Nathan seems to have a peculiar air about him that spells 'Peace on earth, good will to man'; or something is wrong . . . [and] it is bad to forget it." Levine criticized the play's lack of character development, its defeatism, and its lack of anger. Stressing also an absence of political and social focus, and debunking Nathan's view that social protest is bad for art, Levine pointed out that during the Depression it was not only the workers who protested unemployment, but also the small business man and the artist. Levine concluded his report by stating that the play fails because there is no real conflict, making its theme false and its material static.[37]

Here was a bald example of a subjective reader's report. One is not aware in reading it if the conflict is actually missing or missing because it is not the conflict Levine expects.

The New Orleans Project presented three new plays: CaptainWhat-the-Devil, Monsignor's Hour, and African Vineyard. The first production, Captain-What-the-Devil, described by the FTP as an historical romantic comedy written by Zelma Tiden, was presented for one performance March 11, 1937. Tiden, from Shrevesport, Louisiana, attempted to write a play with local color and regional interest. The FTP felt that the play would be particularly suited for "educational audiences," schools, and historical groups.[38]

Captain-What-the-Devil deals with the exploits of Jean Lafitte, a famous pirate during the War of 1812. Lafitte is sought by the Governor of Louisiana. Lafitte's brother has already been captured together with several of his cohorts. The English are preparing to attack New Orleans. To gain his brother's release, Lafitte offers to help the Americans combat the English. To further his plan to gain his brother's release, Lafitte stages a purported kidnapping and holds Felice, the daughter of M. Fernand Mille, hostage until the Americans will guarantee the brother's freedom. The Americans board Lafitte's ship and negotiate the release pending Lafitte's offer of aid. The plan fails because Felice overhears the proceedings of the conference and concludes that Lafitte's offer to help the Americans is a lie. Felice is rescued and relates what she has heard. Lafitte escapes and finds a way to reach the Governor to personally offer to fight for the Americans in exchange for his brother's release.[39]

E.R. Armstrong reported that the author had only a superficial understanding of the incidents portrayed in the play. Armstrong felt that the script was a "silly, trivial, idealization . . . tedious dialogue along with the naive attempt to portray Lafitte would send anyone from New Orleans into spasms of laughter and thoroughly arouse the ire of anyone familiar with the time and place."[40]

Reader Arthur Bond said that it would make an excellent book for an American operetta.[41] The "special reader," the final arbiter of play selection who wrote the official FTP release, stated that the "author has been fortunate in selecting interesting characters combining fact with charming romance. Good light comedy--delightful touches . . . considerable commercial value, and reminiscent of Pursuit of Happiness."[42]

Charles P. Jones, writing in the Times Picayune, commented that the New Orleans Federal Theatre was to be praised for plunging into the "uncharted" territory of a new play; rejecting the option of just one more revival and "leavings of Broadway." He did not question the author's familiarity with her home state, but did doubt her true knowledge of pirates and Lafitte, in particular. He continued that the production was not "entirely good theatre . . . one moment we suspect it of going Gilbert and Sullivan, and in the next, we fully anticipate that General Jackson will clatter across on his metal horse"--which he does.[43] Thomas Edwin Dabney stated in the New Orleans States that the play is "of August possibilities, capably presented, [it] could be better if needless dialogue were cut out and more incidents introduced."[44]

In what may or may not have been common practice in FTP productions regarding script changes (since more abundant information is not available), the director in his production notes indicated that he made significant changes in the script prompted by the Birmingham Play Bureau suggestions. He stated: "Since the authoress did not show any desire to make changes, it fell to the hands of the director. Convinced that the play Bureau's suggestions were sound, these were carried out almost to the letter." The major work performed by the director was on the first act, because the second and third acts were less in need of changes. The many long French speeches were translated into English. Very authoritatively, the director claimed that the author lamented the changes and felt her play was ruined. The director then stated, "This is a cry we have heard in theatre from authors generally, without much reason for it."[45]

Captain-What-the-Devil once again reveals a lack of congruence in the opinions reflected by the three main judging groups of FTP plays: playreaders, "special readers" (Playreading Department Supervisors), and critics in the local press. Armstrong, who may or may not have been familiar with the region, found the play "superficial" and not authentic for New Orleans audiences. The "special reader" viewed it as having "considerable commercial value," and the Times Picayune, praising FTP for doing new plays and not Broadway revivals, did not question the author's understanding of her "regional material."

The next new play produced in New Orleans was Emmet Lavery's one-act "Monsignor's Hour" presented with Eugene O'Neill's "Moon Over the Caribees" and Pearl River's "Hager," March 22, 1937. Already successfully produced in Vienna and Budapest, "Monsignor's Hour" is a strong plea for world peace, which encouraged FTP to recommend it for "advanced amateur groups and Catholic organizations." It tells how a deeply religious Catholic artist visits the Vatican with her fiance, a skeptical young lawyer. She is told that the visit to the Pope is an impossibility for ordinary Catholics. The girl's protests in the art gallery of the Vatican are overheard by an American priest, Reverend Carey, who is studying a painting by an unknown artist, recently discovered by the Pope. Reverend Carey wants to restore the girl's fiance's faith. When everyone leaves the gallery and only the priest remains, a "prelate" comes to gaze at the painting and is fascinated by the painting's mysterious message of peace. The "prelate" states that if he were the Pope, he would publish an encyclical asking for world peace, and that humankind should never fight under any circumstances. Reverend Carey tells the "prelate" about the young couple and their desire to see the Pope. The "prelate" arranges an audience with the Pope for the following day. The next day at the audience, Reverend Carey discovers that the "prelate" was in fact the Pope himself. The Pope then implies that an encyclical urging world peace will be published.[46]

Ruth Morris, in her reader's report, recommended the play for Catholic audiences because of its religious tone. She suggested that general audiences might not be interested "in view of the Pope's last speech about Communists."[47] In that speech the Pope warned against taking the communist path. Zachary Caully wrote: "Needless to say, the implication of this play is one of religion and faith. It offers the centuries-old solution for the woes of mankind, namely the way of God. . . . after twenty centuries of Christianity, we are still in misery . . . and the fault is not entirely with the peoples of the earth."[48]

Thomas Ewing Dabney in the New Orleans States found "Monsignor's Hour" the most interesting of the three one-acts presented: "Its topical influences and importance at times like these should be great. The acting was excellent, and the direction effective."[49] Harnet T. Kane, writing in Item, referred to Lavery's play as a "slight thing, in some ways a tract more intent on presenting its theme than a dramatic story, but it is delicately done, and it has more than usual interest at present. For its problem is peace."[50] Charles P. Jones, in the Times Picayune, called it a "dignified and reverent preachment."[51]

Emmet Lavery's "Monsignor's Hour" was written by a FTP employee, in this case before he became head of the Play Department, where he served from July 1937 through December 1938. As a "peace" play designated for a Catholic audience, it was criticized by Morris and Caully who reveal in their commmments a tendency to fill reports with personal opinions without reflecting upon the play's feasibility for production for a particular audience.

The last new play produced in New Orleans was African Vineyard, written by Hollywood writer Gladys Unger and Walter Armitage, Director of New Orleans Federal Theatre. It was presented December 14-19, 1937. The action takes place in the South Africa of 1913, and reflects the conflict and strife between the English and the Boers. Armitage, himself an Afrikaner, drew upon personal recollections to tell his story. He also directed the play.

The story focuses on the struggle of Eleanor Chalfont, who seeks to build a life for herself and her children after being deserted by her husband. With the money she has saved and after selling some property, Chalfont buys a half-share in a neglected South African vineyard where she has retreated to help heal her son's failing health. There she meets Johannes Stock, a widower with a small daughter, and the son of the Dutch owners of the vineyard.

During the second act, the time period is 1925, and Eleanor Chalfont has prospered in her managing of the vineyard; however, her returned husband threatens to take his son with him unless his wife takes him back. Chalfont is in love with Johannes, but leaves the vineyard for her husband when he threatens to ruin her lover. When the third act begins, the time is 1938; the farm is now the most prosperous in South Africa. It is being managed by Johannes's daughter, Katerina, and Eleanor's son Robert, who have returned from England to take Chalfont's place. Johannes, resentful of Eleanor's leaving him, refuses to sanction Robert and Katerina's marriage. Eleanor returns and arranges the marriage by finally admitting to Johannes the real reason for her leaving.[52] Interwoven in the plot is a conflict occurring because of an interracial relationship involving Pieter and Bertha Stock.

Armitage, in his directorial notes, characterized the story as "a passionate plea for tolerance and understanding of two people of different nationalities who have to live and work together." He also stated in his notes that "throughout the play, there is an intense feeling of possible friction and trouble with the natives, all leading toward a necessary understanding and tolerance between the Dutch and English." The trouble with the natives included the problem of miscegenation. Armitage stressed that another story would be evident to the critics and playgoers of New Orleans, that is, the story as it paralleled the American scene regarding the North and South.[53]

In fact this "story" was alluded to by K.T. Knobloch writing in Item: "The racial drama as shown appeared trivial, the rumblings of the most tremendous of racial dramas--the tragedy of miscegenation with characters like Pieter Stock and old Bertha Stock. Armitage and Miss Unger might have more on their hands [than] the Federal Players [can handle]." Knoblock obviously did not care too much for the play. He began his review by saying, "The bones of a play rattled on the stage of Federal Theatre." He continued, "Fleshed occasionally, and very well fleshed . . . the play was [still] skeletal." He further stated that "There was a play there, to be hewn and mined out by determined and expert re-writing."[54]

Thomas Ewing Dabney was unrestrained in his enthusiasm. Writing in the New Orleans States: "Every curtain call, every burst of applause, every foyer-expressed comment was deserved . . . for excellent construction," its high literary "quality," "lofty conception," and its gripping, "appealing interest." He found the locale new, the local color "rich," and the performances excellent.[55] Charles P. Jones found the script "cleverly hewn and often epigrammatic."[56]

African Vineyard exemplifies the trend in Federal Theatre plays to use another time and setting to reflect contemporary problems. The issues of interracial sexual union are considered explosive by critics even when framed in another time/place context.

After African Vineyard, Armitage wrote the book and music for a musical revue which he also directed. Jambalaya presented January 4-9, 1938, was simply a series of sketches about life in New Orleans.

The new plays presented in Texas, The Last Enemy and Precious Land, were done in San Antonio. The Last Enemy by Frances Nimme Greene and Robert Harvey Green, was presented April 1-3, 1937. The action takes place in 1921 and deals with the perils of a recently discovered, powerfully destructive death-ray to be used in warfare. Dr. Larabee, the elderly and noted scientist who discovered the weapon, wants to promote his discovery, but wishes to restrain its use by an "unprepared generation." The death-ray is entrusted to three men who vow to never reveal what they know. The three who are given the secret are the Larabee's grandson, Larabee's private secretary, and one of Larabee's friends, Tom Alling, an average businessman. Alling wants to keep the secret, as he has vowed. However, the grandson and secretary conspire to destroy the ray's formula because of its potential destructiveness. Berny, the secretary, wants to turn it over to the government. John, the grandson, wants to destroy it by keeping it secret until their death. To defend his plan, John kills Berny. When friends urge a plea of insanity at John's murder trial, he pleads with an old friend, Harriet, to attest to his sanity so that he can be executed. Harriet fails to do so, and John then kills himself.[57]

Reviewing for the San Antonio Light, Howard Le Baron found the play "a dialectical pill of patriotism versus pacifism with a sugar coating of drama." He characterized The Last Enemy as excessively talky and static in its dialogue. He praised Forrest Hofbrecht's excellent interpretation of the grandson, "the neurotic back from the wars, intent on beating the God Mars in the den of the international bankers and munitions makers because of his ghastly experiences."[58]

The Last Enemy was considered "dialectical" in its pacifism by the San Antonio Light. This reaction is indicative of the FTP propensity to produce pacifist plays even when the writing was very obviously mediocre.

San Antonio's next production, Precious Land by Robert Whitehead, was presented May 19-23, 1937. The drama portrays an Oklahoma farmer's unwillingness to sell his land to oil speculators. Jason and Hecuba and their children, Charles and Laura, are living a sedate life on their farm when oil is discovered nearby. Jason will not accept the offers made to buy his farm. However, Jason's son Charles, bitter about the loneliness and drudgery of his life, wants to leave his birthplace and never return. When Charley reaches his twenty-first birthday, Jason gives him

40 acres of land, which Charley immediately sells to the oil company. Charley leaves the farm, followed by Laura, who elopes with an oil worker, a boarder at Jason's home. Jason and Hecuba feel more and more isolated from friends and neighbors who are benefiting from the enormous wealth produced by the discovery of oil. Hecuba attempts to convince Jason to yield to the pressures made by the oil company and is almost successful, but Jason finally decides to stay on his farm. Hecuba remains so that they can live out their lives on the soil they love so passionately.[59]

Playreader Louis Solomon reported that the play revealed interesting local and regional color, reflecting the author's familiarity with the subject matter but that ultimately the script becomes monotonous and lacks a clearly defined point of view. He noted that the play vaguely suggests a "clash between the old and young, between conservatism and progress," but that all of this is not clear. Solomon continued to say that in any case, Jason is "too absurd and unbelievable to represent a respected force or trend of thought," and that an oil field is no longer a "symbol of progressiveness."[60]

Fanny Malkin, in her reader's report, found the play containing "interesting dramatic material," the characters well drawn and not localized with a dialect. She found the dialogue "even, consistent, and good," and the theme "a problem of great social import."[61] Paul Lake stated that the script was "a dry colorless story, lacking in action and dramatic interest."[62] J.A. Greenberg said that he did not feel the land or the people on the land: "They don't live; they are card-board figures moving obscurely in the mind of the author." Greenberg conceded that the author may have felt the land and characters in his "mind and in his imagination" but that he does not have the "talent" or "craftsmanship" or

"genius" to "make them come alive. . . . Therefore, the script is thin card-
board, very fragile." Greenberg did not stop there; he went on to say,

> Precious Land is a stagnant pool with brown and green scum on
> top and a trickle of water underneath. . . . There's drama there,
> and you can't see it, you can't feel it. But if a man came along
> with a microscope, and you looked through it, you might be
> entranced with the vivid life exposed through the glass.[63]

Fleet Munson rejected it by saying: "Thank heavens the five-act play is no
longer traditional. Three acts of this was quite enough thank you.
Rejected: with laughter."[64]

However, a "special reader" must have passed the final word of
approval because the FTP, in its official release, said the play was
"thoughtfully prepared, with a vigorously defined conflict and a
background exclusively and authentic and richly drawn. A frank, vital play
rich in fresh material and human appeal."[65]

The San Antonio Commercial Recorder agreed with the official FTP
assessment and called it "vigorously defined, authentic, rich in fresh
material and warm in human appeal."[66] Ed Neri reported in the San
Antonio Light that the audience reacted enthusiastically and laughed in the
right and wrong places. He liked the scenography: "Precious Land swept
the stage clean of anything trite to build the small roofless South Texas
farm house right on the stage with the realistic oil derrick that jutted up
into the backdrops." He further commented that all was fine, considering
that Federal Theatre always labors "with heavy human conflict and social
problems."[67] Eddie Cope in the San Antonio Evening News lamented that
"For the past several productions, Federal Theatre actors have been rising

high above their dramatic pieces de resistance . . . [and] last night's preview . . . was no exception."[68]

Reactions to Precious Land were extreme examples of how four young playreaders rejected the play only to have the "special reader" refute their observations in an almost diametrically opposed fashion. Greenberg's comments reveal how totally unrestrained the readers were in their humorously mocking commentaries. The San Antonio Evening News indicated what became a somewhat typical response given by critics in the various regions--that of giving credit to the performers and productions, while not showing much respect for the playwriting. In this case, local critics agreed with FTP officials and not the playreaders.

The state that did the most to discover its native soul was Oklahoma. It was in that state where the greatest effort was made to conduct research into the ethnology of an area and to reflect native material in performance. FTP's Research Division in Oklahoma in cooperation with the Drama Department of the University of Oklahoma, researched the history and culture of the Southwest. Various Indian groups did a great deal to provide information. John Dunne, Oklahoma FTP Director, who was also affiliated with the state university, organized performance units to service the entire state, utilizing workers from vaudeville, medecine shows, tab shows, circus, and stock. Dunne used qualified researchers with three playwrights supplied by the National Service Bureau to discover material indigenous to the writers' own states. FTP called for regional source material via radio announcements directed to writers and theatre groups throughout the entire Southwest, and material flowed in from Oklahoma, Texas, Arkansas, New Mexico, and Kansas.[69]

Numerous requests for scripts about Southwestern culture and history were sent to Oklahoma's FTP office, which then furnished plays, radio scripts, and other performance material to over 200 educational institutions and dramatic clubs. A small playwriting group developed into a 66-member unit. Writers were used as supervisors for community centers where actors wanted original material. In a state sponsored radio play contest, seven of the 13 plays selected as winners were written by Federal Theatre writers. John Dunne described the plays in a foreword to one of the Oklahoma Federal Theatre volumes: "The plays are not offered as examples of great literature. They are based on the rich folklore of the Southwest--simple stories of pioneers, cowboys, Indians . . . people who made history."

Among the longer plays developed, the most noteworthy were Dunne's own Beyond Tomorrow, a melodrama about the Wild West after the Civil War, produced in Oklahoma City, February 26, 1937, and John Woodworth's Cheat and Swing, the story of the infamous female desperado Belle Starr, presented in Oklahoma City. Also developed in this group of plays was Robert Whithead's Precious Land, already discussed as a production in San Antonio, Texas.[70] More complete information about Cheat and Swing and Beyond Tomorrow was not located.

To conduct research into native folklore, and record Indian legends, the FTP employed "natives"--Indians living among Indians all of their lives and familiar with "authentic" material. As an example, a descendent of the noted Choctaw Chief, Pushmataha, Mrs. Josephine Usray Latimer worked on legends tracing "tradition, crops, war, courtship, peace, the sun, the moon, nature lore and philosophy." One of Mrs. Latimer's projects was the writing of a history of the "Trail of Tears," drawn from stories told to her by her grandfather, who in 1856 made the trek from Mississippi to Indian Territory. All of the material including "Trail of Tears" was gathered for future dramatizations.[71] A one-act drama, "Riding for the Cherokee Strip," based on pioneer life in Oklahoma, was presented by the Tulsa unit in November 1936.[72]

John Dunne's work and the production of Altars of Steel proved that the South could be more than "moonlight and magnolias" or "Tobacco Road." In fact it was in the South where the single most concerted effort was made to reflect the ethnology and soul of a region as portrayed in the work of the Oklahoma units. The South ended up making some of the most dynamic contributions to FTP's interest in reflecting the "landscape" and "native materials" of a region.

Notes

[1]Flanagan, Arena, p. 81.

[2]Ibid.

[3]Federal One III-1 (April 1978): 1.

[4]John Temple Graves addressing FTP Southern Directors, 7 October 1936, cited in Flanagan, Arena, p. 88.

[5]Jacksonville Journal, 4 September 1936.

[6]Robert Travis Mardi, "Federal Theatre in Florida" (Ph.D. dissertation, University of Florida, 1972), pp. 111-115.

[7]Ibid., p. 451.

[8]Synopsis at George Mason University.

[9]Samuel Steinhardt, Playreaders report, n.d. At George Mason University.

[10]William Beyer, Playreaders report, 5 April 1937. At George Mason University.

[11]Ann Grosvenor Ayres, Playreaders report, 4 January 1937. At George Mason University.

[12]Miami Life, 19 June 1937.

[13]Miami Daily News, 1 March 1938.

[14]Synopsis at George Mason University.

[15]Flanagan, Arena, p. 89. Flanagan cites reactions printed in newspapers but does not indicate which ones or the dates.

[16]Ibid., p. 90.

[17]Federal One III-1 (April 1979): 9.

[18]Miami Daily News, 1 March 1938.

[19]Synopsis at George Mason University.

[20]Louis Solomon, Playreaders report, 3 November 1936. At George Mason University.

[21]Fleet Munson, Playreaders report, 16 November 1936. At George Mason University.

[22]Edmund Fuller, Playreaders report, 16 November 1936. At George Mason University.

[23]Alexander Cutner, Playreaders report, 22 December 1936. At George Mason University.

[24]Converse Tyler, Playreaders report, 19 October 1937. At George Mason University.

[25]Francis Bosworth, Playreaders report, 1 November 1937. At George Mason University.

[26]Miami Daily News, 2 June 1938.

[27]Ibid.

[28]Converse Tyler, Playreaders report, 2 August 1937. At George Mason University.

[29]Synopsis at George Mason University.

[30]Tyler, Playreaders report.

[31]J. Edward Silver, Playreaders report, 2 August 1937. At George Mason University.

[32]Miami Herald, 17 May 1938.

[33]Miami Daily News, 17 May 1938.

[34]_Miami Daily News,_ 17 April 1939.

[35]H. Bond Bliss, an unidentified review of _Whom Dreams Possess,_ n.d. Located in press file for the production at George Mason University.

[36]Synopsis at George Mason University.

[37]Morris Levine, Playreaders report, 7 September 1938. At George Mason University.

[38]Synopsis at George Mason University.

[39]Ibid.

[40]E.R. Armstrong, Playreaders report, 1 October 1936. At George Mason University.

[41]Arthur Bond, Playreaders report, 14 October 1936. At George Mason University.

[42]Ibid.

[43]_Times-Picayune,_ 12 March 1937.

[44]_New Orleans States,_ 12 March 1937.

[45]Director's Notes, Production Bulletin for _Captain-What-the-Devil,_ n.d. At George Mason University.

[46]Synopsis at George Mason University.

[47]Ruth Morris, Playreaders report, 28 December 1936. At George Mason University.

[48]Zachary Caully, Playreaders report, 19 September 1938. At George Mason University.

[49]_New Orleans States,_ 23 March 1938.

[50]_Item,_ 23 March 1938.

[51]Times-Picayune, 23 March 1938.

[52]Synopsis at George Mason University.

[53]Walter Armitage, Director's Notes, Production Bulletin for African Vineyard, n.d., n.p. At George Mason University.

[54]Item, 15 December 1937.

[55]New Orleans States, 15 December 1937.

[56]Times-Picayune, 15 December 1937.

[57]Synopsis at George Mason University.

[58]San Antonio Light, 2 April 1937.

[59]Synopsis at George Mason University.

[60]Louis Solomon, Playreaders report, 14 December 1936. At George Mason University.

[61]Fanny Malkin, Playreaders report, 2 October 1936. At George Mason University.

[62]Paul Lake, Playreaders report, 28 October 1936. At George Mason University.

[63]J.A. Greenberg, Playreaders report, 2 October 1936. At George Mason University.

[64]Fleet Munson, Playreaders report, 30 November 1936. At George Mason University.

[65]Official FTP synopsis at George Mason University.

[66]Commercial Recorder [San Antonio], 12 May 1937.

[67]San Antonio Light, 20 May 1937.

[68]San Antonio Evening News, 20 May 1937.

[69]Flanagan, <u>Arena</u>, pp. 97-98.

[70]Ibid., p. 98.

[71]<u>Oklahoman</u>, 10 August 1936.

[72]<u>Oklahoma City News</u>, 13 October 1936.

CHAPTER IX

THE MIDWEST


(Illinois, Indiana, Michigan, Ohio, Nebraska)


Calling Chicago "as native as a ballgame or a prize fight," Hallie
Flanagan characterized that city as a melodrama if it were to be depicted
in any future cycle play epitomizing the FTP projects. In such a cycle, New
York would be staged as a Living Newspaper, Los Angeles as a musical
comedy, and the South as a folk-play. Censorship problems caused by the
notorious Mayor Kelly were part of the "plots and counter-plots"
constituting the Chicago melodrama.[1]

Hallie Flanagan further described Chicago as the "supply center" for
the entire Midwest, to be used as a "retraining ground" and a place where
"plays should be written, designs created, and equipment built for smaller
units." Iowa University Theatre was to be the "experiment station"
providing courses for FTP personnel seeking retraining. Companies
would be rehearsed in Chicago for tours throughout the villages and small
towns of the Midwest.[2]

In August 1936, the FTP in Chicago announced that it was seeking
play submissions; "American scenes" of any length were especially
welcome. Susan Glaspell, head of the Midwest Play Bureau, emphasized
that she intended to help Midwestern writers avoid the stresses and waste
of time involved in risking the "1,000 to 1 shot of landing in the intricate
maze of producers on Broadway." She planned to reflect the lives and
drama of the Midwest in native folk-lore, native poetry, and indigenous
drama.[3]

Glaspell, along with John McGee, organized the Midwest Play Bureau November 6, 1936, indicating the following intentions:

(a) The collection of manuscripts and published plays dealing with Midwestern themes or of special interest to Midwestern audiences, or written by Midwestern authors.

(b) The selection of producible manuscripts from this group and further development of these in cooperation with the authors.

(c) The recommendation of the best of these scripts for production by the theatres of this region.

(d) The specific recommendation to Hiram Motherwell (Director of the National Service Bureau) of plays which have a general application as well as a regional one.[4]

Chicago's attempt to produce plays by local authors was initiated when the city's project formed a small experimental theatre group established to develop plays for productions in legitimate theatres. The group, formed in February 1936, began rehearsals in March for its first production, James Van Nices's anti-Nazi play, A Cry for Life. Rehearsing in a small loft, the group's efforts were hampered by a lack of space. When Chicago's FTP director, George Kondolf, attended a "test" performance given for him to determine the group's professional viability, his response was negative, indicating that he felt the directors were too "little theatre" and "arty" in their approach. Scripts for the group were not forthcoming, so Kondolf decided to replace the unit's directors in July 1936 with Kay Ewing, who was Acting Director of the Vassar Experimental Theatre.[5]

Ewing directed the first main stage production of the newly formed Experimental Unit as part of a nationwide cycle of religious plays. Marcus Bach's Within These Walls was presented at the Blackstone Theatre, January 27-February 13, 1937. Originally produced at the University of Iowa, the play depicts a young trappist monk grappling with his conscience which urges him to forsake the world of the flesh and assume the vow of silence. Gail Borden of the Chicago Daily Times said, "As a play of 'special appeal,' Mr. Bach's drama is a good workman-like job; it is written with considerable feeling; it is handsomely produced, and it is intelligently directed by Kay Ewing."[6] Hazel McDonald of the Chicago American called it a "dish of caviar," after FTP's past efforts of catering "too indulgently to popular taste."[7]

Soon after the successful production of the play, Within These Walls, the Chicago Project began having problems with censorship. Chicago's Mayor Kelly, upholding his reputation as the overseer and protector of public morals and conscience, decided to ban Meyer Levin's Model Tenement, a play telling how a grocer desires to improve his life by building a "model tenement." A construction worker who helped build the tenement, and also one of its tenants, is evicted. Neighbors protest the eviction, and during a violent melee, a boy is shot. This event causes the nearly bankrupt grocer to attempt suicide, and though he is saved from committing suicide, his problems persist. The conclusion conveys the message that only a thorough-going change in the social and economic system will correct social problems.[8]

Model Tenement was to open at the Great Northern Theatre. However, Mayor Kelly's "right hand man," Victor Klebba, prompted the play's censorship by citing its "dangerous and subversive ideas."[9] Further supporting the censorship, Kelly phoned WPA headquarters in Washington, calling the play "seditious." Later in 1936, Hymn to the Rising Sun, the Paul Green play successfully presented by the Experimental Theatre in New York, was banned in Illinois by the state's WPA Director, Robert Dunham.[10] A year later when Hallie Flanagan asked Mayor Kelly why he cancelled <u>Model Tenement</u>, Kelly answered: "Don't get me wrong, I can stop plays about sex that would cause crime among our boys and girls."[11]

Chicago gained nationwide notoriety for its first big original show, a musical comedy revue, <u>O Say Can You Sing</u>. The hit had a history-making run of seven months, December 12, 1936-August 21, 1937. The book and lyrics were by Sid Kuller and Ray Golden, with music by Phil Charig. George Kondolf was highly instrumental in launching and motivating the project. He wanted to show that Chicago could do a Broadway-type musical revue as well or better than any done in New York. The format and storyline of <u>O Say Can You Sing</u> influenced the writing of <u>Sing for Your Supper</u>, done by the Popular Price Theatre in New York when Kondolf was brought there for the specific purpose of repeating the same type of show as <u>O Say Can You Sing</u>, a production about Uncle Sam becoming a theatrical angel.

Hallie Flanagan characterized the show as being very regional: "Chicago was distinctly itself, creating its own new patterns out of its own material and suited to its own city." She called it a "made in Chicago" show--"Chicago as Chicago." With a blustering bravado, the show depicting the WPA in show business, revealed that "No antiadministration paper could laugh more at Federal Theatre than did Federal Theatre itself."[12]

FTP described the storyline of <u>O Say Can You Sing</u> as follows:

Newsboys broadcast the information that Uncle Sam goes into show business. Actors, singers, dancers receive the news. Mr. Hamfield, a prominent theatre man, now secretary of entertainment, is introduced to the secretary of the budget and announces his plans to put actors back to work. In front of the Federal Theatre office, he encounters and leaves a one man trio. Later, in his office he meets a directorial genius with a new method of acting. His secretary encounters a magician and a singer, who are seeking employment. Mr. Hamfield turns down a proposition from the secretary of the budget to place his wife in a Federal show and thereby draws the enmity of the budget director. The latter then has Hamfield brought before the Supreme Court on charges of unconstitutionality but fails to have him nullified. The budget director holds back funds for the Federal Theatre, and the actors rally to support Hamfield. Hamfield appears before his home town to state his case. Back in his office, Hamfield reminisces on the careers at stake in his struggle with the director of the budget. Brought before the Senate, Hamfield is vindicated.

Scenes from the Federal Theatre productions weave in and out as Hamfield endeavors to establish his project. Modern and satiric ballets, tap dancers, choruses, specialty numbers, new songs and singers are revealed.[13]

Critical response to O Say Can You Sing was mixed. Although the show was given a great deal of attention in the press, reviewers were only luke-warm to the revue, which they considered "loud and lavish," "brassy," "boisterous," and "vulgar." According to Flanagan, "It was distinctly not a critic's show. It was a people's show."[14]

The New York incarnation of O Say Can You Sing in Sing for Your Supper was far more difficult and far less successful. It was Kondolf's New York commercial orientation which inspired him to do O Say Can You Sing in Chicago. However, when he took over the position of Director of the New York City Regional Federal Theatre, he encountered a host of difficulties working against Sing for Your Supper's opening and possibility for success. Where Chicago critics were somewhat scandalized by O Say Can You Sing's "vulgarity," New York critics dismissed Sing for Your Supper as a nervy, weak, and mediocre attempt to imitate a Broadway musical. Both shows became known as people's, not critic's, shows. However, Federal Theatre's experience with these two musicals revealed how FTP's work in one region influenced its work in another.

The next new play presented by the Chicago Project was Howard Koch's Lonely Man described by FTP as a modern dramatic fantasy. It opened at the Blackstone Theatre, May 16, 1937, and ran through August 28. It tells the story of David Hildebrand, a "reincarnated" Abraham Lincoln returning to Lincoln University in the 1930s--seeking a job as a professor. He arrives just at the time mine owners in the neighborhood and the College Board of Trustees are urging the faculty and students of the university to be silent about a number of abuses suffered by the miners. During his interview, Hildebrand evades all questions about his past in a clever and skillful manner, is hired, and soon becomes not only a very effective teacher, but also acts as the attorney for a miner fired for "spreading views inflammatory to the mine owners." When the aroused students seek to invade the jail and liberate the miner, Hildebrand argues against violence. Enduring attacks by strike breakers, Hildebrand finally wins over the radical students and faltering university president to his benign purposes. He then quietly leaves.[15]

Press comments were moderately favorable. Variety said, "It marks the high mark for production on the part of the WPA theatre group and, along with other efforts of the Chicago FTP, ranks as solid theatre. WPA has done many fine things, but this rates with the best."[16] The Chicago Herald Examiner claimed, "The FTP deserves plenty of credit for its fine production of a difficult play."[17] The New York Times reported that audiences were hailing the production enthusiastically.[18]

Lonely Man was part of FTP's campaign promoting historical plays with "updated" material linking characters and situations from American history to problems of contemporary society. Howard Koch, the author, indicated that Lonely Man was about a young Lincoln "returning to the modern world to find that the slaves were still not free; in other words they were taking different forms now. They were 'wage slaves'. . . . People generally oppressed . . . wanted to [be] free again."[19]

Koch was the head of the first fledgling FTP Playwriting Unit in New York. Reflecting on the subject of Lonely Man, and how in the play, labor and academics united in a common struggle during the Depression, Koch stated,

> I think it still is a hope . . . that intellectuals will finally have some influence on . . . our soul. . . . Now at the time we felt we were a part of a decision. What we did was important, that we could create a theatre which could say things which would help people, which would answer some of the social questions which were brought up by the Depression.[20]

Lonely Man was also noteworthy because a non-Federal Theatre employee, Robert Milton, was engaged to direct the show because he owned the rights. He could be brought in under the FTP ruling allowing 10 percent of production staffs to be comprised of non-Project personnel. Milton engaged John Huston to play the role of the reincarnated Lincoln under the same arrangements.[21]

Lonely Man was the final work to be presented by a regular drama group in Chicago during George Kondolf's tenure as Director. In

September 1937, Kondolf left Chicago to assume the position of Director of the New York City Project. Harry Minturn replaced him.

The last new play produced in Chicago was another Marcus Bach script, Mister Jim, at the Selwyn Theatre, July 4-9, 1938. Presented as a try-out test for a commercial run at an increased admission price of $2.00, Mister Jim was set among desert ranchers in the Southwest. While he was on a Rockefeller Foundation Grant to conduct research in New Mexico, Bach wrote Mister Jim. A tenant rancher, Jim neglects his work in order to satisfy his mystical yearning to write songs like the "Psalms of David." Threatened by eviction, Jim is saved when he discovers a cave which has the potential for becoming a big tourist attraction. The government rewards Jim for his discovery by giving him a new job as the writer of guides to be sold to visitors coming to the cave to see a new touristic center of interest.[22]

Charles Collins, writing in the Chicago Tribune, characterized Bach's work as derivative: "The author has borrowed an epileptic halfwit character from Of Mice and Men, and keeps him on stage in a chronic state of jitters to the acute discomfort of the audience. . . . The rest of the work sounds like a blend of all the folkloric and hillbilly plays ever written." Collins also stated that Mister Jim was a "non-play," with "words minus action." He further disparaged the play by stating: "The play has less dramatic value than anything the project has staged in Chicago . . . It is cold and dead at birth . . . Any first nighter . . . would brand it with the dreadful word failure."[23] Claudia Cassidy agreed that it was "trite, tiresome, and unpardonably reminiscent."[24]

The production of Mister Jim exacerbated an on-going controversy about FTP's incursions into the domain of commercial theatre. Highly derivative and "amateurish," Mister Jim provoked vituperative critical reaction which was unanimously negative.

Previewers especially lambasted the FTP for boosting ticket prices for such a mediocre play and production. Claudia Cassidy stated: "Not only does it fail disastrously to measure up to commercial standard, but it is far inferior to several productions which have played the regular federal houses at modest prices."[25] Variety also lamented FTP's incursion into the Loop area of Chicago, causing unfair competition with commercial theatre.[26] Mister Jim received what was probably the most negative critical rejection of any FTP play due to derivative content. This became an "example" of a play illustrating FTP's "ineptitude."

One play rejected by George Kondolf for Chicago production was Every Where I Roam by Arnold Sundgaard, later produced on Broadway by Marc Connelly in December 1938. Sundgaard, who worked in the Midwest Playreading Bureau, recalled that the small group of readers consisted of approximately five writers, then including Alice Gerstenberg, Sidney Blackstone, and Fanny McConnell. They met twice a week to discuss their reports, compared them, and then discussed their conclusions with Susan Glaspell. Plays were sent from all parts of the Midwest in various forms and degrees of quality. Sundgaard remembered that the condition of the manuscripts was often unusual: "They didn't even know what a script really looked like. Some of them were handwritten, sent from farmers in Minnesota or North Dakota and from towns like Grand Forks, or Lincoln, Nebraska." Sundgaard stated that the Midwest Play Bureau was conscientious about doing comprehensive reader's reports, copies of which would be sent back to the authors, and that Glaspell tried to encourage writers whose plays were rejected.[27]

Recalling his work on <u>Every Where I Roam</u>, Sundgaard remembered that he was inspired to write the play while working on the magazine, <u>Midwest</u>. He found one cover particularly inspirational and used it as a basis for the play. According to Sundgaard, Kondolf rejected the play because Kondolf's orientation was the commercial, Broadway theatre, and also because the play reflected populist sentiments, which were much too far to the left for Kondolf. Sundgaard stated that he and Glaspell attempted to foster innovative, experimental work, since Glaspell's orientation was that of the Provincetown Players, where she worked with Eugene O'Neill. Sundgaard regreted that the Midwest units did not do the kind of regional plays they had planned.[28]

Recommended for a writing position by his mentor at Yale University, Walter Pritchard Eaton, Sundgaard worked with the FTP during the period from December 1936 through 1938, and was then disqualified because he became an "employed" writer after having written two plays and a novel. To gain his original employment by the Chicago Federal Theatre, Sundgaard recalled hitchhiking to Chicago, Thanksgiving 1936, with fifty cents in his pocket, renting a room at the Delano Hotel for twenty-five cents a night, and the next day walking to the FTP office at the corner of Rush and Erie. "You've no idea what the Depression was like. It was cold, and I went out to a high school . . . and I got in line with all the other unemployed people . . . blocks, long blocks of people . . . in that dismal cold. There was a smell of fumigation . . . the smell of poverty."[29]

Chicago Project employees described Chicago as offering special advantages for FTP writers. According to Sundgaard, work with the Chicago FTP was especially exciting for young writers:

We could drift into a rehearsal for a dance troupe or a vaudeville troupe there. We'd go around to different theatres . . . or to . . . Federal symphony rehearsals. There was a ferment there in Chicago for any young person . . . and then in the evening . . . We'd congregate and see Studs Terkel . . . Meyer Levin was an editor at Esquire at that time . . . It was Bohemia; for me one of the really exciting periods of my life.[30]

Ohio's major contribution to the category of new plays was Ohio Doom by Harold Igow. It opened in Cincinnati on November 22 and played a week of performances until December 2, 1938. The program for the production stated that Ohio Doom was a second play (the only one produced) in a projected "Transitional Trilogy" reflecting the changing times in America since the 1920s: "It attempts to fuse the rhythm of the machine with that of the soil, through social organization and integration." It is the story of Tom Garner who, after working for years in the Ford plant in Dearborn, Michigan, arrives homes in Ohio for his grandmother's funeral. Finding the family farm in a state of decay and the farmers backward and superstitious, Garner wants to employ some of the efficiency techniques of the auto assembly line to improve the farm's condition and productivity. Encouraged by the fact that chain farming had already been introduced in the country with some success, Tom attempts unsuccessfully to persuade his town to adopt it. Just as he is to return to work again in the Ford plant, a barn is destroyed by a fire for which he is blamed. The fire causes Tom's father to have a stroke. Tom's younger brother torments him by claiming that their father caused the fire to keep Tom on the farm. This ploy forces Tom to remain at home and rebuild the barn with the help of neighbors. As the work begins, Tom's father attempts to watch the construction, but as he approaches the windows to watch, he dies. However, he dies knowing that his son, Tom, is "where he belongs."[31]

The Cincinnati Enquirer said Igow "has the spirit of a poet, but when he puts his ideas into dramatic form, he can't keep out of a rut bordered with cliches about urban and rural life." The reviewer further stated:

> Mr. Igow is impressed with the need for farmer cooperatives to prevent independent farmers from being swallowed up in a tenantfarming system dominated by city Capitalists. . . . Mr. Igow's play has the merit of holding your interest. Its short-comings are in its pretense to set forth a real situation in Ohio by creating the false impression that nobility of character . . . is limited to rural areas like "Yellow Creek."

The reviewer criticized another impression given by the play: "[It] . . . errs in making its principal pastoral characters poetic souls frequently ready to spout forth with the latest flash from a recent communion with Nature. . . . Ohio Doom doesn't reveal Mr. Igow as the capable playwright he may become with more practice.[32]

Ohio Doom reflected a FTP tendency to offer plays romanticizing rural life and at the same time extolling the virtues of "social progress" in urban industrial areas despite the machinations of "city capitalists." New playwrights were not always deeply familiar with their "native landscape" and strove in their efforts, however feebly, to write about the "land" and the "people" self-consciously.

Detroit was Federal Theatre's center of gravity in Michigan. Little else happened outside that industrial metropolis. Two new plays were done by the Detroit FTP: William Beyer's I Confess and Arthur Miller's They Too Arise. The FTP promoted I Confess as a script with, exceptional comic value. The background and material is universally fresh and topical, and has never been used before in this way. . . . Very amusing, rapidly paced and without a single taboo. Would give offense to no one. . . . Dialogue is crispy and funny, treatment is original.[33]

The play tells the story of what happens when Ernie Walters loses his job as an orchestra musician. Supported by his wife, Amy, he sits around all day playing his trombone. To supplement their income, the couple take in a boarder, Diane Dennis, who works as a graphologist (a handwriting analyst). Diane and Amy enter a "confessional magazine" story contest—to "tell their lives" in a highly fictionalized manner. Ernie is made the main character in their story, but despite the clever contrivances, the story is rejected. The surprise ending reveals that Ernie has also entered the contest and has won the prize with his "confession."[34]

Francis Bosworth, head of the Playreading Department of FTP, was the first to promote the script. In a memorandum, he wrote, "Here is a grand mighty comedy written in the manner of Beggar on Horseback. This is a real challenge to an experimental theatre, yet contains no taboos and would be enjoyed as good entertainment by any audience.[35] According to FTP guidelines, a good play did not go against the taboos or mores of a community.

I Confess was first considered and rejected as a vehicle for New York's Experimental Theatre, as indicated by reader, Louis Solomon: "Essentially a yarn of the Broadway-hoofer type, and not a very good one at that, which no amount of flashbacks and hocus-pocus staging can disguise. . . . In any event, not the type of script suitable for the Experimental Theatre."[36]

The author directed the production, assisted by the technical crew in giving the performance some clever staging. A circular, revolving platform was used:

> The preliminary scene and the last scene take place on the permanent setting, which is the living room. During the end of the first scene . . . the lights black out, and the rhythm of the typewriter is heard in the dark. At this point, the house curtain is lowered, and during an intermission of a minute and a half . . . the revolving platform is turned to the first flash-back scene.[37]

I Confess represents a FTP attempt to avoid controversy by doing "commercial" plays; however, the choice is ironic since Bosworth had recommended the script for an Experimental Theatre production. Comments by Bosworth reveal what for FTP, and perhaps generally for the time, was considered commercial or "experimental." Since no specific guidelines were provided to readers by FTP Playreading Department supervisors, it is difficult to know what would constitute experimental, or even conventionally "good" criteria for that matter.

Arthur Miller's first play, written while he was a student at the University of Michigan, won the Avery Hopwood Award in 1936 and first prize in the Bureau of New Plays Contest in 1937. They Too Arise was first produced by the Hillel Players at the Lydia Mendelsohn Theatre in Ann Arbor, Michigan, and deals with the struggles of a middle-class Jewish family during an industrial strike. Its first and only performance in Detroit was October 23, 1937, at the Jewish Community Center. The decision to present the play at the Jewish Center followed Detroit FTP's new 1937 policy of bringing productions directly to the various groups and organizations of the city. In the cast were Jay Michaels as Abe Simon, the "reactionary" father, and Hy Foreman as Arnold, the younger son.[38]

They Too Arise relates how clothing manufacturer Abe Simon loses his business because he refuses to help strike breakers during a clothing workers' strike. An opportunity to save himself is given to Simon when Roth, a rich manufacturer visits him expressing a desire to have Simon's son, Benny, marry Roth's daughter, Helen, so that the young couple can take over the business when Roth retires. Benny is willing to marry the girl to save his parents from poverty, despite the fact that he does not love her. However, Abe rejects the offer when he learns that Roth has used strike breakers and has also denied him his customers. Simon orders Roth to leave the house.[39]

There was a great variance of opinion regarding the play's promise as reflected in several playreaders' reports. Leo Schmeltsman characterized They Too Arise as "A plotless, incoherent, undramatic and uninteresting piece. It has a few lines of good humor and smooth but juvenile and pointless dialogue."[40] Another report, signed "Fuller," included the comment: "This is a sincere social play taking cognizance of the economic impass which makes it impossible, in many cases, for sincere employees to combat the oppressors within their own ranks and survive . . . needs a good bit of cutting."[41] Playreader John Rimassa indicated: "The author uses what sounds like authentic dialogue, but has kept his play upon a monotonous level, has failed to include any drama, humor, or melodrama." Rimassa found the result "very dull dull talk," derivative of Awake and Sing without the "theatrical ingredients," making the play "very life-like" but dull.[42] Fanny Malkin remarked: "The author has no knowledge, training or dramatic sense; not enough to write a play. Results: incoherence, very poor dialogue using Jewish dialect, dreadful method of characterization."[43]

A reader's report signed "Lipschutz," qualified <u>They Too Arise</u> as "an exceedingly promising play, just fitted for the Anglo-Jewish Theatre." Despite the fact that Lipschutz found "weaknesses in dramatic structure" and the dialogue "often heavy," he stated that the play was "really dramatic for all these weaknesses . . . characters are convincing." He also stated that the script was the most convincing he found while working for the Play Bureau.[44] However, a later report signed by Benjamin Ressler, Leo Schmeltsman, and Lipschutz characterized the play as,

> merely an attempt at playwriting . . . some ability for dialogue, but his ideas are pitifully immature. Construction is hopeless . . . The development and climax are unconvincing. While the author should be encouraged, his present effort is still too poor a play to deserve production consideration.[45]

A curiously unsigned report gave glowing praise to Miller's drama. This "reader" stated that the play had "definite promise" and was written with simplicity, "honesty and conviction." The report also stated:

> Every character is lifelike and individual, and none of the Simons is a carbon copy of any other Jewish stage family. The development . . . is told with power, and natural effect. . . . The dialogue has vitality, authenticity, and abundant humor, and characters are fresh and well-rounded. . . . bitingly genuine, rich in sentiment, though never lapsing into sentimentality, and reaches its evolving conclusion with true artistic restraint.

The report continued to say that the author "writes from the heart and has something to say." The final recommendation urged that the play be given "immediate try-out" since it was an original approach to the contemporary picture.[46] Arthur Miller was a writer in the Playwriting Department, and also a playreader at the time.

In another unsigned synopsis and comment on <u>They Too Arise</u>, in the "official" format used by the Play Bureau, the play was described as "an universal script, written with an understanding concept of the labor problems current in the clothing industry. . . . several finely wrought characters . . . sensitive observations of Jewish life." It was recommended for Jewish labor audiences and "all adult socially alert groups."[47]

A look at the "behind-the-scenes" contrivances in the consideration of <u>They Too Arise</u> shows how far the lack of congruence could go among Federal Theatre arbiters. It is not clear who the "special" readers were in this case, but the fact that there was so much variance of opinion among the young readers and the "official" view is curious. One can only speculate about Arthur Miller's role in this occurrence.

In any case, none of the FTP plays presented in Michigan or Illinois were by local writers reflecting their "native landscape." The work in Detroit was very New York: a comedy by a New York author, using a New York locale. The Miller play was by a New York writer portraying labor strife in New York's garment center.

Susan Glaspell never succeeded in reflecting the native folklore, native poetry, or indigenous drama of the Midwest as she had planned. However, the Midwest Play Bureau was one of the most serious and diligent in its effort to realize its other aims. A great deal of nationwide attention was focused on the Chicago Project when it produced <u>Lonely Man</u> and Arnold Sundgaard's <u>Spirochete,</u> a Living Newspaper about syphilis. Despite the failure to realize her aims, and despite the FTP's "melodramatic" problems with censorship, Glaspell helped create an atmosphere which, with the general social climate in Chicago, made that city an exciting place for a writer to live and work. It was in Detroit, not

New York, where Arthur Miller was given the first professional production of one of his plays. Probably one of the greatest ironies of the FTP enterprise was Arthur Miller's rise to fame despite the very mixed and very negative messages given to him by his peers and mentors. When one contrasts the history of the professional production of Miller's first play and that of Marjory Stoneman Douglas's <u>Gallows Gate</u>, remembering that <u>Miami Life</u> predicted a brilliant future for Douglas, one is struck by the realization of how tenuous FTP's role was in finding, nurturing, and launching real talent.

Notes

[1]Flanagan, Arena, p. 136.

[2]Ibid., p. 131.

[3]Chicago Daily News, 22 August 1936.

[4]Peoria Star, 3 May 1937.

[5]Susan Glaspell, George Kondolf, and John McGee, Memorandum to Hallie Flanagan, 6 November 1936. Record Group 69, United States National Archives, cited in John Charles Koch, "The Federal Theatre Project: Region IV--A Structural and Historical Analysis of How It Functioned and What It Accomplished" (Ph.D. dissertation, University of Nebraska, 1981).

[6]Chicago Daily News, 29 January 1937.

[7]Chicago-American, 29 January 1937.

[8]Synopsis at George Mason University.

[9]Victor Klebba to Robert Dunham, Illinois WPA Director, 4 January 1936. Record Group 69, United States National Archives, cited in Koch, p. 193.

[10]Lee Stanleigh, Daily Worker, 24 December 1936.

[11]Flanagan, Arena, p. 136.

[12]Ibid., p. 138.

[13]Synopsis in Production Bulletin, n.d., n.p. At George Mason University.

[14]Buttitta and Witham, p. 145; Flanagan, Arena, pp. 139-140.

[15]Synopsis at George Mason University.

[16]Variety, 26 June 1937.

[17]Herald Examiner [Chicago], 17 May 1937.

[18]New York Times, 18 June 1937.

[19]Interview with Howard Koch, conducted by John O'Connor, n.d. Tape at George Mason University.

[20]Ibid.

[21]Ibid.

[22]Synopsis at George Mason University.

[23]Chicago Tribune, 5 July 1938.

[24]Journal of Commerce [Chicago], 5 July 1938.

[25]Ibid.

[26]"WPA Takes Over the Selwyn," Variety, 29 June 1938.

[27]Interview with Arnold Sundgaard, conducted by John O'Connor, 5 September 1976. Tape at George Mason University.

[28]Ibid.

[29]Ibid.

[30]Sundgaard, quoted in Federal One II-2 (August 1977): n.p.

[31]Synopsis at George Mason University.

[32]Cincinnati Enquirer, 23 November 1938.

[33]Synopsis at George Mason University.

[34]Ibid.

[35]Francis Bosworth, General Memorandum to Playreading Department, 29 June 1936. At George Mason University.

[36]Louis Solomon, Playreaders report, 15 July 1936. At George Mason University.

[37]Technical Report, Production Bulletin, n.d., n.p. At George Mason University.

[38]Detroit Times, 17 October 1937.

[39]Synopsis at George Mason University.

[40]Leo Schmeltsman, Playreaders report and synopsis, n.d. At George Mason University.

[41]Fuller, Playreaders report, 9 February 1937. At George Mason University.

[42]John Rimassa, Playreaders report, 4 January 1937. At George Mason University.

[43]Fanny Malkin, Playreaders report, 7 December 1937. At George Mason University.

[44]Lipschutz, Playreaders report, n.d.

[45]Benjamin Ressler, Leo Schmeltsman, and Lipschutz, Playreaders report, n.d. At George Mason University.

[46]Unsigned Playreaders report, n.d. At George Mason University.

[47]Official synopsis at George Mason University.

CHAPTER X

THE WEST

(California, Colorado, Oregon, Washington)

According to Hallie Flanagan, the Western region reflected best the spirit of its territory. Speaking of Federal Theatres west of the Mississippi, Flanagan claimed: "They were more free and easy, more exuberant and gutzy. They picketed less and laughed more." FTP had to urge restraint in the West, unlike New York where "We were always moving heaven and earth to get shows open." One of the Western directors informed Flanagan that FTP did not have to worry about union regulations because theatre people in the West would work night and day to get a show on. It was precisely this spirit that enabled California to produce 398 shows as compared to New York City's 242.[1]

Flanagan noted a further difference in the spirit generated on the two coasts. She reflected that the attitudes of western theatre workers was completely different from New York workers, who more typically regarded Project supervisors as members of "management" pitted against the interests of the working classes. In the West, clashes of any sort between Project workers and officials were considered more of a family quarrel: "Here, as in the South, people on the Project saw us off on trains, gave special performances after hours, often running through their entire repertory."[2] It was probably because of this special feeling in the West that Federal Theatre was able to accomplish there some of its most creative, innovative work.

Denver, Seattle, Portland, San Francisco, and San Diego selected their plays and planned their programs through the regional service bureau in Los Angeles. Unlike the FTP units in Louisiana, Oklahoma, or North Carolina, which were linked to their communities and serviced them by providing celebrations and special events, Denver (under the direction of Karon Tillman and Michael Slane) remained exclusively a theatrical organization. Denver never produced what would be considered a "local" or "regional" play.[3] The two new plays it produced were Me Third by Mary Coyle Chase, a local journalist, and This Pretty World by Converse Tyler.

Me Third was presented at the Baker Federal Theatre in Denver, November 27-December 12, 1936, and was produced on Broadway, re-titled Now You've Done It. Chase later wrote the very commercially successful Harvey. Me Third's story centers around the exploits of Harlan Hazlett, a very egocentric man, catered to by his wife, sister, and mother, and his plans to run for the office of County Attorney. His motto is "God first, the other fellows second, and me third." This "sign of goodness" inspires his wife Stella to sacrifice to help Harlan get elected. The Hazlett family hires a maid, who as it turns out is a reform school graduate, because they want to give the household "tone." However, Sandra, the maid, knows too much about the straying infidelities of the important men in the community, information which Harlan uses to blackmail his way into the nomination for office. Meanwhile, Sandra conspires to get her friend, Joe, a job as the family gardener. Joe falls in love with Stella and devotes himself to the task of exposing the family secrets. Succeeding in his strategy, Joe is then exposed as a millionaire hiding from his mother and her intense insistence that he run for mayor. Stella becomes thoroughly disgusted and decides to get a Reno divorce in order to attach herself full-time to Joe. During this time, Harlan discovers after all of the votes are tabulated that he has come in third in the campaign.[4]

Two readers' reports rejected the play in no uncertain terms. Tralie McCann wrote:

> This is neither fish nor fowl. The author says it is a farce, but the only farcical thing about it is the outline of the plot, which might be made into a real farce with proper handling. As it is, it is a hopeless mass of situations and ridiculous characters who never are funny.[5]

Edmund Fuller was less kind:

> One of the most abysmally stupid plays this reader has plowed through in a long time. If anyone would do so simple a thing as explain to me the phenomenon of the changing sex of the character named Orville or Orletta, I would be greatly comforted. The play is poorly written and is puerile in conception. It is unsuited to either professional or non-professional production.[6]

Me Third was produced because a "special reader" approved it as very commercial. Reviews were very favorable. A. de Bernardi did not agree with the playreaders' judgment of Me Third, stating in the Denver Post that it "has all the essential elements of a first class commercial farce comedy . . . with some re-writing could rank with such commercial successes as Strictly Dishonorable and Baby Cyclone."[7] Alberta Pike, writing in the Rocky Mountain News, said, "We've got a full fledged playwright in our midst." She described how the enthusiastic capacity crowd "half of it swathed in diamonds, poured down to the WPA theatre . . . by the car barns, looking for entertainment." According to Pike, the crowd was entertained in "large doses from a laugh-filled near-farce that is full of fresh ideas, witty lines and guffawproducing situations . . . Me Third . . . one of the best first plays I've seen in years."[8]

The success of Me Third spurred theatre activity in Denver generally. Because Chase was a local author, the press in her city warmly supported her. Critics in Denver were generally very encouraging to Federal Theatre doing new plays, to the point that Lee Casey, based on the success of Me Third, said in the Rocky Mountain News: "In its brief existence the Federal Theatre in Denver has done more toward the development of playwriting than has been accomplished by various little theatre movements thus far."[9] It was this spirit of support that also prompted Alberta Pike to credit FTP with helping to revive "the road" by creating interest in theatre: "A hearty and healthy revival of the road seems to be indicated in reports from Broadway producers and from local impressarios. Inland America . . . is willing to spend [money] on the spoken drama."[10] Me Third was considered to be a catalyst for inspiring interest in theatre and playwriting.

Me Third revealed an instance in which the differences in opinions expressed by FTP playreaders and local critics were extreme. This revealed the fallibility of the FTP selection process. The fact that the play was viewed so negatively by the playreaders, received so respectfully by local critics, and later produced by the commercially minded Broadway producer, Brock Pemberton, was a graphic example of how radically different the viewpoints could be regarding judgments of FTP plays.

The next new play, This Pretty World, depicted how an average family is ruined by the economic upheaval of the Depression. It was an example of a play written off Project time by a member of the Play Bureau- -in this case, the Playreading Supervisor. The show played at the

Lawrence Street Playhouse, March 12 through April 4, 1938. In this study of survival in New York City during the hard times of the Depression, the Haleys, an intelligent, middle-class couple, have suffered the humiliation of being "on relief" but gain back some selfrespect when Mr. Haley is given back his former position. His salary, supplemented by help from his daughter, Doris, and his son, Bud, who worked in a CCC camp, is not sufficient. Bud is discouraged when he cannot find a job, and is further disillusioned when he discovers that his sister, Doris, has left her boyfriend, Jim, to become her boss's mistress to improve things economically. Bud, in total despair, joins up with a disreputable group in the neighborhood consisting of strong arm racketeers. One night, having been trapped in a "set up," he kills a man in self-defense. Bud is convicted of the murder and, while waiting for execution, marries his girlfriend, Dot, who is pregnant. Dot gives birth to their child at the exact time of Bud's execution. Bud's parents are devastated, and Doris, enraged by the events, realizes that she has been selfish in her concern only with herself and joins forces with Jim to help others change their lives. The meaning is clear: crime does not pay.[11]

The Monitor stated that This Pretty World was a good example of FTP's desire to present plays by American authors relevant to the economic and social conditions of the times, in locales with which the authors were familiar.[12] The Rocky Mountain News reported that the play reached audiences, which were unanimous "in the opinion that it is the most interesting and exciting drama to be seen in a long time."[13] The Denver Democrat praised the play, indicating that Tyler succeeded in using "subtle lines" and a "contrasting set of situations" to expose how the "loathsome, degrading, brutalizing, and crime-breeding poverty . . . [that] distorts the lives of the young." The reviewer was pleased that Tyler "does not rail at wealth, or suggest reforms, nor does he throw a sop to silly sentimentality by a Pollyannish ending." The ending was provocative for the reviewer: "The play should make men think . . . surely there is some way out of this labyrinth of shattered hopes, broken lives."[14]

The Denver production of This Pretty World was an example of how much latitude directors were given in "doctoring" scripts. In the production bulletin for This Pretty World, director, Michael Andrew Slane indicated in his "Director's Report" a number of changes he made in the script while working on the production, stating that he changed the script so that Bud, not Doris, became the protagonist. There were several cuts made in the second act. In the third act, scenes with "extraneous material" about capital punishment were eliminated to give the play a sharper focus. Slane pointed out that Doris appeared to be too much of a mouthpiece for the author, too much of a union propagandizer. Tyler was admonished to promote his propaganda in action not in long "dissertations": "These preachings are boring to the audience no matter how left-wing the audience may be. This is especially true of a Midwest audience, which is anything but left-winged [sic]."[15]

Considering statements made by the Denver Democrat and the play's director, in his "Director's Report," one can assume that perhaps to some extent it was the director's play "doctoring" which made it more acceptable to local critics. One can conjecture that, in the "doctoring" process, the "propaganda" was muted, and the play became less a "dissertation" to the extent that it "does not rail at wealth, or suggest reforms." In this case even the suggestion of reforms would have been less acceptable to a "Midwest audience which is anything but left-winged."

This was a production well targeted for its audience as a result of the great freedom given directors to "doctor" plays. Even the fact that it was written by the head of the Playreading Department did not deny the director his authority in the rewriting of the script.

California is where some of FTP's most original and creative work was done. In its issue describing FTP in California, Federal One (a publication of the Research Center for the Federal Theatre Project at George Mason University) cited Hallie Flanagan's assessment: "It was the clearest and least expensive plan under which we worked." Headed by Howard Miller, California was one of the most productive and efficient regional organizations, with units in Los Angeles, San Francisco, Oakland, San Bernardino, Riverside, and San Diego. Los Angeles was the most vital, creating French, Yiddish, and Negro units, and others which produced classical, modern, religious, and experimental drama. Dance drama and musical revues were especially popular in Los Angeles, which was the FTP Western Region clearing house. Georgia Fink headed the Regional Service Bureau and supplied scripts and publications to the 18 Western region states. The Research Bureau compiled extensive historical informational guides including Plays and Pageants of the West.[16]

Beginning in the fall of 1937, cutbacks in personnel and administrative reorganization slowed production and diminished the California FTP's vitality. This lasted for a year-and-a-half, and by the end of 1938, the Oakland, San Bernardino, and Riverside Federal Theatres were terminated, leaving the San Francisco, Los Angeles, and San Diego units still operating, but at reduced effectiveness.[17]

California's dramatic units did the most to produce new Federal Theatre plays. Stock plays were favored at first, but when the national office applied pressure to change this policy, the California units began doing more modern and experimental productions.[18]

The most noteworthy unit attempting creative, original work was the Southwest Unit of Los Angeles under the leadership of Virginia Farmer, who had been associated with the Group Theatre in New York and the Provincetown Players. Farmer's goal was to interpret the life and history of the Southwest. She used the Stanislavsky method training gained from the Group Theatre to develop scenarios for plays, utilizing improvization, animal exercises, and other techniques. Farmer's approach employed collective collaboration in creating performance material. This "composing" method was a way of getting an actor to work for a collaborative group-creation rather than for his own selfaggrandizement as a performer.[19]

For its first production, the Southwest Unit chose Roadside, a revival by Lynn Riggs, presented at the Musart Theatre in Los Angeles, April 8-May 8, 1938. The unit's general intentions, explained in a program note for Roadside, were that, while the unit was developing as a repertory group, it would produce old and new plays from and about every section of the country-reflecting subject matter and themes portraying the lives of the people.[20] The program for The Sun Rises in the West stated some other goals of Farmer's group: "Although emphasizing any regional material, the Theatre of the Southwest is open to plays on the American scene which interpret their subjects in modern and progressive terms."[21]

The most significant work done by the Southwest Unit was The Sun Rises in the West, playing at the Mayan Theatre July 1-August 28, 1938. Chronicling the trek of pioneers traveling westward to California, the production was prepared as a collaborative effort by members of the unit, who contributed ideas, analyzed them collectively, and then developed a scenario. During rehearsals, actors created additional characters and situations. As a result of improvization, scenes were written, revised, and re-written by the authors in collaboration with the actors and director, who offered further criticism and suggestions. When the final version of the script emerged, the authors listed were Donald Murray, Theodore Pezman, and Rena Vale.[22]

The Sun Rises in the West relates the saga of a pioneering family who in 1851 begin a venture toward California seeking to discover gold. While in Nebraska, the Gillen's caravan meets prospectors returning from California telling tales of easy wealth. Abraham Gillen, repelled by these stories, decides to remain in Nebraska's wilderness to start a new life with his pregnant wife. Several generations of Gillens are born in Nebraska. In 1929, A. Gillen III is a prosperous farmer. Just before the Crash of '29, his son, Matt, lured by gold fever, goes to live in California. When the banks fail, the impoverished family of A. Gillen goes to settle on a few acres in Colorado, where they are confronted by dust storms. Gillen, a rugged individualist, will not cooperate with the Farmer's Association in Colorado and sells his remaining cattle to an exploitative speculator. In despair, Gillen sets out in search of Matt in California. Reaching Sacramento, the Gillens are confronted by tourists, dirt-storm refugees, hunger, and people giving a California "hard sell." This gives them no peace. The story becomes an updated 1930s version of the Gold Rush. At the camp for migrants in Sacramento, David Gillen is "galvanized into action" and helps the Gillens unite with others to find security.[23]

In her "Director's Report," Virginia Farmer stated that the theme of the play, the "spine," was the "fight for security--against an active background of migration and possession, dispossession and migration." Farmer indicated that her original plan for the staging of The Sun Rises in the West was to do the production in a semi-circular seating arrangement, with three main playing areas, using one "indicatory set piece or unconventionally painted traveler curtain." Lighting would be used to spot and highlight playing areas, fading to black at the end of scenes. These plans changed because of the staff and budget cuts occurring during the entire year the group worked on the production. A small proscenium theatre, the Musart, was finally used for the presentation.[24] In his "Technical Report," Art Director Frederick Stover described the scenography as employing "Small set units suggesting part interiors or exteriors, set against a blue cyclorama; the stage [was] framed by a cut-out proscenium in semi-circular form. Side stages were used . . . so that no changes were necessary."[25]

Critical reaction to the production was varied, but, in general, the Los Angeles area critics were among the most supportive of Federal Theatre workers, their aims, and accomplishments. The Hollywood Variety did not like the play's message, its purported bias: "It no doubt was plotted as a telling blow to Capital, but it comes far from accomplishing the purpose for which it is aimed."[27] However, the Herald Express called it "the most unusual and certainly most important play so far produced by the Los Angeles Federal Theatre Project. . . . It deals uncompromisingly with a drama of American life that tends to slip by us in the new's headlines, but hits with terrific impact when presented with fidelity of character and event as in the play."[28] The Los Angeles Examiner commented favorably on the acting and directing and found the plot "well woven" and the production moved "with brilliant pageant-like effect from the westward trek of the first California bound settlers to the transient labor of today's fruit field."[29]

Showing strong support for the FTP writers, Hollywood Life stated: "The average WPA writer has seen enough of unjustified poverty to make him an authority on the subject. Group action is likely to be his remedy." The reviewer praised the scripting and production of The Sun Rises in the West: "Mass movement and clear-cut writing comprise a stirring piece of writing." He also praised Eddison Von Ottenfeld's original score: "naive, profound, and melodious [music] punctuated this very artistic presentation."[30] The collaborative process of creating the script was praised by the Los Angeles Journal: "A blessed relief . . . is the absence of a 'star system.' Complete freedom of expression prevails among the members of the cast with a definite trend toward the development of a collective theatre."[31] The Wilshire Press lauded the content and form, and stressed that the collective writing was based upon records in social service files in addition to personal contact with workers in the fields to tell the story of the 250,000 California migrant workers in a "terse, hard-hitting" manner utilizing the "cinematic techniques of the Living Newspapers."[32]

California critics indicated a definite respect for the aims and purposes of the Southwest Unit. Virginia Farmer had very solid credentials in the professional theatre and brought her "experimental" background and experience while working with the Group Theatre and Provincetown Players to her work with the Southwest Unit in a dynamic and innovative manner. Her collaborative writing of scripts was very new for the time, and it is ironic that Los Angeles area critics were so appreciative. Here was an artist defying the "star system" in a place where the tradition was possibly most deeply entrenched. The combination of Farmer's background, talent, and way of working helped produce work of such a high caliber that no excuses had to be made for toddering "amateurism" or "artiness." Farmer's creative "professionalism" gained for her respect from all those who knew of, or evaluated, her work.

During the Spring of 1939, the Southwest Unit began work on the Living Newspaper, Spanish Grant. However, this, like many other projects, was never produced because of the Federal Theatre Project's termination in June 1939. Although they were not new plays produced for the first time by FTP, the Southwest Unit also presented Class of '29, The House of Connely, and Susan Glaspell's The Inheritors.

Conrad Seiler's Censored, a comedy-drama, opened March 30 and played through May 1, 1936. This satire attacks censorship by depicting how a realistic, brawling war play is produced and suddenly closed by the Vice-Squad, and then re-written by a moral reformer in a totally benign form. The play-within-a-play begins as World War I is being fought in the trenches by two pirates, Red and Tubbs. On the front line facing death, all they speak of is "wine, women, and song." While on furlough, Red murders his Lieutenant in a jealous fight over a French girl, Lizette. At this point, police officers and the ViceSquad enter to stop the play-within-a-play. During Act II, a trial is held to determine what constitutes stage decency. All arguments for decency are presented to the jury, which suggests that the play continue only if rewritten by Miss Clutterbuck, an authoress of many "clean" plays. This is accomplished as Act III becomes Act I during the structural transformation in the rewritten version. Act III reveals Red, Tubbs, and Lizette as characters of "high morals." Red is given the

Lieutenant's commission as a sop for losing the romantic contest, and Tubbs wins Lizette's hand. The dramatic action is interrupted by chorus members so that the entire scene takes on the quality of a "lady-like operetta."[33] Unfortunately, further information about the production was not located.

Around the Corner, by Martin Flavin, was presented July 15-26, 1936. This social drama depicted how the destructive effects of the Depression almost totally destroy a typical American family. Fred Perkins, a successful hardware merchant in a small Midwestern town, is despairing and nervous after having lost his business. Mary, his wife, is also agitated but not nearly as resigned and defeated. Mary and Fred's son, Joe, had become a petty criminal after losing a civil service job. Joe's brother, Amos, the County Sheriff, has come to live with the family to help financially, while a married daughter, Sally, having arrived for a brief visit, stays two months. Dave, who becomes romantically involved with Sally, enters the family circle destitute and unemployed. The tension in the family increases until it reaches a climax when Dave, after losing a job at a box factory, is provoked by Joe and Sally's desperation to stage a robbery at the train station. Feeling guilty, Dave surrenders to Amos, who breaks his oath of office and decides to give the young people another chance.[34]

Readers' reports for Around the Corner provoke curiosity as to why the play was selected for production because some of them were emphatically negative. Henry Bennett rejected the script with the following assessments: "Martin Flavin is too expert a craftsman to write an utterly impossible play, but this dismal picture of the times seems to lack any particular virtues." Bennett found the dialogue flat, the characterization "sketchy" and "unconvincing." The theme disturbed

Bennett: "The Author plumps for ruggedly individual effort as the way out of depression, but his argument is sadly illogical, unless the truth is that his play should be taken as a subtle satire."[35] Bennett disliked both the theme and the writing, leaving it unclear if his dislike of the point of view affected his regard for the writing. However, another reader, Lee Harnett, disagreed with Bennett regarding the quality of the writing: "Technically, the play is faultless--indeed brilliant. From the very opening, it moves in a sure straight line, with swift compactness, to its closing scene." Harnett agreed with Bennett about the author's theme and viewpoint. He stated: "Your reader, however, frankly disagrees with the viewpoint expressed by the author. Its implication, is, unmistakeably, that the lesson of the times is patience--patience with the existing society exactly as it stands--patience until it begins to work again."[36]

In the case of Around the Corner, Lee Harnett revealed an ability to differentiate between his dislike for the theme and point of view and his respect for the other aspects of the writing. Harnett's approach was not highly evident in other FTP's playreaders' reports. The young readers frequently reflected the opinion that reforms were not enough to improve social conditions. However, it was always apparent that these misgivings were over-ruled by the FTP official position which promoted reformist views. They also did not indicate what type of social changes should have replaced "reformism."

Lars Killed His Son, by Lawrence J. Bernard, described as a tragedy-drama, was presented at the Musart in Los Angeles February 1828, 1937. The action of the play takes place in Norway during the 1930s and tells the story of Lars Baregan, who enters a court room after proceedings are over and surrenders himself to the Magistrate and Prosecutor for having killed his son. Offering no motive for the crime, he is taken to a cell where he reads the Bible. The police torture Lars in an attempt to force him to reveal a motive for the murder, however, Lars resists the pressure. Meanwhile, the Coroner indicates that there were two sets of Lars's footsteps going to the shed where the son, Fergus, was killed. Character witnesses testify that Fergus was worthless. The motive for the murder remains a mystery as even Lars's good friend, Mortensen, cannot convince Lars to speak truthfully. Mortensen visits a greatly suffering Lars in his jail cell, but is still unable to force him to talk. During this time, Anne, Lars's wife, dies suddenly--an event which forces Lars to tell the true story. The final scene is the re-enactment of the tragic shooting. Lars has gone to the shed to reprimand Fergus for drinking. Fergus accuses Lars of causing his brother's death because of his coldness and lack of understanding. Lars attempts to halt Fergus's accusatory statements and then runs from the shed. Alone in the shed, Fergus shoots himself. The motive for the "killing" is now clear. Mortensen informs Lars that he will soon be free, however, Lars is left in a deeply despairing and sorrowful state.[37]

The Los Angeles Evening Herald referred to Lars Killed His Son as the most touching play ever presented by FTP, "a masterpiece that reaches deep into one's heart."[38] The Los Angeles Evening News disagreed, saying that the play was uneven and in need of revisions: "insufferably dull for two acts whose only virtue is that they do build for the climatic third." Both reviewers found the dialogue banal.[39]

San Bernardino's only new play was The Great Gay Road by Norman MacDonald, presented by FTP to American audiences for the first time after it had a very successful, long run in London. The story concerns how a soldier of fortune drifts along on "the great gay road of life," meeting happiness and then despair while associating with the entire spectrum of the social world in London--everyone from the slum dwellers to the elite of the English nobility. The charismatic soldier is accepted into high society as one who authentically belongs. Nancy, the niece of Sir Crispen Vickery, sees in this man the answer to her romantic dreams. The soldier of fortune is presented as having a dozen personas: vagabond, Don Juan, nobleman, thief and others. The "glamorous" man's true identity is revealed at the end.[40]

Critics in San Bernardino were impressed with The Great Gay Road. The show especially impressed the reviewer for the San Bernardino Sun Telegram-Riverside News, who liked it not the least because it "created a sensation in the London show world," and also because it was considered an "artistic three act-play."[41] However, it had been strongly rejected by two FTP playreaders, who found little to redeem what they considered a grossly inferior script. Milton Luban indicated in his report: "Rejected with great glee. A stupid, boring piece of writing. Author apparently is overcome with awe at the mention of a gentleman. Dialogue is stilted and inane. For his sake, I trust the author will never try to be his conception of a gentlemen." In the space where readers indicated the audiences for which plays might appeal, Luban stated, "Half-wits."[42]

Charles Gaskill obviously despised the play:

> The piece is so machine-made that it creaks constantly. One is aware of what will happen almost from the first, and being so aware is instantly depressed--for it's nothing to write home about. The dialogue--curiously pretentious in places--is very poor. One dislikes all of the characters--since none of them is a

truthful human --or rather truthfully a human. Clearly enough, when one dislikes the hero, one automatically dislikes all.[43]

Then Gaskill indicated that he thought it would appeal to the following audiences:

> At that, I am sorry to say, I really believe the stuff would appeal to lovers of what we call HORSE OPERY [sic]. In neighborhoods predominately composed of house-girls, valets, tub-ladies, and so on, it would go big. A five an' ten show [sic].[44]

The director indicated in his Director's Report that the show had appeal because, "While the subject matter of this production is out-dated and of no social significance, the atmosphere and actions are beautiful."[45] The director described the audience reaction as follows:

> The Great Gay Road was well received and was considered a beautiful and artistic play by most of the members of our audiences. On the other hand, a few did not enjoy the bill at all, and a few criticized it because it was an English play.[46]

FTP's decision to produce The Great Gay Road was curious for many reasons. Despite Federal Theatre's commitment to doing new American plays, some foreign plays like The Great Gay Road were offered if they were recommended by play agents because of a successful and glamorous run in a European capital. Local FTP directors in San Bernardino County obviously knew what would appeal to local critics and audiences. An out-dated, non-socially significant play would do just fine as long as it could be billed as having a "sensational" London run. However, some members of the audiences objected to a foreign play being presented. The script with no social significance did not appeal to the two readers quoted. A play about a glamorous "gentleman" living among the high and low life of London was judged to have no appeal for FTP audiences. Perhaps this was another case of the subjective opinions of FTP playreaders being of very little consequence in gaging the appropriateness of plays for various audiences. Subjective biases were evidently overruled in this case also by the "special reader."

Hallie Flanagan had characterized Los Angeles as a musical. Musical revues were a vital part of the activity in Los Angeles and provided that city with some of its greatest successes and notoriety. The first revue presented there was Follow the Parade by Gene Stone and Jack Robinson, directed by Eda Edson. The show was written to utilize the talents of the many vaudevillians out of work in California. Eda Edson wanted to help revive vaudeville and to assist in giving it new, fresh ideas so that it would have the same relevance in the thirties that it had in the twenties. Flanagan agreed with Edson: "We know that too often vaudeville is a dreary succession of outworn acts. I think it is our job . . . to work out new and exciting ways to use vaudeville techniques." These sentiments motivated the creation of Follow the Parade as a way of making vaudeville entertaining to audiences of the Depression era.[47]

During the first act of Follow the Parade, unemployed vaudevillians decide to produce a new show using vaudeville talent, classifying it as a topical satirical musical revue:

> Vaudeville performers congregated in a typical theatrical boardinghouse are reliving the glories of their past life in an attempt to reconcile themselves to being "out of the parade" with the new innovations of radio, etc. Jimmy Ross, a young stage director, has an enthusiastic plan for restoring vaudeville by a new type of presentation--differing from the typical musical revue in that his show concerns itself with the important events of the day, and its comedy is a commentary on topics that

concern the world at present. Jimmy sells his show to Moe Kornblum, who decides to produce it. Following a back-stage rehearsal, the opening night finds Moe in a state of trepidation over the outcome of his venture, although his unerring theatrical sense tells him the show has "box office."[48]

Opening April 12, 1936, and running until August 2, the revue was warmly received and won great praise from audiences and critics. Not only did it attract wide audiences, proving that vaudeville was perhaps making a comeback, it drew favorable comments from Variety which indicated that Follow the Parade was competing with the motion picture industry--in its own territory:

This is the biggest 50c [sic] worth of entertainment ever doled out in these precincts. Two and a half hours of music, hoofing, and specialties, with all else thrown in to give it the stature of a Broadway revue. . . . In that cast can be singled out names that meant something in the halcyon days of vaudeville. . . . Let the cinematics try to match it for 50c.[49]

Follow the Parade was so successful that it enjoyed a fourteen week run in Los Angeles and was then sent by the United States government to represent America at the Texas Centennial in Dallas.

Based on the success of Follow the Parade, a series of original revues written by Stone and Robinson were presented. Revue of Reviews was the next musical to captivate Los Angeles audiences. Presented January 14-March 28, 1937, it was similar in format to Follow the Parade in that it was a series of sketches, not a book show with a conventional plot. In the revue format, it employed as a unifying idea, the satirizing of popular magazines of the day. Particular leading magazines of the time were spoofed. One of the biggest crowd pleasers was the satire on dance magazines titled, "America Takes up the Dance," spoofing the Mary

Wigman and Kurt Jooss ballets by broadly making fun of their "ridiculously formalized dance of the workers."[50]

Time magazine was lampooned in a political sketch. The Evening News described the content and stage action of the other sketches as follows:

> Of quite a different nature, but almost as well received, was the act inspired by House Beautiful. By extending their principle and stipulating that "this issue features Dresden china," Authors Stone and Robinson were able to include in their show a tableau of porcelain figures that come to life and perform graceful dances. The costumes in this number, incidentally, are extremely well executed.
>
> Several of the other acts in "Revue of Reviews" also have real merit. There's the rib on Physical Culture magazine, whose publisher, it appears, doesn't approve of people who catch colds. There's the sketch inspired by Travel, notable for the catchy "It's a Small World After All" and impressionistic settings. There's another good tune sung to ingenious lyrics in the travesty on advertising copywriters. "Rhythm of the Breeze," an extraneous number which starts off the second act, also incorporates a good song.
>
> So, for that matter, does the amusing blackout based on Love Stories magazine and incorporating a ditty sung to varied lyrics by three couples. And as a final item on the credit side of the "Revue of Reviews" ledger must be put the dancing of Davey Jamieson.[51]

Although audiences were very enthusiastic, some of them returning more than once to see the show, certain critics found weaknesses in the revue as a whole. The Script reported that the music was of only average quality, lacking a real point of emphasis. A lack of good musical talent was lamented: "No matter how clever the material, nor how decorative the trimmings, no musical revue can survive without 'personalities,' and there is scarcely a single member of this cast who projects himself effectively."[52]

Gene Stone and Jack Robinson's Ready Aim Fire, a musical comedy, anti-war satire, followed Revue of Reviews. This was the most ambitious and most publicized musical to be done in Los Angeles. It differed from the other revues in that it was a book musical with a conventional plot and storyline. Presented October 22, 1937, and running through January 9, 1938, the story was described by FTP:

> Dictator Schmaltz of the mythical country of Moronia is perturbed by anti-war propaganda by banner bearing strikers who interfere with his preparedness program. Krupenheimer "the power behind the Dictator" calls on him to do something about those "damn pacifists," or they will ruin the country. A good war is what the country needs; it would help business. He overcomes Schmaltz's objection to war by proclaiming that their forefathers went out and got shot first and asked questions afterward. . . . That's patriotism. A Cabinet meeting is called by the puppet king, the Ministers declaring unanimously that the people refuse to get shot. In their hour of need, they are rescued by Franz Schulz, a football enthusiast just returned from America. What do they think brought America into the last war? The sinking of the Lusitania? No! A popular song: "Over There" did it. That is what is needed in Moronia right now. A telegram for help is dispatched to "Bugs" Magee and Harry Hinkle, a team of Hollywood song writers whom Franz has met, and preparations are made immediately to give them an official welcome.
>
> In the meantime Dictator Borsht of the neighboring state of Berzerkia, traditional enemy of Moronia, hears the sensational news that Moronians are to be stirred up by a new war song instead of the funereal sounding national anthem of which no one knows the words. He thereupon dispatches the beautiful spy

Sonya on a secret mission to Moronia to steal the song. Sonya, accompanied by the charming Princess Louise, disguised as her maid, burglarizes the song-writers' apartment, but finds nothing but old trash. Louise, posing as a chambermaid, is surprised by Franz, who falls in love with her. Sonya enters with the composers, who are rather tipsy from imbibing too much, finds the hiding place of the song and steals it. Thus Berzerkia comes into possession of a war song before anyone in Moronia has even heard it; slightly changed, it is broadcast to the excited Berzerkian populace. Unfortunately, Moronia is on the same radio-hook-up, and Hinkle and Magee are thrown into a cell for their carelessness and await execution for high treason. At the last minute, before a firing squad, Magee has an inspiration. He's found a sure-fire-hit-title for a sure-firesong: "READY! AIM! FIRE!" They are reprieved and decorated by Dictator Schmaltz, who now declares war upon Berzerkia. In the second act, Franz is heard as one of the actors in the Krupenheimer radio hour. Hinkle and Magee trick young men into entering the army by promising them strip-tease-acts by Gypsy Nora Lee. Krupenheimer manages the two hostile dictators like puppets . . . Franz, longing for Louise, escapes into Berzerkia, only to find that Dictator Borsht has first claims on her. Desperate, he returns to Moronia, and by singing "No More War" over the combined network, effectively, ends the war and enmity forever.[53]

Critical response was favorable. The Los Angeles Times viewed Ready! Aim! Fire! as an improvement upon Revue of Reviews in the quality of its writing, its music by Claire Leonard, and in the performances. The Times stated that the show was a "rollicking satire on war" performed with all of the qualities "needed to make a hit with the public." Qualities making the show a hit were its "verve, humor, whimsy, freshness, novelty, lively music and dances, pretty girls and a fine male chorus."[54]

Two a Day was the most ambitious venture in doing a musical, and one that called a great deal of attention to the special work Federal Theatre was doing in Los Angeles to revive vaudeville and to entertain with extravagantly produced musical comedies. Written by Stone and Robinson, it was a cavalcade of 50 years of vaudeville history presented in 30 rapidly shifting scenes. With a cast of 100, the show covered the period of vaudeville's history from 1890 through 1938:

Act I
This calvacade of vaudeville begins with the days of Pat Rooney and the Hickman Brothers in 1890 and ends with the radio programs of 1938. The great personalities of vaudeville are shown in bits of their "acts," interspersed by the outstanding news flashes in the march of time from 1890 to 1938, via spot pickups aided by the loudspeaker.

The Chicago World's Fair of 1893 is brought into the picture with its entertainment concessions and exhibits of the latest inventions of the day: Edison's X-ray, the cream separator, etc.

Thence, the action moves to 1897 and the heavyweight championship fight of St. Patrick's Day, won by Bob Fitzsimmons over James J. Corbett; then 1898 in Miner's Bowery Theatre in New York where the amateur night first award is given to a boy named Eddie Cantor. At the same time the news that the United States Battleship Maine has been sunk in Havana Harbor rouses the indignation of the nation.

The influx of immigrants from Germany brings about the familiar "little German band" on city streets and inspires the "Dutch comic" in vaudeville, as best exemplified by Weber and Fields. Lillian Russell was the reigning stage beauty of the time.

A family scene, introducing Mr. and Mrs. Evans, informs you that eggs in 1899 have risen to eight cents a dozen. With the cost of living so high, Mr. Evans is fortunate in earning the magnificent salary of $10 per week. The Evans decide to eat out that night at the swankiest cafe in town, indulging in the deluxe

25c dinner, after which they plan to attend Hammerstein's Music Hall where a new magician named Houdini is featured along with the Cherry Sisters and their "worst act in vaudeville," Marie Dressler and Harry Lauder.

In the year 1901 the assassination of President McKinley brings to the presidency of the United States the colorful Theodore Roosevelt.

In 1903 the first airplane flights are attempted, one by Professor Langley which failed and, two months later, another by the Wright Brothers, a success.

The Iroquois Theatre fire which took the lives of 488 people broke out during a performance of Eddie Foy in "Mister Bluebeard"; Carrie Nation was then hatchetating around from saloon to saloon; and no future threat to the popularity of vaudeville was apprehended in the new form of entertainment known as moving pictures, just flickering into existence.

And in 1907 vaudeville was being dressed in dazzling clothes by Florenz Ziegfeld. Beautiful girls and gorgeous sets succeeded in glorifying vaudeville as well as the American girl.

For the patriotic finale, follies girls, dancing to national airs, are dressed to represent states of the union, wearing miniature battleships for head dresses.

Act II

In 1910 the most beloved act playing the boards was Gus Edward's "School Days"; an up and coming young song writer named Irving Berlin was composing a tune called "Everybody's Doin' It" which he hoped would be as successful as "Alexander's Ragtime Band"; with the advent of ragtime came the craze for dancing: the "Turkey Trot," the "Grizzly Bear," the "Bunny Hug" and, finally, the "Tango," as introduced by Vernon and Irene Castle.

By 1914 the Evans family owns a Ford. Jokes inspired by the lowly "tin lizzie" are common in vaudeville, at home, and in the saloon. Mrs. Evans is too busy playing "whist" daytimes to have time to cook for her husband. Mr. Evans thanks God that women have not yet won the right to vote, and decries the way they'd rule the world. But Mrs. Evans points out that, with Europe on the verge of war, the masculine rule hasn't been anything to boast about.

In the year 1915, the sinking of the Lusitania is the event of most interest to America, and in 1917 war is declared with Germany. The liberty bond campaign starts with famous stage folk participating. Elsie Janis goes abroad and is shown entertaining doughboys in a French canteen.

In 1920 the year's greatest accomplishment seems to have been the Prohibition Amendment.

In 1926 vaudeville is pictured at its height, its performers in the money. Cross word puzzles have become the chief diversion of the Evans family with the money to be won playing the stock market a choice subject of conversation.

In 1928 the stock market is flying high, and the song is "Buy! Buy! Buy!" But, by 1930 the dirge has changed to a frantic "Sell! Sell! Sell!," and the market crashes.

In the midst of the depression, the same vaudeville performers, earning $350 per week in 1926, can scarcely spare a nickel for a brother, and bookings are few and far between.

And in 1938, in the Evans home, at the mention of vaudeville, the granddaughter of Mr. and Mrs. Evans asks: "Grandpa, what is vaudeville?" As Grandfather Evans attempts to explain, the great personalities of the vaudeville era parade onto the scene for the grand finale.[55]

Critics and audiences reacted very enthusiastically to Two a Day as a show, and also as an attempt to revive vaudeville. It played to packed, sold-out houses, causing many to observe the irony in the fact that vaudeville was having a "come-back" in Hollywood, the town responsible for killing it. Vaudeville's "re-birth" was seen by many as due to a great extent to WPA patronage. In one of the strongest endorsements of federal support of the arts, and specifically with regard to its role in reviving a dying theatrical form, the Hollywood Citizen News stated, regarding Two a Day:

> And when vaudeville comes back it will owe its renaissance to the WPA. To the Federal Theater projects. Art, and for that matter, artifice, flourish best under a system of patronage. History has proven that fact endlessly. Artists are as a rule not money makers and something the other needs. In the present age the American government is acting as patron of the arts, for private capital cannot do it. Private capital's resources are not broad enough to gamble on a renaissance in vaudeville. Private capital's resources are needed too badly in other directions. The American Government, by levering vaudeville into the public's consciousness, will definitely reestablish vaudeville as one of the pillars of the amusement world. In a short time vaudeville will be so well-established again that it will not need its patron. It will step boldly out on its own again. It will become a private enterprise. Vaudeville will not be a government project any longer. Vaudeville will have come back.[56]

San Francisco's highly anticipated and noted contribution to the production of new plays was the first production of George Savage's See How They Run, winning play of the Dramatists' Guild Play Contest. The social drama reflected labor conditions during the 1930s and opened at the Alcazar Theatre, running September 9-17, 1938. It tells how a liberal college president risks the fulfillment of his life's ambition to win a strike for the workers at the Maynard Milling Company. Capital, represented by the company's president, the Mayor, and the local bank president meet to devise a way to resolve the conflict. They conclude that the best solution would be to force Johnson, president of the State University, to sway public opinion against the workers by threatening to withhold money from a fund set up by the founder of the milling company. Two labor leaders vie for the commanding position. Meanwhile, Gus Schultz, a labor leader-racketeer watches enthusiastically. One leader, Aino Laukening, arouses the rank and file of the union into action. During the melee, Aino is killed, and the other leader, Steve McDougal, is badly hurt. Steve gets to Johnson before the groups representing Capital, and the racketeers. Johnson asks to meet with the racketeers and capitalists. A microphone is planted in the room, and as the group talks, the entire discussion is broadcast to a large crowd at a football game waiting to hear opening remarks. Exposed, the capitalists are only too eager to concede to the worker's requests.[57]

Ben Russak, head of the Playreading Department, in his remarks made as a judge in the Dramatists Guild Play Contest, called the play a "tour de force" because "the author has created out of melodramatic material, a drama of great power. . . . However . . . the chief fault lies with the superficial characterization--in an easy definition of character motivation."[58] Converse Tyler, reviewing the play for the contest, indicated that it had vitality and an exciting story, and further stated "Although it is tough-fibered . . . it succeeds in being fair-minded to a considerable degree."[59] Reader Jeannette Druce said: "There is not a woman in the cast . . . [the author is complemented] in resisting the conventional impulse to clutter up a masculine and intensely virile script with a sticky romance."[60] Playreader M. Porter, commenting on its suitability as a contest entry, indicated that the play reminded him of a John Howard Lawson "lesser masterpiece" and that "all it needs is a step-ladder on the stage to give it a 'constructivist technique.'" He found the play "weighed down with dialogue and the characters undeveloped."[61]

Perhaps the "constructivist" approach in the playwriting was also something that inspired the director, who, in his "Director's Report," stated that in front of synthetic photographic murals of a civic center and an industrial plant he placed "Six colored workers dressed in varying shades of blue [who] were used as strikers . . . radical workers in varying shades of red, and yellow dog workers dressed in yellow. An attempt was made to indicate the polyglot nationalities of the workers." The director further commented that the play was "wildly applauded" by labor and radical audiences but that it "bored everybody else."[62]

John Hobart, in the San Francisco Chronicle said,

> Although the problem [of the ending] is solved glibly, by calling in the National Labor Relations Board as though it were the marines . . . It is an interesting play but suffers from a certain didactic dryness that gives it the air of a symposium or a lecture-platform discussion.[63]

Robert Lee, in the San Francisco News, found the subject matter over-worked:

> Nothing new is said for capital or labor, and there's no solution offered to today's industrial problems. . . . But as entertainment, there's some argument in favor of the production. . . . Characters are well-drawn, lines are robust, if not always brilliant . . . the situation interesting.[64]

Commenting on the congressional investigations then being held into FTP activity conducted by Representative Martin Dies, the Call Bulletin stated:

> How far the government project will permit propaganda to be injected into its presentation, if at all, is yet to be revealed. What it has to say of communism will be of special interest, in view of

a congressional inquiry into asserted radicalism in the Federal Theatre Project beginning August 11, [1938].[65]

Wood Sloane of the Oakland Tribune was not too concerned about any "subversive" undercurrent in the play, saying that the collegiate viewpoint of the play would be very acceptable to a general audience but that a more radical group might be disappointed that possible propaganda in the play was subordinated to the dramatic action.[66]

In his autobiographical sketch, George Savage, the author of See How They Run, credits FTP for inspiring him to use Living Newspaper techniques in his play, that is, the interspersing of short, episodic scenes into the narrative.[67]

See How They Run vividly revealed a wide range of conflicting opinions about a play's content and form. Following the 1930's trend to write in a "committed" manner--social plays with labor-strife themes --,George Savage also attempted to enrich his material with techniques borrowed from the Living Newspapers. This, along with the fact that the script inspired the director to use "constructivist" techniques, made this production innovative for a FTP show. FTP readers found the characterizations weak; however, the San Francisco News said that they were "well drawn." The San Francisco Chronicle regarded the play as "didactic" and "dry," but the Oakland Tribune considered the "possible propaganda" subordinate to the dramatic action. Again, critics were encouraging to FTP, emphasizing that the form of this play was better than the content, illustrating the perfect FTP play: social, but not radical; always "fair-minded."

San Francisco's contribution to the production of an original musical comedy was noteworthy because of the experimental way it revealed its

plot. Swing Parade, arranged by Max Dill, Richard Melville, and Gene
Stone, with music by Nat Goldstein and lyrics by Richard Melville and Del
Foster, was a book-show with a series of sketches about show business.
Using over 100 performers, it played from April 15-June 30, 1937. FTP
described it as follows:

> A musical comedy of catchy songs, dances and comedy, a topical
> satire, a modern or reminiscent slice of San Francisco scenes. A
> television illusion, specialty performers, soloist, stirring
> choruses, attractive chorines, held together by a slender thread
> of continuity to make sense and give excuse for action.

Prologue:

Act I
Scene 1 "Swing Parade" starts on its ramble from a theatrical
boarding house. Here, stranded actors are trying to
bolster their spirits and find outlet for their talents,
meanwhile keeping in trim by practising their
specialties in the boarding house parlor.
Scene 2 shifts to a stage box in which Moe Kornblum, producer,
has an office. Business has been bad. Max is disgusted
and greets crisply a young author who presents his
play "Swing Parade" for his consideration.
Undaunted, the author describes its possibilities with
such fervor that Moe too becomes enthused and
determines to take a chance and put it "over."
Scene 3 shows backstage preparing for the opening of the new
play. Great activity among actors, dancing girls,
carpenters, electricians, stage-hands. Moe, nervous
and excited tries to look after everything and
everybody, thereby getting into all kinds of comical
difficulties. His wrath increases as peels of laughter
emanate from the members of his company.

Act I     the opening night. The play is on. A unique innovation is introduced: Each number of the act is called to the attention of the audience by television broadcasting. The announcer's face enlarged and projected upon a screen is seen in natural coloring.

Scene 1   to the tune of "Follow Swing Parade"--sung by an actor from the side of the stage as the curtain rises--the entire company, entering from the lobby, joins in the song, swings down the aisle of the theatre and onto the stage as the illuminated Golden Gate Bridge bursts into view and the famous China Clipper drones her way over the waters.

Scene 2   higher education takes a jolt in a street scene in Berkeley; two educated, uniformed street cleaners are discussing Shaw, opera, Voltaire and philosophy; two passersby, well dressed swells--not so intellectual-- weigh the pros and cons of Grand Opera and decide it is a worthless waste of time to listen to the great artists, then carelessly toss to the pavement two tickets they had bought. The tickets are a find for the street cleaners of higher musical taste.

Scene 3   the announcer takes the audience to Moscow, to a beautiful night scene in a Russian street. Snow is falling (this effect is produced by a clever manipulation of lighting); there is St. Petersburg, the winter palace, lights glistening upon the palace windows, sleighs arriving filled with gay, laughing young men and women, brilliant flashes of color in costume, fast moving music, rapid dancing, comedy, pep.

Scene 4   a ludicrous conversation takes place between a wellappearing citizen and a contentious, argumentative man of the town.

278

Scene 5 in Africa. A weird, wild, barbaric ceremonial dance, to the accompaniment of tom-toms, is in progress in jungle land, and the fantastic antics of the natives, urged on by the gayly adorned witch doctor and an alluring princess, give opportunity for a realistic bit of acting by the colored folk.

Scene 6 a street in New York. A clever piece of pantomime involving four people. Without a word being spoken, this skit, for over ten minutes, held the tense interest of the audience, broken at intervals by chuckles of laughter. A very creditable performance.

Scene 7 in Hawaii. A dozen fair girls dance the hula-hula on Waikiki Beach while the most "real" waves sweep its shore. In one of their numbers, they swung poi balls (or gourds) such as are used by natives of the Islands when celebrating one of their festival dances.

Act II
Scene 1 from far-away Hawaii, the announcer switches "just like that" to Toyland. Old familiar nursery stories come tumbling pell-mell before your eyes. Cinderella's pumpkin with the little mouse on top, the witches cauldron and the two hideous witches who turned Prince Charming into a frog, the funny paunchy guards, the patchwork girl, the red devil and the fairy godmother are all there. The wooden soldiers (a dozen young girls in military costumes) do their famous drill dance (recalled many times by the audience). The funny little Penguins with their Eskimo waddled across stage from their igloo and with their quaint dances and taking songs nearly broke up the show on opening night. The quintuplets, each in her own high chair wheeled in by her nurse, gave evidence that they could sing and dance in a very captivating way. Sure, as

always, of their audience, they answered to several encores.

Scene 2   prison--Alcatraz.   A take-off on the oft-repeated stories about the luxurious lives lived by the wealthy convicts.

Scene 3   "Black and White Rhythm," a dance ensemble, enabled nine colored men dancers to do some fast-stepping tap routines, on different levels. A spectacular effect. They wore full-dress suits and topper, one half of the suit wholly black and the other half white, turned alternately toward the audience as they danced.

Scene 4   "Three Men On a Bench" illustrated the usual boast of one man to another as to his "boss" status in his own family and the meek attitude of each when surprised by the sudden appearance of their respective wives.

Scene 5   "Chinatown Then and Now" showed Grant Avenue of twenty years ago with its odd stores, oriental atmosphere and pedestrians attired in costumes of the far East mingling with modern American citizenry; then an up-to-date Chinese Cafe with sight-seeing tourists, patrons, entertainers, colorful dancing and decorative furnishings. The theme running through this sketch is the betrothal of a baby girl and boy of opposing factions in the tong controversy, culminating in their marriage in later years.

"Stu" Stewart, a drunk, entering and leaving the various scenes at odd moments caused many laughs by his clever understandable pantomime, "unconscious" expression and comical slump of body.

A melophone, a soprano, and a violinist, playing and singing, between acts, from two upper stage boxes was a highlight of the show.[68]

The experimental use of the television machine to reveal the storyline was described by the Supervisor of the Sound Department as follows:

The whole plot of "SWING PARADE" was based upon an imaginary tour with a Television machine, on a screen where an announcer was seen in pure and natural color and enlarged to six by five feet. This was achieved by the ingenious use of a special, chemically coated, transparent screen set at right angles in the middle stage left box. The screen was stretched on frames and lined around the edges with black velvet. Everyone in the theatre was able to see the picture, and according to newspaper reports, it was a decided sensation in theatrical experimentation.[69]

Swing Parade was very enthusiastically received by audiences and critics. It played to responsive and appreciative full houses every night of its run.[70]

Probably the most earnest and organized attempt at establishing an ongoing Playwriting Unit occurred in Tacoma, Washington, in the form of the Tacoma Playwrights' Theatre, under the leadership of Clarence Talbot. The Puget Sounder outlined the aims of the unit, stating that the FTP was seeking plays about the Northwest, "vital plays, which speak to Northwesterners in their own idiom about things which concern them." The article continued to indicate that the Playwrights' Theatre generally produced "sketch" productions of plays by Northwest authors every two weeks. The unit's production policy would be to prefer plays reflecting regional subject matter about contemporary or pioneer life. Scripts were to be sent to Guy Williams, FTP Washington State Director. Promising scripts would be given "sketch productions" by a professional Tacoma Theatre company; however, no royalty would be paid to authors. Listed in the article were those scripts already presented to mixed critical reaction: William A. Kimball's "Spring Afternoon," Harold McGrath's "Men at Work," George Savage's "All My Life," Garland Ethel's In His Image, Glen Hugh's The Leading Man, and Girl Wants Glamour by Ralph Dyar.[71]

These plays and M.D. by Clarence Talbot will be reviewed here. In a very strict sense, none of the plays with the exception perhaps of M.D., had a very significant intention other than to entertain an audience with relatively light fare. Primarily, they were presented to show-case the work of Northwest writers. However, the plays hardly presented at all Northwestern themes or characters, and it could be said that, at this early point in the development of the unit, the specific purpose was just giving local authors an opportunity to see their work performed by a professional company.

Guy Williams, head of the Drama Department at the University of Washington and FTP State Supervisor for Washington, helped establish the Tacoma Playwrights' Theatre by implementing the Federal Theatre policy for creating producing units in cities where the Project would build its organization. Williams had the Drama League in Tacoma sponsor the playwriting unit, locating it in a small building in the Old Town of Tacoma; "down by the old fishing wharves. It was [two] two-story buildings side by side. One of them we built the theatre in, and the adjacent one we used for rehearsal halls, construction hall, offices and so forth."[72] The Tacoma and Seattle Projects were eventually consolidated.

An evening of one-acts directed by Clarence Talbot--consisting of "All My Life," "Men at Work," and "Spring Afternoon"--was presented June 12 and 13, 1936. "All My Life" was described by FTP as a "middleclass story of a mother and daughter, complex." A mother lives vicariously through her daughter whose burning ambition is to be a poet. The daughter receives a poetry prize; however, her moment of glory is destroyed when it is discovered that the poem she submitted as a contest entry was a poem her mother, Griselda, had written 25 years earlier. The daughter is exposed as a plagiarist, and the mother is then given the acclaim for having written the prize-winning poetry. She becomes recognized as a writer of talent, fulfilling her life-long dream of finally achieving recognition for her creativity.[73]

"Men at Work" is described as a "tense tragedy." Three characters: Duffy, Neely, an old diver, and Dirk, an apprentice diver in love with May, Duffy's daughter, are trapped within a Caesson-bell lying on the sea bed. When all communication is cut off, the old man attempts to calm the others. The men draw straws, and Neely wins the right to flee to safety but instead pushes Dirk up the ladder to enable him to escape. Duffy and Neely try in vain to save themselves.

"Spring Afternoon," a light comedy, takes place in a beach cabin where Vera and Frank depict a married couple whose stability is threatened when Vera's former lover, Steve, appears to create disharmony.[74]

Girl Wants Glamour, a "contemporary domestic drama," is the story of Mabel, an imaginative, spirited 20 year old suffering from the repression and monotony of living in a small Midwestern town. She works as a secretary to support herself and her maiden aunt. Mabel escapes boredom by reading tawdry, sensational, adventure and romance magazines. These escapes into fantasy make it increasingly more difficult for her to choose between her childhood sweetheart and an elderly, wealthy man. The play deals with how the vicarious thrills gained from reading the magazines make Mabel sexually aroused and restless. However, at the end of the play, her sound judgment returns.[75]

Revealing how plays of the type were viewed in the regions at the time, the Tacoma News Tribunal referred to Girl Wants Glamour as a "Melodrama of the deep, throaty, twitchy variety given in the cowboy and love 'interludes.'"[76] Interludes were not defined.

M.D. by Clarence Talbot, Director of the Tacoma Playwrights' Unit, was presented January 12 and 13, 1937. Based on actual facts, the play was dedicated in the program to the medical profession "with prayer and respect." The plot revolves around the discovery by Dr. Gerry Jefferys, a very dedicated and compassionate physician, of a new anesthetic, and the bizarre way it is tested. Dr. Hugh Jefferys, Gerry's son, is accidentally killed in a shoot-out on the street. Hugh's father learns of the event when he hears the news report on the radio. One of the gangsters shot during the shoot-out comes to Dr. Jeffery's office for treatment. Jefferys knows that the gangster is the man who has shot his son and decides to inject him with the anesthesia he has discovered, hoping to test its effects, and also to kill the hoodlum in revenge. The anesthesia does not kill the gangster who is able to leave the office and be picked up by his gang of buddies who throw him out of the car as they drive toward a hide-out. The wounded gunman is picked up by the police and taken to a hospital where, in a delirious state, he reveals all of the incidents of the shooting. The gang is captured, and Dr. Jefferys is declared a hero. However, the disconsolate physician is barely able to carry on, greatly suffering the loss of his son.[77]

Playreader M. Murray commented: "Construction good. . . . Actions fast, would hold interest. Shows sacrifice and constant help doctors [give] to mankind."[78]  However, Jeannette Druce said: "This isn't a good play, admirable as its intentions are. It really isn't exciting. . . . The story lacks purpose and unity. . . . There is no conflict."[79] Paul Lake agreed that it was "poorly dramatized, loosely held together by small talk and weakly reinforced with meaningless incidents."[80]  A report signed "Beyer" stated that "the plot and characterizations are hopelessly amateurish. . . . The doctor is an impossible character . . . would be laughed off the boards."[81] Based upon these comments, one could wonder if it would have been produced if Talbot were not the head of the Playwriting Unit. Perhaps the absence of available reviews for M.D. in FTP files indicates that the critics agreed.

Glen Hughes--university professor, playwright, and Seattle's FTP head--was the author of the next play to be produced by the playwriting unit. Too Lucky, a farcical social comedy, was presented July 7-8, 1936. The Tacoma News Tribune gave a good description of the plot but said little about the play in terms of its strengths and weaknesses in content and form, or how it was received by the Tacoma audience:

> The Marsh family . . . represented the typical lives of a manufacturing tycoon of the early 1930s--who stood only two shirts and a pair of socks distant from the breadlines. Mrs. Marsh was the queen bee and the children were the drones. Having nothing to do with their hands, possessing nimble brains, the children developed naturally enough into beardless Groucho Marxes, full of the very devil and eager to spill out. This much family should have been old man Marshes rightful proportion of misery on earth, and doubtless would have in normal times, but the depression bore tragedy upon rich and poor alike. Thus the Marshes supported enough flotsam and jetsam relatives to sink the British fleet. But in the end the

Marshes recover their bearings, the worthless children decide to go forth and develop callouses. . . . That stern realist, Horatio Alger, couldn't have portrayed life more truly.[82]

Typical of the Tacoma Playwrights' Unit's attempt to avoid plays dealing with searching studies of social problems, Too Lucky, a play showing a typical family's struggles during the depression, became a "farcical social comedy" instead of a "social tragedy." This group was not interested at all in "social" or "relevant" plays and did nothing even to make an attempt in the direction of experimentation in form or content. This regional group of the Northwest made a concerted effort to avoid controversy and the reality of the depression.

In His Image by Garland Ethel, a drama of "social reform," was presented at the Little Theatre, September 1, 1936, for one performance. The story was described by FTP as follows:

> Maw Boyer, and her son and daughter, Henry and Mary, are dry-land farmers in the North Central part of the state of Washington. Maw Boyer believes that the world is coming to an end and thus stifles her daughter's attempts to live a normal life. The play is an episodic character study of how her daughter, Mary, revolts against her mother's religious intolerance and determines to get a bit of romance in her life.[83]

Exemplifying what critics in the Northwest region considered an unusual play, the North End News called In His Image one of the most "different" dramas ever attempted by the Tacoma Playwrights' Theatre and strongly urged theatregoers to see it. The review indicated that the "startling" play revealed how "religious fanaticism warped the lives of three people." It was further characterized as "gripping" and "realistic."[84] The Times stated that it was "one of the most dynamic dramas ever to be offered to Tacoma audiences. . . . This play is highlighted by a Freudian dream scene that will be one rib-tickling scene that will amuse everyone who see it."[85]

The last play offered by the Tacoma Playwrights' Theatre was The Leading Man by William Alden Kimball, presented August 6-8, 1936. The FTP described the play in the following manner:

> The play is concerned with the marriage of an egotistical, bombastic and completely self-centered and self-indulgent Hollywood leading man. Being a scenario writer as well as an actor, and equally ham at both, he is continually being misunderstood and persecuted in his own self-prejudiced mind. Added to his own vocational difficulties are the personal difficulties that arise in the shape of a none too fastidious past that is always interfering with his relations with his wife, a very charming and capable girl who is to the manor born.
>
> Having been completely spoiled by his mother and the adulation of his fans, his every reaction is personal, petty and almost childish. Although insanely jealous and unnecessarily insisting on absolute fidelity from his wife, he insists that it is not only his perogative but his nature to be a dilettante and that she must understand and make allowances. This she will not do, for although she loves him, her standards are on a much higher plane, so she leaves him.
>
> Finally, circumstances in the guise of his secretary, his director, and his fans prove to him what an ass he is and reconciliation is made with the able assistance of the stork.[86]

Critics in the various regions were generally not very revelatory regarding a play's content and form. They did not concern themselves too much with dramaturgy, and instead, frequently made titillating statements to amuse and entertain their readers. This was particularly true in Tacoma. Reviewing The Leading Man, the Tacoma New Tribune indicated that the satiric play was based upon the real life of a Hollywood leading man, but did not indicate which one. The review further stated that the theatre group scored a "smacking-good hit," supporting the claim: "Time and time again, it has been contended there is nothing like a little fairy in the house to promote happiness, engender good feeling and place faith, hope and charity in what otherwise would become a drab existence."[87]

The plays presented by the Tacoma Playwrights' Unit were neither "native" or socially relevant. They were conventional plays used as vehicles for Northwest writers to show their work. Recalling his tenure with the Playwrights' Unit, Clarence Talbot justified his choices:

> We didn't run into the controversial area. We ran into more of an apathetic area because the audiences that we were playing to . . . still were not looking upon the theatre as a sounding board for either social or political messages, or any nouveau concept [Flanagan] was trying to inculcate in the theatre picture.[88]

Talbot further supported his play choices and reflected attitudes shared by other regional directors:

> Now, in the larger cities, Los Angeles, New York, Mercury Theatre, you know, all the rest of the jazz, you were playing the numbers racket. You had enough people that would go to the theatre regardless of what was being shown if here's something new. Well, let's go see what it is. But if you got into the provinces of the United States, and I'm speaking in terms of provincial attitudes, people . . . expected something they could understand in the area of conventional theatrical entertainment. They wanted mysteries, they wanted comedies, they wanted romantic stories.[89]

These were attitudes shared by many of FTP regional directors and producers, attitudes which, according to Talbot, conflicted with the national office because "recommendations" from Hallie Flanagan were perceived as "tantamount" to a directive:

> So those of us in the field, when Hallie Flanagan sent out a recommended list of plays for a season or "We urge that you give your consideration" type of memo, . . . [we] interpreted that as almost a mandate. That this season you will do plays from this list only. Don't think for yourself. These are the ones that we have cleared the rights [for] at the national level. These we can get for you. These we've got royalty agreements [for] and that it'll only cost so much to do, and you will do a play from this list was our interpretation of it.[90]

This policy displeased Talbot, and although he was able to have his play M.D. produced, he later resigned, due to his disagreements with Flanagan, whom he characterized as someone whose "skirts had never been sullied by the crass commercialism of the professional theatre. . . . a woman in charge of a national program who honestly did not have any knowledge, any depth of knowledge, of what the needs of the professional performer were. And she expressed this on many occasions."[91]

Probably the most authentically regional play to be presented in the Western region was one that exploited the variety-type entertainment offered in the early Oregon dance halls during the "gay nineties." Portland presented Timberline Tintypes August 12-September 3, 1938. Written by Yasha Frank, it was a farce-melodrama "based on the popular entertainment features offered by vaudevillians and 'legit' troupers to a group of loggers and tavern-frequenters in the days of early Oregon."[92] FTP further described the farce melodrama:

> As the play opens, a group of persons are assembled on the stage, which has for its setting an early Oregon Dance Hall in a tavern. Several loggers enter from the front of the theatre and

engage in an argument. They approach the stage through the audience and ascend the stage, on which a wrestling match ensues.

Various "bits" of a popular appeal of a bygone period are featured, such as "The Face on the Bar Room Floor," "Father, Dear Father, Come Home with Me Now," etc. Vaudeville skits are presented on the elevated Music Hall Stage in the rear. Ensemble numbers included selections by a group of singing waiters, the "Flory Dory Double Octette," "Bertha's Buxom Beauties" and others.[93]

Presented at Timberline Lodge, the production aroused a great deal of nostalgia among the older members of the audience, who remembered the type of popular entertainment being celebrated in Frank's recreation of the theatrical entertainment of Oregon's frontier days.

The show was a big hit as a celebration of the West's unique brand of entertainment. Critics and audiences were equally enthusiastic about this production. The review that made the most searching comments about the show as a significant recreation of Oregon's past popular entertainment traditions was the one in the Labor New Dealer:

> . . . fun-poking ranging from subtle satire to the more obvious hokum bordering on burlesque . . . What must have been the Worst of ham vaudeville in the last decades before the turn of the century is transformed here into a darn swell Best of 1938 . . . this monkey-glanded presentation of old-time beer-parlor variety acts with all their exaggerated histrionics, rises toward the finish in a hilarious crescendo of dance, music, songs and antics.[94]

The Western region not only produced the greatest number of shows of all of the regions, including New York City, but it was also the area where a wide range of performance possibilities was explored, experimented with and presented to enthusiastic audiences sharing the enthusiasm reflected by FTP workers. The gamut ran from the collaborative scripting done by Virginia Farmer with her Southwest Unit to the very conventional and commercial work performed by Clarence Talbot and his Tacoma Playwrights' Unit. There was still something of the frontier and pioneering spirit that abounded in the way the Western units embraced the Federal Theatre and all of the opportunities it offered. As Hallie Flanagan claimed, "The variety show was the backbone of western show business, and drama was in the thick of things."[95]

Notes

[1]Flanagan, Arena, p. 272.

[2]Ibid., p. 273.

[3]Ibid., p. 294.

[4]Synopsis at George Mason University.

[5]Tralie McCann, Playreaders report, n.d.   At George Mason University.

[6]Edmund Fuller, Playreaders report, n.d.   At George Mason University.

[7]Denver Post, n.d.

[8]Denver News, 28 March 1938.

[9]Rocky Mountain News, n.d., quoted in Flanagan, Arena, p. 295.

[10]"WPA Theater Gets Credit of Revival of the Road," Rocky Mountain News, 4 April 1937.

[11]Synopsis at George Mason University.

[12]Monitor [Denver], 18 March 1938.

[13]Rocky Mountain News, 27 March 1938.

[14]Denver Democrat, 2 April 1938.

[15]Michael Andrew Slane, Director's Notes, Production Bulletin, n.d., p. 6.  At George Mason University.

[16]Federal One I-3 (August 1976): 1.

[17]Ibid., p. 2.

[18]Ibid.

[19]Ibid., p. 5.

[20]Ibid., p. 6.

[21]Ibid.

[22]Program for The Sun Rises in the West. At George Mason University.

[23]Synopsis at George Mason University.

[24]Virginia Farmer, "Director's Report," Production Bulletin, n.d., pp. 6-7. At George Mason University.

[25]Frederick Stover, "Technical Report," Production Bulletin, n.d., p. 8. At George Mason University.

[26]Judson O'Donnell, Playreaders report, 12 May 1938. At George Mason University.

[27]Hollywood Variety, 2 July 1938.

[28]Herald Express [Los Angeles], 2 July 1938.

[29]Los Angeles Examiner, 2 July 1938.

[30]Hollywood Life, July 1938.

[31]Los Angeles Journal, 2 July 1938.

[32]Wilshire Press, 18 July 1938.

[33]Synopsis at George Mason University.

[34]Synopsis at George Mason University.

[35]Henry Bennett, Playreaders report, 12 March 1937. At George Mason University.

[36]Lee Harrett, Playreaders report, 19 March 1937. At George Mason University.

[37]Synopsis at George Mason University.

[38]Los Angeles Evening Herald, 19 February 1937.

[39]Los Angeles Evening News, 18 February 1937.

[40]Synopsis at George Mason University.

[41]San Bernardino Sun Telegram-Riverside News, 30 April 1936.

[42]Milton Luban, Playreaders report, 3 September 1936. At George Mason University.

[43]Charles Gaskill, Playreaders report, 28 August 1936. At George Mason University.

[44]Ibid.

[45]"Director's Report," Production Bulletin, n.d., n.p. At George Mason University.

[46]Ibid.

[47]Federal One I-3 (August 1976).

[48]Synopsis, Production Bulletin, n.d., n.p. At George Mason University.

[49]Variety, n.d., quoted in Flanagan, Arena, p. 279.

[50]Los Angeles Evening News, 15 January 1937.

[51]Ibid.

[52]Script, 23 January 1937.

[53]Synopsis, Production Bulletin, n.d., p. 1. At George Mason University.

[54]Los Angeles Times, 23 October 1937.

[55]Synopsis, Production Bulletin, n.d., pp. 1-3. At George Mason University.

[56]Hollywood Citizen News, 7 November 1938.

[57]Synopsis at George Mason University.

[58]Ben Russak, Playreaders report, 6 December 1937. At George Mason University.

[59]Converse Tyler, Playreaders report, 5 November 1937. At George Mason University.

[60]Jeannette Druce, Playreaders report, 9 November 1937. At George Mason University.

[61]M. Portner, Playreaders report, 18 August 1937. At George Mason University.

[62]Alan Williams, "Director's Report," Production Bulletin, n.d. At George Mason University.

[63]San Francisco Chronicle, 8 September 1938.

[64]San Francisco News, 7 September 1938.

[65]Call Bulletin [San Francisco], 1 August 1938.

[66]Oakland Tribune, 20 September 1938.

[67]George Savage, "Autobiographical Sketch," Production Bulletin, n.d., n.p. At George Mason University.

[68]Synopsis, Production Bulletin, n.d., pp. 1-4. At George Mason University.

[69]Supervisor of the Sound Department, "Technical Report," Production Bulletin, n.d., p. 11. At George Mason University.

[70]Japanese American News, 9 April 1937.

[71]Burke Ormsby, Puget Sounder, 14 October 1936.

[72]Interview with Clarence Talbot conducted by Karen Wickre, 21 July 1977, p. 2. Tape at George Mason University.

[73]Synopsis at George Mason University.

[74]Synopsis at George Mason University.

[75]Synopsis at George Mason University.

[76]Tacoma News Tribune, press clipping in Production Bulletin, n.d., n.p. At George Mason University.

[77]Synopsis at George Mason University.

[78]M. Murray, Playreaders report, 16 February 1937. At George Mason University.

[79]Jeannette Druce, Playreaders report, 25 February 1937. At George Mason University.

[80]Paul Lake, Playreaders report, 18 February 1937. At George Mason University.

[81]Beyer, Playreaders report, 15 January 1937. At George Mason University.

[82]Tacoma News Tribune, press clipping in Clipping File, n.d. At George Mason University.

[83]Synopsis at George Mason University.

[84]North End News [Tacoma], press clipping in Press Notices File, n.d. At George Mason University.

[85]Times [Tacoma], press clipping in Press Notices File, n.d. At George Mason University.

[86]Synopsis at George Mason University.

[87]Tacoma News Tribune, press clipping in Press Notices File, n.d. At George Mason University.

[88]Interview with Clarence Talbot, p. 8.

[89]Ibid.

[90]Ibid., pp. 9-10.

[91]Ibid., p. 8.

[92]Synopsis, Production Bulletin, n.d., p. 1. At George Mason University.

[93]Ibid.

[94]Labor New Dealer, 26 August 1938.

[95]Flanagan, Arena, p. 271.

# CONCLUSION

It is now over fifty years since Hallie Flanagan dreamed her impossible dream of creating a "federation of theatres" growing and flourishing throughout America. Flanagan dreamed of rescuing the American theatre from the economic calamities of the Great Depression and the numerous corrupt practices plaguing it before the Crash of '29:

> The list of such practices was long: gambling in theatres as real estate; syndicates fostering a cross-country touring system; a monopoly booking system; the "star" system; long-run shows that destroyed repertory; type casting that stifled an actor's development; the staging of the "tried and true" rather than the work of a new playwright with ideas. The result was predictable--an art stumbling toward maturity had been transformed into a primarily commercial enterprise.[1]

Hallie Flanagan wanted to go beyond calamity and create something America never had before--a government endowed people's theatre that would not cater just to the tastes and spending power of an urban elite but play to every segment of the population regardless of age, class, race, or ethnic background in rural and grass-roots communities, in parks, hospitals, prisons, and schools. Federal Theatre's triumphs and achievements were many and very impressive. In addition to being a forum for new plays, it created an increasing and expanding number of avenues for a variety of other performance experiences.

The Federal Theatre Project was not, however, a spawning ground for new playwrights. As Irwin Rhodes, FTP Counsel, recalled:

> We simply had a bunch of young playwrights who were being supported by the U.S. government at a time of great need. And I

would like to think that many of the people got their first start at that time, their encouragement, but it wasn't anything like that.[2]

One of the few exceptions would be Arthur Miller, whose They Too Arise was produced in Detroit. Some of the directors of various FTP units--including Clarence Talbot, Emmet Lavery, Virgil Geddes, and Converse Tyler--managed to have their plays produced by Federal Theatre, assisted probably by the fact that they were in strategic executive positions. However, none of the plays authored by these playwrights were written by them on Project time.

For several complicated reasons, FTP was also not a spawning ground for new plays of any enduring significance. In fact one is hard pressed to think of plays presented to American audiences for the first time in professional production by Federal Theatre that are still being produced--or even remembered, for that matter. There is the occasional exception, like Murder in the Cathedral, but very few others. The study of the FTP as a forum for new plays is not the study of a great era of dramatic literature or of a momentous school of dramatic writing. It is the study of what was done under less than ideal circumstances, and severe time restraints, in an experiment which attempted to bring to America an experience it had never had before.

Flanagan dreamed of reviving the American theatre from its "terminal," moribund state by offering something new, daring, and hopefully enduring to the American public. However, her theatre was dangerous in many ways and was doomed from the start by a set of built-in conflicts and contradictions which prevented Federal Theatre from producing an impressive number of new plays of any great or lasting importance. Writing was not a top priority for FTP; putting unemployed actors back to work was. FTP playwrights did not want to write plays on Project time because the government would then own the copyright. The "rental" fees the government was willing to pay playwrights for the rights to do their plays were not enticing enough to attract the most talented, experienced, and dynamic writers. The Dramatists' Guild encouraged the FTP to stage revivals. Actors' Equity demanded an arrangement with FTP that made rehearsing and opening shows difficult for the most creative and experimental playwrights and directors. Federal Theatre could not advertise and had to rely on press reviews and word-of-mouth advertising to promote its shows. As a result, FTP was always at the mercy of journalists representing factional segments of the Project's audience. Consequently, Federal Theatre was dangerously placed in a no-win position as a focal point of controversies about art and politics. The WPA enterprise was temporary; everything had to be done in the quickest and most expedient manner. In trying to impress government officials that the FTP was spending federal funds wisely on a steady stream of performances, unit directors hastily presented unprepared scripts, causing the quality of the writing to suffer. When offered employment in the commercial theatre, the most talented workers frequently left shows during rehearsals or after openings. Regional directors preferred stock productions, not the new and "relevant" plays Hallie Flanagan "suggested."

FTP's greatest achievement was that it created a vast new audience to which it offered an extremely diversified number of performance experiences. Although FTP's new plays were not always memorable, the forum Federal Theatre created for new plays and other productions was gigantic in scope and pleasing to a new, working-class audience. FTP offered free or low priced theatre to 500,000 spectators weekly during its four year existence. Thirty million theatregoers, 65 percent of whom were seeing theatre for the first time, attended FTP performances.[3]

About the new audience FTP was creating, Flanagan stated: "Our function is to extend the boundaries of theatre-going, to create a vigorous new audience, to make the theatre of value to more people."[4] Describing the new audience, Orson Welles was moved to say: "It was eager. To anyone who saw it night after night as we did, it was not the Broadway crowd . . . One had the feeling every night, that here were people on a voyage of discovery in theatre."[5] Richard Lockridge, drama critic for the New York Sun, described the audience:

> The Works Progress Administration has brought into the legitimate play-house a new, vociferous and rather engaging audience.
>     It is an audience which I suspect is not over-familiar with the stage of flesh and blood, and it has had moments of rather startling naivete. But it is an engaging audience. Its face is not frozen. It is not sitting on its hands. When it hisses, it is not self-conscious, and when it cheers, it means it. It is young, lively and I suspect hard-up.
>     Probably the low admission fees charged at the Works Progress Administration plays have had a large part in bringing it out of the neighborhood movie houses--it is an eager audience.[6]

FTP did attempt to give each region an opportunity to develop its own "indigenous drama and native expression--a drama reflecting its landscape, regional material," and plays about each region's "past and present." Notable examples were Feet on the Ground, produced in the Eastern Region, John Dunne's work on Oklahoma folklore for the

Southern Region, and Virginia Farmer's Southwest Unit's <u>The Sun Rises</u> <u>in the West</u>, presented in Los Angeles. The Midwest Region was the least successful in reflecting its "native material." These were all creative, useful, and innovative ways to employ writing talent.

Flanagan wanted the projects initiated by FTP to continue after the primary aims of the WPA were accomplished. She even dreamed that FTP would eventually develop into a vital national theatre and that its presence would continue indefinitely. Theories about FTP's rise and fall still linger. An opinion persists that perhaps Federal Theatre could have continued if it had not mixed art and politics. However, most observers of the events preceding and following FTP's demise generally concede that the Project was doomed because ultra-conservative congressmen wanted to attack and discredit the Roosevelt Administration and get rid of WPA. Federal Theatre became a convenient scapegoat in that campaign; Flanagan has described in <u>Arena</u>, her history of the Project, the cogent details of the killing of Federal Theatre. The House Committee to Investigate Un-American Activities (HUAC), probing into alleged communist subversion in FTP in 1938, was the beginning of the end for Federal Theatre.

FTP was so much a part of the temper of the thirties that it is hard to imagine what kind of theatre organization it would have been had it not dealt with political and social issues. About radicalism and FTP, Eric Bentley speculated that without the radical politics perhaps it could have continued:

> But then, what would it have been? Continued as what? And not as something that would have interested her [Flanagan] and those whose enthusiasm she won. I mean for many people's

tastes, she wasn't radical enough. . . . She got it both ways. I thought that was an inept criticism, irrespective of the right and wrongs of radicalism because that was where it got its identity, through being bold. If it had not been bold, and she'd just explained to Senator Dirksen, you know, that Up in Mabel's Room is all right and is not a naughty play about communistic love, then what would it have been--just another summer stock operation.[7]

Flanagan frequently reflected upon FTP's role in portraying American life during the 1930s. In one of her statements, she clearly enunciated Federal Theatre's special mission:

The Federal Theatre is a pioneer theatre because it is part of a tremendous re-thinking, re-building and re-dreaming of America. . . . These activities represent the new frontier in America, a frontier against disease, dirt, poverty, illiteracy, unemployment, and despair, and at the same time against selfishness, special privilege and social apathy. And in the struggle for a better life . . . Federal Theatre . . . becomes not merely a decoration but a vital force in our Democracy.[8]

When FTP was referred to as the "red" or "leftist" or "dangerous" theatre in the thirties, "leftism" conveyed a different, less damning, set of connotations. John Gassner discussed those connotations as follows:

And the label of "leftism" was not used pejoratively, as it came to be used in the 1950s, but in a vaguely complimentary sense by proponents of liberalism. "Leftism," for them, was the banner under which one fought against fascism and Nazism and for human decency and social reforms soon to be incorporated in the law of the land without commitment to the overthrow of capitalism and the establishment of a "dictatorship of the proletariat."[9]

An artist's political affiliation, or the affinities of artists in a political movement, should not damn their creations, nor the artistic stature of any new movement in art. Michael Kirby reflected upon this issue in discussing the Italian futurist theatre and its link to Italian fascism: "The value of art, however, is not measured by political standards. Appreciation of a piece is not dependent upon knowing the beliefs of its creator. Great art is not necessarily produced by heroes, nor are 'villains' unable to create major works."[10] The irony in this is that now when FTP is discussed, the "political drama" of its rise and fall seems to be of paramount importance. A full discussion of FTP and its relationship to art seems to be an after-thought, as if its achievements (the over 1,000 productions) of a non-political-social character were somehow of no importance.

What have we learned from the Federal Theatre Project experience, particularly with regard to financing the arts and the nurturing of new plays and playwrights? One would have to make a guess in trying to determine whether the following statement was made in 1936 or 1986 and to estimate its relevance to where we are today:

> It has become more and more apparent each year that the theatre as an art cannot be self-supporting. In fact, strictly speaking, it is no longer self-supporting as an individual enterprise. Trustification is rapidly taking place in the theatre, as in every other form of business or industry.[11]

Elmer Rice made that statement as he helped create the FTP's New York City Project in 1936. Have things changed at all for the better or the worse? This is what Don Shewey said about theatre in New York City in 1986 in his article "Regrouping of American Theatre," appearing in the Village Voice:

> It's true that Broadway is dying. Costs are so high that fewer shows are produced. Tickets are so expensive that most people go on special occasions rather than habitually. And without the

sense of continuity--of carrying on a dialogue with a
knowledgeable audience--artists have no incentive to brave the
market-place with anything but commercial product.
OffBroadway is scarcely better. . . . Off-Off Broadway is a sorry
sight, too. . . . the production of new plays Off-Off, a
oncefruitful source of new material for the American Theater,
[is] now largely relegated to reviving moldy-oldies like Dial M
for Murder.[12]

Writing about "Theatrical Life Far from Broadway," Jack Viertel

observes little change in the entire country since 1936. It seems as if we are

in a time-warp as Viertel describes it:

[There are] two serious and deepening problems that interlock,
and that have always been at the heart of the American theater's
dilemma--money and vision. At this point, with public support
for the non-profit arts at a low ebb, there is simply not enough
cash washing through the industry to keep anyone in it for very
long. A young writer can entertain no reasonable expectations
for a life in the theater.[13]

Perhaps this is the reason why when Marsha Norman made her

acceptance speech for the Pulitzer Prise she received for her play, 'Night,

Mother, she said words to the effect that writing for the theatre is

tantamount to an act of charity. Hardly anyone can make a living writing

for the theatre.

And where will there be to go for those who want to think or hope

that a life in the theatre is still possible when theatre ceases to exist in New

York City because artists can no longer afford the astronomical rents they

are forced to pay for spaces in which to work? Erika Munk clearly

indicated that death is imminent for the arts in New York, as she reported

in her grimly documented article, "New York to the Arts: Drop Dead,"

appearing in the Village Voice:

Everyone knows that real estate is Manhattan's obsession: we're consumed by the spaces we're living in, leaving, or looking for. . . . Almost everyone also knows that skyrocketing rents are having a catastrophic effect on the city's cultural life: The gentry don't make art or ideas, and the way things are going, pretty soon no one else will be home. Without a drastic change Manhattan will be finished as America's creative center.[14]

Clearly, something in the way we establish our national priorities is not entirely friendly to the idea of the arts thriving in our massively productive technological society.

Invoking the spirit of Hallie Flanagan and the Federal Theatre Project, but at the same time avoiding its mistakes, may be a step forward in creating a viable way for playwrights to live and work. Jack Viertel suggests a modest solution, a beginning which would possibly avoid some of the pitfalls in which Federal Theatre found itself:

If every sufficiently budgeted regional theatre in the country would put two playwrights on staff at . . . $50,000 a year, and steal from their production budgets, their travel budgets, even heaven forfend, the money that is spent instead to read the latest script by the local dentist, what kinds of writers might those theatres command? If every empty seat . . . were given away to every willing student every night, who knows how many of those students might want someday to actually buy a ticket? Certainly it is a scheme that smacks of desperation, even mild insanity, perhaps brought on by the arrival of the afternoon mail: a third "Big Chill" script and a musical about King David "in the style of 'Kismet,' but can be performed on two synthezizers with a cast of five." Surely we must take action soon.[15]

We definitely must take action soon. What we must do is resurrect the boldness of Hallie Flanagan's vision, her willingness to play dangerously in the arena of art and money.  What is needed is the spirit of the time when Harry Hopkins and Hallie Flanagan attempted to develop strategies that would allow artists a way to begin to live a decent life.  As Hopkins said to Flanagan when they talked about setting up the Federal Theatre Project and everything seemed possible: "This is America, the richest country in the world.  We can afford to pay for anything we want.  And we want a decent life for all the people in this country.  And we are going to pay for it."[16] Those dreams were never fully realized under the circumstances existing at the time, but it was a beginning, a new way of using the resources and wealth of America.  Flanagan realized that FTP was important more as a lesson for the future than for its accomplishments in the past:

> Its significance lies in its pointing to the future.  The ten thousand annonymous men and women--the et ceteras and the and-soforths who did the work, the nobodies who were everybody, the somebodies who believed it--their dreams were not the end.  They were the beginning of a people's theatre in a country whose greatest plays are still to come.[17]

Notes

¹Mathews, p. 23.

²Interview with Irwin Rhodes.

³Federal One V-I (February 1980): 1-3.

⁴Ibid., p. 1.

⁵Ibid., p. 5.

⁶Ibid., p. 4.

⁷Interview with Eric Bentley conducted by Mae Krulak, 12 May 1976. Tape at George Mason University.

⁸O'Connor and Brown, p. 26.

⁹John Gassner, "Politics and Theatre," foreword to Himmelstein, p. ix.

¹⁰Michael Kirby, Futurist Performance (New York: Dutton & Company, Inc., 1971), p. 4.

¹¹"The Federal Theatre Hereabouts," New York Times, 5 January 1936.

¹²Village Voice, 10 December 1985, p. 14.

¹³New York Times, 1 June 1986.

¹⁴Village Voice, 27 May 1986, p. 18.

¹⁵New York Times, 1 June 1986.

¹⁶Flanagan, Arena, p. 28.

¹⁷Ibid., p. 373.

APPENDIX A


FEDERAL THEATRE PROJECT ADMINISTRATION

1935-1939


Part One - General administration of the FTP as outlined and prepared by the staff, Special Collections at George Mason University.


Part Two - Organization and basic profile of the National Service Bureau as outlined by FTP, 10 January 1939.

FEDERAL THEATRE PROJECT ADMINISTRATION
NOVEMBER 1935

Harry Hopkins : Adm. of WPA :

Jacob Baker : Asst. Adm. of WPA :

Hallie Flanagan : Nat'l.Dir. :

Lester Lang : Deputy Dir. A.A. in D.C. :

Bureau of Research and Publication :

Rosamond Gilder :

| | | | | | |
|---|---|---|---|---|---|
| N.Y.City | N.Y.State | New England | NJ-PA Reg. | Ohio Reg. | VA. Carolinas | South |
| J. Askling Dir. | P. Barber Reg.-State Dir. | H. Motherwell Reg.Dir. | J. Deeter Reg.Dir. | F.McConnell Reg.Dir. | F. Koch Reg.Dir. | J. McGee Reg.Dir. |
| E. Rice Dir. | G. Gotts Asst.St. Dir. | G. Whitecomb Asst.Reg. Dir. | H. Shoeni Asst.Reg. Dir. | | | |
| P. Barber Asst.Dir. | | | | | | |

| Central | Prairie | South Western | North Western | California | D.C. | |
|---|---|---|---|---|---|---|
| T.W.Stevens Reg.Dir. | E.C.Mabie Reg.Dir. | C.Meredith Reg.Dir. | G.Hughes Reg.Dir. | G.Brown Reg.Dir. | Hallie Flanagan | |
| | E.K.Davis Asst.Reg. Dir. | E.D.Bryant Asst.Reg. Dir. | G.Williams Asst.Reg. Dir. | J.H.Miller Asst.Reg. Dir. | | |

BUREAU OF RESEARCH AND PUBLICATIONS
Rosamond Gilder

| Theatre Research K. Clugston, Dir. | Play Reading E. Hull, Dir. | Publications P. de Rohan, Dir. | Press Department P. Perlman | Regional Offices |
|---|---|---|---|---|
| A. Play Lists | A. Play Reading: F. Bosworth | A. Federal Theatre | | |
| 1. Non-royalty: Terwilliger | 1. Script Reading: H. Meadow | B. Publications | | |
| 2. Catalogue: Feldman | 2. Americana: E. Evans | 1. Loose leaf cat. of plays | | |
| Assts: | 3. Play Readers | 2. Special play lists & bibliog. studies | | |
| R. Tibbits | B. Contracts and Plays Rentals: R. Lange | 3. Magazine or bulletin | | |
| Z. Liden | 1. Contracts | | | |
| 3. TAN Index: Ayers | 2. Res. on Copyright & royalty: McNamara Moynehan | | | |
| 4. Translations | | | | |
| 5. Children's: R. Tibbets | | | | |
| 6. Amateur: Z. Liden, P. Arnow | | | | |
| 7. Christmas Lists: M. Worthington, R. Lewis | | | | |
| 8. Regional drama: R. Morris | | | | |
| B. Special Res. | | | | |
| 1. European Th. | | | | |
| 2. Early Th. | | | | |
| 3. Negro Th. | | | | |
| 4. Puppet | | | | |
| 5. Pageants | | | | |
| 6. One-Act | | | | |
| 7. Children's | | | | |
| 8. Vaudeville | | | | |
| 9. National Th. | | | | |

FEDERAL THEATRE PROJECT ADMINISTRATION
JANUARY/FEBRUARY 1936

Harry Hopkins
Adm. of WPA

Jacob Baker
Asst. Adm. of WPA

Hallie Flanagan
Nat'l.Dir.

Lester Lang
Deputy Dir.
A.A. in D.C.

William Farnsworth
Asst.Natl.Dir.
as of 2/1936

Bureau of Research and Publication
Rosamond Gilder, Dir.

Kate Drain Lawson
Dir. Fall 1936

Katharine Clugston

| N.Y.City | N.Y.State | New England | NJ-PA Reg. | Ohio Reg. | VA. Carolinas | South |
|---|---|---|---|---|---|---|
| E. Rice Dir. | G. Gotts Reg. Dir. | | | | | |
| P. Barber Dir. Feb.1936 | | | | | | |

| Central | Prairie | South Western | North Western | Cali-fornia | D.C. | |
|---|---|---|---|---|---|---|
| | | | | G. Fink Reg.Dir. | Hallie Flanagan | |

FEDERAL THEATRE PROJECT ADMINISTRATION
MAY 1936

Harry Hopkins: Adm. of WPA

Jacob Baker: Asst. Adm. of WPA

Hallie Flanagan: Nat'l.Dir.

William Farnsworth: Deputy Dir. A.A. in D.C.

Bureau of Research and Publication: Rosamond Gilder, Dir.

Kate Drain Lawson: Dir. Fall 1936

| Region I | Region II | Region III | Region IV | Region V |
|---|---|---|---|---|
| H. Motherwell (Jan-Apr) | | J. McGee | T.W. Stevens (until May 13) | J.H. Miller, Asst.to Fed.Dir. |
| W. Stahl (April) | | F. Koch, Reg.Adv. | E.C. Mabie, Reg. Adv. | G. Hughes, Reg. Adv. |
| CT: G. Don Dero | DE: E. Porter, A.A. | AL: V. Haldene | IL: E.K. Davis, St.Dir. | CA: G. Brown, St.Dir. |
| MA: L. Gallagher | J. Zerbe, Proj.Sup. | AR: J. McGee, Asst to Fed.Dir. | G. Kondolf, Dir, Chicago | CO: K. Tillman, Proj.Sup. |
| ME: A. Hickey | DC: E. Porter | FL: D. Lynch, St. Dir. | IO: C.W. Jeffries, Proj.Sup. | OR: B. Whitecomb, St.Sup. |
| NH: A. Snow | IN: L. Nouvelle, St.Dir. | LA: B. Szird, Proj. Sup. | MS: W.R. Perry, Proj.Sup. | WA: G. Williams, St.Dir. |
| J.B. Mack | NJ: H. Schoeni, Spec.Rep. | OK: J. Dunn, St. Dir. | NB: A. Howell, St.Dir. | |
| NY: C. Gotts, St. Dir. | OH: L.E. Lang, St.Dir, | NC: M. Dirnberger, St. Dir. | E. Strong, Proj.Sup. | |
| G. Patmerton, Asst.St.Dir. | PA:L.J. Howard, April '36 St.Dir, after J. Deeter | TX: C. Meredith, St. Dir. | O. Lieben, Proj.Sup. | |
| NYC:P. Barber | | | | |
| RI: J. Hughes | | | | |

FEDERAL THEATRE PROJECT ADMINISTRATION
NOVEMBER 1936

Harry Hopkins : Adm. of WPA

Ellen Woodward : Asst. Adm. of WPA (July 1936)

Hallie Flanagan : Nat'l.Dir.

William Farnsworth : Asst.Nat'l.Dir. (Feb. 1937) : E.E. McLeish (Feb. 1937-)

National Play Bureau : Francis Bosworth, Dir.

Formerly : Bureau of Research and Publication

Play Policy Board (Feb. 1937) : Hiram Motherwell : Chairman : Competition (Dir)

| Region I | Region II | Region III | Region IV | Region V |
|---|---|---|---|---|
| W. Stahl | | J. McGee | G. Kondolf Reg. Dir. | J.H. Miller G. Fink Dir.,Reg.Serv.Bur. |
| CT: G. Don Dero | DE: J. Eckman, Dir, Women's & Prof.Proj. WPA | AL: V. Haldene | IL: G. Kondolf, St. Dir. | CA: G. Gerwing St.Dir & L.A. |
| MA: L. Gallagher | | FL: D. Lynch | MI: J.W. Stannard, St.Sup.Prof. & Serv.Proj. | CO: K. Tillman, St. Dir. |
| ME: A. Hickey | | GA: | NB: O. Lieben St.Dir. | OR: B. Whitecomb, |
| NH: J.B. Mack | DC: C. Holt | LA: L. Fletcher | | |
| NJ: L. Siniot | IN: L. Nouvelle | NC: H. Bailey | | |
| NY: G. Gotts | OH: F. Raymond | OK: J.W. Dunn | | |
| NYC:P. Barber | PA: L.J. Howard | TX: F. Marron | | |

FEDERAL THEATRE PROJECT ADMINISTRATION
SEPTEMBER 1937

Harry Hopkins : Adm. of WPA

Ellen Woodward : Asst. Adm. of WPA

Hallie Flanagan : Nat'l.Dir.

William Farnsworth : Asst.Nat'l.Dir.
J.H. Miller : Dep. Dir., D.C.

National Service Bureau : (July 1937)
John McGee
Comb:
Nat'l. Play Bureau & Play Policy Board

Special Productions :
1. National Radio : Programs
2. Information
3. Children's : Theatre
4. World's Fair and : N.Y. Fair

| P. Barber Dir.-N.Y.C. | O. Ness Asst.Dir.-West (Gerwing sent East) | John McGee Asst.Dir.-South | G. Gerwing (temp) Asst.Dir.,-East | H. Ashton Asst.Dir.-Mid-West |
|---|---|---|---|---|
| | Reg.Serv.Bur. G. Fink, Dir. | Reg.Serv.Bur. F.N. Greene, Dir. | Reg.Serv.Bur. | Reg.Serv.Bur. |
| | State Dirs. | State Dirs. | State Dirs. | State Dirs. |
| | CA: G. Gerwing | AL: E.S. Western | CT: G. Don Dero | IN: closed 6/37 |
| | CO: K. Tillman | FL: D. Lynch | DE: closed 6/37 | IO: C. LaRue |
| | OR: B. Whitecomb | GA: | ME: A. Hickey | MI: F. Morrow |
| | WA: G. Williams | LA: R.H. Parker | MA: J.B. Mack | NB: closed 6/37 |
| | | NC.: H. Bailey | NH: J.B. Mack | OH: Frartlon |
| | | | NJ: L. Siniot | |
| | | | NY: C. Hopkins | |

E.K. Davis
Asst.Dir-IL.

NATIONAL SERVICE BUREAU
JOHN McGEE

Business Manager:
L.A. Rubinstein
(now Rhodes)

1. Publications: P. de Rohan
2. Personnel: P. Dekher
3. Publicity: T. Mountz
4. Clearance, loan, contracts, travel

| Play Dept. Emmet Lavery (7/37-12/38) | Technical Dept. | Production Dept. | Reference Dept. |
|---|---|---|---|
| 1. Play Reading: Converse Tyler | 1. Lectures and Exhibits: Francis Bosworth Pierre Loving Janet Aster | 1. Test Production Unit: Halsted Welles | 1. Library: Geo. Terwilliger Barnet Braverman |
| 2. Translating: Benson Inge | 2. Technical Exp.: Richard Rawls George Hyde | 2. Music and Folklore: Herbert Halpert | 2. Script Dept.: Etelka E. Eden |
| 3. Research: Helen Crowe | | | |
| 4. Playwriting: Ben Russak | | | |

FEDERAL THEATRE PROJECT ADMINISTRATION
1938

Harry Hopkins
Adm. of WPA

Ellen Woodward
Asst. Adm. of WPA

Hallie Flanagan
Nat'l.Dir.

W.P. Farnsworth
Asst.Nat'l.Dir.

J.H. Miller
Dep. Dir., D.C.

National Service Bureau
Emmet Lavery
(12/28/37)

Special Productions:
1. National Radio Programs
E. Roberts, Dir.
2. Information
3. Nat'l.Children's
Y. Frank
4. Fairs

N.Y. City
G. Kondolf, Dir.

Western Region
(Los Angeles & San Francisco)
O. Ness, Reg.Dir.

Southern Region
J. Lentz

Midwestern Region
(Chicago)

Eastern Region
B. Sloan, Reg.Dir.

FEDERAL THEATRE PROJECT ADMINISTRATION
FEBRUARY 1939

Harry Hopkins : Adm. of WPA :

Ellen Woodward : Asst. Adm. of WPA :

Hallie : Flanagan : Nat'l Dir. :

J.H. Miller : Dep. Dir., D.C. :

National Service :
Bureau :
Emmet Lavery :
Director :

Special Productions :
1. National Radio
   Programs :
   E. Roberts, Dir. :
2. Information :
3. Nat'l. Children's :
   Y. Frank :
4. Fairs :
   Scheitler :
   H.G. Graham :

| Western Region (San Francisco) O. Ness, Reg. Dir. | Southern Region (New Orleans) J. Lentz | Midwestern Region (Chicago) H. Minturn, Reg. Dir. (Sept. 1938) | Eastern Region (New York City) B. Sloan, Reg. Dir. |
|---|---|---|---|
| State Dirs. | State Dirs. | State Dirs. | State Dirs. |
| S.CA: A. Leftwich | FL: D. Lynch | MI: V. Haldene | CT: C. LaRue |
| N.CA: C. Tocuum | GA: S. Thomas | OH: F. Raymond | ME: A. Hickey |
| CO: K. Tillman | LA: R.H. Parker | | MA: J.B. Mack |
| OR: B. Whitecomb | NC: J.A. Walker | | NH: A. Snow |
| WA: E. O'Connor | OK: J.W. Dunn | | NJ: C. Hopkins |
| | | | NY: M. Petri |
| | | | PA: |

N.Y. City
G. Kondolf, Dir.

Southern
California
(L.A.)

# NATIONAL SERVICE BUREAU

## B_A_S_I_C    P_O_L_I_C_I_E_S

As defined in a memorandum
from the Director of the National
Service Bureau, Federal Theatre,
to the Supervisors of National
Service Bureau on Jan. 10, 1939.

**W.P.A. FEDERAL THEATRE**
National Service Bureau

HALLIE FLANAGAN
Director F.T.P.

J. HOWARD MILLER
Deputy Director

PAUL EDWARDS
Admin. Off.
Federal Project #1

EMMET LAVERY
Director

IRWIN A. RUBINSTEIN
Bus. Manager

---

**ADMINISTRATION**
JOSEPH MOSS
Administration
Ass't.

**TECHNICAL DEPARTMENT**
RICHARD B. RAWLS
Director
GEORGE G. HYDE

**TEST UNIT**
HALSTED WELLES
Director
WILL T. GOODWIN

**CONTRACTS AND REQUISITIONS**
ANNA FALLER
Personnel
PAUL DECKER
Supplies
THOMAS REDIGAN
Mail & Mess.
WILLIAM RUBIN
Loan & Travel

**PLAY DEPT.**
BEN RUSSAK
Acting Director
Playwriting
Play Reading
CONVERSE TYLER
Translations
BENSON INGE
Vaudeville

**LIBRARY**
GEO. TERWILLIGER
Acting Director
Research
HARRIET MEYER
Records
EDWARD HOPTER
Inquiries

**PUBLICATIONS**
PIERRE DE ROHAN
Director
Editing
HERBERT HENRY

**MUSIC DEPT.**
HERBERT HALPERT
Acting Director
Music Clearance
HARRY JOSEPHSON
Music Copying
SIMEON JURIST
Folk Songs

**EXHIBITIONS DEPARTMENT**
FRANCIS BOSWORTH
Director

To carry out these policies, seven general departments were functioning. Eight departments were to now administer the work of the Bureau with a slight rearrangement.

| Departments at Present | Departments Revised |
|---|---|
| <u>Play Department:</u>   Lavery | <u>Play Department:</u>   Russak |
| Play Writing - Russak<br>Play Reading - Tyler<br>Translations - Inge (on leave)<br>Vaudeville<br>Community Service - Terwilliger | Play Writing - Russak<br>Play Reading - Tyler<br>Translations<br>Vaudeville |
| <u>Administration:</u>   Moss | <u>Administration:</u>   Moss |
| Contracts - Faller<br>Supplies - Redigan<br>Personnel - Decker<br>Loan & Travel -<br>Typing - Eden<br>Music - Halpert<br>Editing - Henry<br>Records - Hopter<br>Mail &<br>Messengers - Rubin | Contracts - Faller<br>Supplies - Redigan<br>Personnel - Decker<br>Loan & Travel -<br>Typing - Eden<br>Mail &<br>Messengers - Rubin |
| <u>Research:</u>   Meyer | <u>Library:</u>   Terwilliger |
| Creative -<br>Functional - | Research - Meyer<br>Records - Hopter<br>Inquiries - Terwilliger |
| <u>Test Productions:</u>   Welles | <u>Test Productions: Welles-Director</u> |
| <u>Technical Dept.:</u>   Rawls | <u>Technical: Rawls - Director</u> |
| <u>Exhibitions:</u>   Bosworth | <u>Exhibitions & Lectures: Bosworth</u> |
| <u>Publications:</u>   de Rohan | <u>Publications: de Rohan</u><br>Publications - de Rohan<br>Editing - Mr. Henry |
| | <u>Music Dept.: Halpert</u><br>Folk Songs - Halpert<br>Music Copying -<br>Music Clearance - Josephson |

APPENDIX B

A LIST OF NEW PLAYS PRODUCED BY THE FEDERAL
THEATRE PROJECT AS DOCUMENTED IN THIS STUDY

African Vineyard
  Author: Gladys Unger and Walter Armitage
  Director: Walter Armitage
  Designer: William Perkins
  Other:

First Production:          New Orleans, LA          December 14-19, 1937
                           (Playhouse Theatre)

Subsequent Productions:  none


"All My Life"
  Author: George Savage
  Director: Clarence H. Talbot
  Designer: not available
  Other: Presented in an evening of one-acts with "Men at Work" and
      "Spring Afternoon"

First Production:          Tacoma, WA          June 12 & 13, 1936
                           (The Little Theatre)


Altars of Steel
  Author: Thomas Hall-Rogers
  Director: H. Gordon Graham
  Designer: Josef Lentz
  Other:

First Production:        Atlanta, GA              April 1-8, 1937

Subsequent Productions:  Indianapolis, IN         May 24-29, 1937
                         Miami, FL                Feb. 28-Mar. 19, 1938
                         (Federal Theatre)

American Holiday
  Author: Edwin L. and Albert Barker
  Director: Halsted Welles
  Designer: Tom Adrian Crascraft
Other:

First Production:          New York, NY          Feb. 21-Mar. 14, 1936
                           (Manhattan Theatre)

Subsequent Productions: Birmingham, AL          December 27-31, 1936


American Wing
  Author: Talbot Jennings
  Director: Arthur Ritchie
  Designer: Paul Cadorette
Other:

First Production:          Salem, MA              March 14, 1938
                           (Empire Theatre)

Subsequent Productions: Holyoke, MA              August 6, 1938
                        Manchester, NH           July 10-13, 1938
                        San Francisco, CA        June 29-July 11, 1936


Around the Corner
  Author: Martin Flavin
  Director: Jerome Coray
  Designer: Frederick Stover
Other:

First Production:          Los Angeles, CA        July 14-26, 1936

Subsequent Productions: Atlanta, GA              February 8-11, 1937
                        Chicago, IL              Feb. 19-Apr. 8, 1937
                        Detroit, MI              February 17-28, 1937
                        New Orleans, LA          February 18, 1937

|  | Peoria, IL | February 10-15, 1937 |
|---|---|---|

**Backwash** (produced on Broadway as <u>Kickback</u>)
Author: Edwin H. Blum
Director: Felix Basch
Designer: Rollo Wayne
Other:

First Production:          New York, NY          May 16-June 6, 1936
                           (Willis Theatre)

Subsequent Productions:    none

**Ballad of Davy Crockett**
Author: Hoffman R. Hays
Director: John Lyman
Designer: Ward MacLane
Other:

First Production:          New York, NY          May 21, 1936
                           (Majestic Theatre)

Subsequent Productions:    none

**Battle Hymn**
Author: Michael Gold and Michael Blankfort
Director: W.E. Watts
Designer: Scott McLean
Other:

First Production:          New York, NY          May 22-July 25, 1936
                           (Daly's Theatre, re-
                           named Experimental)

Subsequent Productions: San Francisco, CA        Jan. 28-Feb. 27, 1937

Beyond Tomorrow
  Author: John W. Dunn
  Director: not available
  Designer: not available
  Other:

First Production:              Oklahoma City, OK    February 26, 1937

Subsequent Productions:  none


The Big Blow
  Author: Theodore Pratt
  Director: Anton Bundsman
  Designer: Samuel Leve
  Other:

First Production:              New York, NY          October 1, 1938
                               (Maxine Elliott)

Subsequent Productions:  Boston, MA            May 30, 1939
                               Chicago, IL           March 2, 1939
                               Los Angeles, CA       May 24, 1939


Captain-What-The-Devil
  Author: Zelma Tiden
  Director: Jack Kingsberry
  Designer: not available
  Other:

First Production:              New Orleans, LA       March 11, 1937
                               (Jerusalem Temple)


Censored
  Author: Conrad Seiler
  Director: Alvin Laughlin
  Designer: not available
  Other:

| First Production: | Los Angeles, CA<br>(Mayan Theatre) | March 30-May 1, 1936 |
|---|---|---|
| Subsequent Productions: | Denver, CO<br>(Estes Park Theatre) | June 6-30, 1936 |
| | San Francisco, CA<br>(Columbia Theatre) | May 11-21, 1936 |

## Chalk Dust
Author: Harold H. Clarke and Maxwell Nurnberg
Director: James Light
Designer: Howard Bay
Other:

| First Production: | New York, NY<br>(Experimental Theatre) | March 4-May 2, 1936 |
|---|---|---|
| Subsequent Productions: | Birmingham, AL | June 16-Sep. 21, 1936 |
| | Boston, MA | Aug. 31-Sep. 19, 1936 |
| | Chicago, IL | Apr. 28-May 27, 1936 |
| | Cincinnati, OH | Nov. 22-Dec. 4, 1936 |
| | Detroit, MI | Aug. 18-19, 1936 |
| | Holyoke, MA | Aug. 19-22, 1936 |
| | Los Angeles, CA | May 12-June 27, 1936 |
| | Miami, FL | January 25-30, 1937 |
| | San Bernardino, CA | May 4-9, 1937 |
| | San Francisco, CA | June 15-July 11, 1936 |

## Cheat and Swing
Author: John Woodworth
Director: not available
Designer: not available
Other:

First Production:      Oklahoma City, OK

Subsequent Productions: none

The Cherokee Night
    Author: Lynn Riggs
    Director: Anton Bundsmann
    Designer: Samuel Leve
    Other:

| First Production: | New York, NY (Studio Theatre) | July 25, 1936 |
|---|---|---|

Subsequent Productions: none

Class of '29
    Author: Orrie Lashin and Milo Hastings
    Director: Lucius Moore Cook
    Designer: Tom Adrian Crascraft
    Other:

| First Production: | New York, NY (Manhattan Theatre) | May 15-July 4, 1936 |
|---|---|---|

| Subsequent Productions: | Bridgeport, CT | August 12-29, 1936 |
|---|---|---|
| | Cambridge, MA | August 18, 1936 |
| | Denver, CO | March 10-20, 1937 |
| | Des Moines, IA | April 22-25, 1937 |
| | Omaha, NE | February 2-14, 1937 |
| | Waterloo, IA | March 17-21, 1937 |
| | Wilmington, DE | Dec. 13, 1936-Apr. 3, 1937 |

Created Equal
    Author: John Hunter Booth
    Director: John Hunter Booth
    Designer: Paul Cadorette
    Other:

| First Production: | Boston, MA | June 27-30, 1938 |
|---|---|---|

(Copley Theatre)

Subsequent Productions: Newark, NJ — Nov. 26-Dec. 10, 1938
Springfield, MA — May 24-28, 1938


## Dance of Death
Author: W.H. Auden
Director: Emile Beliveau
Designer: not available
Other: Music, Clair Leonard

First Production: New York, NY — May 19-June 6, 1936
(Adelphi Theatre)

Subsequent Productions: none


## Feet on the Ground
Author: H.A. Archibald
Director: not available
Designer: not available
Other:

First Production: Reading, PA — June 22-Dec. 23, 1936

Subsequent Productions: none


## Follow the Parade
Author: Gene Stone and Jack Robinson
Director: Eda Edson
Designer: Frederick Stover
Other:

First Production: Los Angeles, CA — Apr. 12-Aug. 2, 1936
(Greek Hollywood
Playhouse/Mayan
Theatre)
Subsequent Productions: Milwaukee, WI — Sep. 30-Oct. 16, 1936

|                    |                 |
|--------------------|-----------------|
| Portland, OR       | (not available) |
| Seattle, WA        | (not available) |
| Tampa, FL          | May 23, 1938    |
| (Rialto Theatre)   |                 |

## The Gallows Gate
Author: Marjory Stoneman Douglas
Director: not available
Designer: not available
Other:

| First Production: | Miami, FL | June 14, 1937 |
|-------------------|-----------|---------------|

Subsequent Productions: none

## Girl Wants Glamour
Author: Ralph E. Dyar
Director: Clarence H. Talbot
Designer: Blanche Morgan
Other:

| First Production: | Tacoma, WA        | September 17, 1936 |
|-------------------|-------------------|--------------------|
|                   | (Little Theatre)  |                    |

Subsequent Productions: none

## The Great Gay Road
Author: Norman McDonald
Director: William E. Felts
Designer: Scenic design, William Kloos
Other:

| First Production: | San Bernardino, CA | May 5, 1936 |
|-------------------|--------------------|-------------|

Subsequent Productions: none

Help Yourself
  Author: Paul Vulpius
  Director: Agnes Morgan and Halsted Welles
  Designer: Tom Adrian Crascraft
  Other: Adapted from the Hungarian by John J. Coman

First Production:        New York, NY          Jan. 14-May 23, 1937
                         (Adelphi Theatre)

Subsequent Productions:  Atlanta, GA           April 25, 1938
                         Boston, MA            August 25, 1937
                         Bridgeport, CT        Aug. 30-Sep. 4, 1937
                         Cincinnati, OH        March 15, 1937
                         Denver, CO            Feb. 24-Mar. 6, 1937
                         Des Moines, IA        Apr. 28-May 2, 1937
                         Drexel Hill, PA       October 18-23, 1937
                         Los Angeles, CA       Jan. 14-May 23, 1937
                         Omaha, NE             March 2-14, 1937
                         Peoria, IL            December 16-20, 1937
                         Philadelphia, PA      September 16, 1937
                         Salem, PA             July 12-17, 1937
                         San Bernardino, CA    October 12-16, 1936
                         San Francisco, CA     Mar. 22-Apr. 10, 1937
                         Seattle, WA           Sep. 20-Oct. 5, 1937
                         Springfield, MA       January 19, 1937
                         Syracuse, NY          September 24, 1936
                         White Plains, NY      September 28, 1936
                         Wilmington, DE        Apr. 8-May 15, 1937

Hymn to the Rising Sun
  Author: Paul Green
  Director: Arun Faxman
  Designer: Robert Chertov and Theodore Fuchs
  Other:

First Production:        New York, NY          May 6-July 10, 1937
                         (Experimental Theatre)

Subsequent Productions:  none

I Confess
  Author: William Beyer and T.W. Stevens
  Director: William Beyer
  Designer: Stephen Nastfogel
  Other:

First Production:          Detroit, MI              May 4-June 20, 1936
                           (Lafayette Theatre)

Subsequent Productions:  Los Angeles, CA            February 4, 1937


If Ye Break Faith
  Author: Maria M. Coxe
  Director: Roy Elkins
  Designer: Charles B. Garlinger
  Other:

First Production:          Miami, FL                June 20-July 2, 1938
                           (Federal Theatre)

Subsequent Productions:  Denver, CO                 Nov. 23-Dec. 4, 1938
                           (Baker Theatre)
                           Jacksonville, FL         November 17-23, 1938
                           (Durkee Field Theatre)
                           New Orleans, LA          November 21-26, 1938
                           (St. Charles Theatre)


In Heaven and Earth
  Author: Arthur Goodman and Washington Pezet
  Director: J.J. White
  Designer: Cleon Throckmorton and Rollo Wayne
  Other:

First Production:          New York, NY             March 26, 1936
                           (Willis Theatre)

Subsequent Productions:  none

## In His Image

Author: Garland Ethel
Director: Clarence H. Talbot
Designer: not available
Other:

| | | |
|---|---|---|
| First Production: | Tacoma, WA (Little Theatre) | September 1, 1936 |

Subsequent Productions:  none

## It Can't Happen Here

Author: Sinclair Lewis and John C. Moffitt
Director: Vincent Sherman
Designer: Tom Adrian Crascraft
Other: At the Adelphi Theatre

| | | |
|---|---|---|
| First Production: | New York, NY (Suitcase Theatre) | Oct. 27, 1936-Jul. 2, 1937 |
| | New York, NY (Biltmore Theatre) | Oct. 27, 1936-May 1, 1937 |
| | New York, NY (Adelphi Theatre) | Oct. 27, 1936-Feb 13, 1937 |
| Subsequent Productions: | Atlanta, GA | May 1937 |
| | Birmingham, AL | Oct. 27-Dec. 2, 1936 |
| | Boston, MA | Oct. 27, 1936-Jul 25, 1938 |
| | Bridgeport, CT | Oct. 27-Nov. 14, 1936 |
| | Chicago, IL | Oct. 27, 1936-Jan 23, 1937 |
| | Cincinnati, OH | Jan. 28-Feb. 17, 1937 |
| | Cincinnati, OH | Mar. 21-Feb. 27, 1937 |
| | Cleveland, OH | Oct. 27-Nov. 6, 1936 |
| | Denver, CO | Oct. 29-Nov. 21, 1936 |
| | Des Moines, IA | May 5-16, 1937 |

| | |
|---|---|
| Detroit, MI | Oct. 27-Nov. 14, 1936 |
| Hartford, CT | Nov. 30-Dec. 12, 1936 |
| Indianapolis, IN | Oct. 27-Nov. 7, 1936 |
| Los Angeles, CA | October 27-28, 1936 |
| Los Angeles, CA | Oct. 27-Dec. 13, 1936 |
| Miami, FL | Oct. 27-Nov. 2, 1936 |
| Newark, NJ | Oct. 27, 1936-Feb 25, 1938 |
| Omaha, NE | Oct. 27-Nov. 14, 1936 |
| Paterson, NJ | April 18, 1937 |
| Peoria, IL | March 20-28, 1937 |
| San Francisco, CA | Oct. 27-Nov. 28, 1936 |
| Seattle, WA | Oct. 27-Nov. 6, 1936 |
| Tacoma, WA | Oct. 27-Nov. 17, 1936 |
| Yonkers, NY | October 27, 1936 |

Jambalaya
    Author: Walter Armitage
    Director: Walter Armitage
    Designer: William Perkins
    Other:

First Production:          New Orleans, LA          January 4-9, 1938
                           (Playhouse of the
                           Federal Theatre)

Subsequent Productions: none


Jefferson Davis
    Author: John McGee
    Director: Henry Stillman
    Designer: not available
    Other: Produced under the personal supervision of Kay McKay

First Production:          New York, NY          February 18-20, 1936
                           (Biltmore Theatre)

Subsequent Productions: none

## Lars Killed His Son
Author: Lawrence J. Bernard
Director: Robert Peel Noble
Designer: not available
Other:

First Production:            Los Angeles, CA          February 18, 1937
                             (Musart Theatre)

Subsequent Productions: none


## The Last Enemy
Author: Robert H. and Frances Nimmo Greene
Director: J. Burt Burton
Designer: Stanford MacNider
Other:

First Production:            San Antonio, TX          April 1, 1937
                             (San Pedro Playhouse)

Subsequent Productions: Atlanta, GA              May 12-19, 1937
                        Jacksonville, FL         April 7-12, 1937


## The Leading Man
Author: William Allen Kimball
Director: Clarence H. Talbot
Designer: Blanche Morgan
Other:

First Production:            Tacoma, WA               August 6, 1936
                             (Playwrights' Theatre)

Subsequent Productions: none


## Life and Death of an American

Author: George Sklar
Director: Charles K. Freeman
Designer: Howard Bay
Other:

First Production:           New York, NY         May 19, 1939
                            (Maxine Elliott)

Subsequent Productions: none


The Lonely Man
    Author: Howard Koch
    Director: not available
    Designer: Clive Rickabaugh
    Other:

First Production:           Chicago, IL          May 16, 1937
                            (Blackstone Theatre)

Subsequent Productions: none


Lucy Stone
    Author: Maud Wood Park
    Director: Elliot Duvey
    Designer: Paul Cadorette
    Other:

First Production:           Boston, MA           May 9, 1939
                            (Copley Theatre)

Subsequent Productions: none


The Machine Age
    Author: William Sully
    Director: Frank Merlin
    Designer: Victor Zaroff and Walter Walden
    Other:

First Production:        Brooklyn, NY        Apr. 30-May 29, 1937
                                (Majestic Theatre)

Subsequent Productions: none

## M.D.
Author: Clarence H. Talbot
Director: Clarence H. Talbot
Designer: Jack McPheden
Other:

First Production:        Tacoma, WA        January 12, 1937
                                (Federal Theatre)

Subsequent Productions: none

## The Man in the Tree
Author: John Woodworth
Director: Roy Elkins
Designer: Josef Lentz
Other:

First Production:        Atlanta, GA        Jan. 31-Feb. 5, 1938
                                (Atlanta Theatre)

Subsequent Productions: Miami, FL        May 16-28, 1938
                                (Federal Theatre)

## Me Third
Author: Mary Coyle Chase
Director: Michael Andrew Slane
Designer: Pancho Gates
Other:

First Production:        Denver, CO         Nov. 27-Dec. 15, 1936
                                (Baker Theatre)

Subsequent Productions: Los Angeles, CA     December 11, 1936
(Hollywood Playhouse)
San Francisco, CA    March 21, 1938
(Alcazar Theatre)

"Men At Work"
Author: Harold McGrath
Director: Clarence H. Talbot
Designer: not available
Other: Presented in an evening of one-acts with "Spring Afternoon"
and "All My Life"

First Production:       Tacoma, WA     June 12, 1936
(Little Theatre)

Subsequent Productions: none

Mister Jim
Author: Marcus L. Bach
Director: Edward Vail
Designer: Clive Rickabaugh
Other:

First Production:       Chicago, IL     May 16, 1937
(Blackstone Theatre)

Subsequent Productions: none

Monsignor's Hour
Author: Emmet Lavery
Director: not available
Designer: not available
Other:

First Production:       New Orleans, LA    March 22-27, 1938
(Federal Playhouse)

Subsequent Productions: none

A Moral Entertainment
　　Author: Richard Maibaum
　　Director: Arthur Ritchie
　　Designer: Paul Cadorette
　　Other:

First Production:　　　　Roslyn, NY　　　　Apr. 30-May 5, 1938
　　　　　　　　　　　　(Four Seasons
　　　　　　　　　　　　Playhouse)

Subsequent Productions: Boston, MA　　　　Dec. 27, 1938-Jan. 7,
　　　　　　　　　　　　　　　　　　　　　1939
　　　　　　　　　　　　Bryn Mawr, PA　　June 18, 1938
　　　　　　　　　　　　Hartford, CT　　　April 20-22, 1939

Mr. Jiggins of Jigginstown
　　Author: Christine Langford
　　Director: J. Augustus Keogh
　　Designer: not available
　　Other:

First Production:　　　　New York, NY　　　December 17, 1936
　　　　　　　　　　　　(Labor Stage)

Subsequent Productions: none

Murder in the Cathedral
　　Author: T.S. Eliot
　　Director: Halsted Welles
　　Designer: Tom Adrian Crascraft
　　Other:

First Production:　　　　New York, NY　　　March 20-May 2, 1936
　　　　　　　　　　　　(Manhattan Theatre)

Subsequent Productions: San Francisco, CA    November 13-26, 1938
(Alacazar Theatre)

## Native Ground
Author: Virgil Geddes
Director: James Light
Designer: Howard Bay
Other:

First Production:    New York, NY    January 27, 1937
(Venice Theatre)

Subsequent Productions: none

## No More Frontiers
Author: Talbot Jennings
Director: not available
Designer: not available
Other:

First Production:    Bridgeport, CT    April 13-24, 1937
(Park Theatre)

Subsequent Productions: New York, NY
(Suitcase Theatre)
San Francisco, CA    June 27-Jul. 9, 1938

## No More Peace
Author: Ernest Toller
Director: Franklin Raymond
Designer: not available
Other:

First Production:    Cincinnati, OH    April 23, 1937
(Emery Auditorium)

Subsequent Productions: Indianapolis, IN    May 24, 1937
    Lawrence, NY    June 3, 1938
    New York, NY    January 28, 1938
    (Maxine Elliott)
    Director:    Designer:
     EdwardVail;    Samuel Leve
    Roslyn, NY    June 3, 1937-June 4,
    (Four Seasons Playhouse)   1938
    Director:    Designer:
     Charles Hopkins;   Experimental Theatre,
                Vassar College

## Ohio Doom
Author: Harold Igo
Director: not available
Designer: not available
Other:

First Production:    Chicago, IL    October 20, 1936

Subsequent Productions: Cincinnati, OH    November 22, 1938

## On the Rocks
Author: George Bernard Shaw
Director: Robert Ross
Designer: Clive Rickabaugh
Other: Music, Phil Charig; Music arranged by Emil Soderstrom and
    David Scheinfeld

First Production:    New York, NY    June 15, 1938
                (Daly's Theatre)

Subsequent Productions: none

## Oh Say Can You Sing
Author: Sid Kuller, Ray Golden and Phil Charig
Director: H. Gordon Graham
Designer: Clive Rickabaugh

Other:

| First Production: | Chicago, IL | Dec. 11, 1936-Aug 21, 1937 |
|---|---|---|
| Subsequent Productions: | Tampa, FL (Centro Asturiano) | June 13-20, 1937 |
| | Seattle, WA (Royal Theatre) | August 5-9, 1937 |

One More Spring
   Author: Lulie Hard McKinley (adapted from novel by Robert Nathan)
   Director: Roy Elkins
   Designer: Joseph L. Lentz
   Other:

| First Production: | Jacksonville, FL (Duval St. Theatre) | June 16, 1937 |
|---|---|---|

Subsequent Productions: none


Path of Flowers
   Author: Valentine Katayev
   Director: Turner Bullock
   Designer: Robert Chertov and Theodore Fuchs
   Other: Translated by Irving De W. Talmadge

| First Production: | New York, NY (Daly's Experimental Theatre) | September 17, 1936 |
|---|---|---|

Subsequent Productions: none


Precious Land
   Author: Robert Whitehead
   Director: J. Burt Burton
   Designer: Stanford MacNider

Other:

First Production:          Oklahoma City, OK   April 1936

Subsequent Productions: San Antonio, TX       May 19-21, 1937
(San Pedro Playhouse)


## Professor Mamlock
Author: Friedrich Wolf
Director: Harold Bolton
Designer: George Phillips
Other: Translated from the German by Anne Bromberger

First Production:          New York, NY       April 13-24, 1937
(Daly's Theatre)

Subsequent Productions: Boston, MA         February 10, 1938
Los Angeles, CA    August 5-26, 1938


## Prologue to Glory
Author: Elsworth Prouty Conkle
Director: Lee Bulgakov
Designer: Walter Walden
Other:

First Production:          New York, NY       March 17, 1938
(Maxine Elliott)

Subsequent Productions: Chicago, IL        Nov. 9, 1938-Jan. 7,
1939
Cincinnati, OH     May 8-27, 1939
Los Angeles, CA    June 16-Jul 17, 1938
New Orleans, LA   Jan. 23-Feb. 5, 1939
Philadelphia, PA   Dec. 19, 1938-Jan. 7,
1939
Portland, OR      Jan. 29-Feb. 12, 1939
San Francisco, CA  May 16-June 11, 1938

Ready! Aim! Fire!
    Author: Gene Stone and Jack Robinson
    Director: Lorin Raker
    Designer: not available
    Other: Music, Clair Leonard; Choreography, Myra Kinch

    First Production:          Los Angeles, CA      Oct. 22, 1937-Jan. 9,
                               (Hollywood Playhouse/        1938
                               Mayan Theatre)

    Subsequent Productions: Tampa, FL              March 6-26, 1938
                            (Rialto Theatre)


Revue of Reviews
    Author: Gene Stone and Jack Robinson
    Director: T.M. Paul
    Designer: not available
    Other: Dance Direction, Myra Kinch

    First Production:

    Subsequent Productions:


Rhapsody in Two Flats
    Author: Edgar L. Hay
    Director: William Tennyson
    Designer: not available
    Other:

    First Production:          Miami, FL            March 5-13, 1937

    Subsequent Productions: none


See How They Run
    Author: George Savage
    Director: Alan Williams

Designer: not available
Other:

First Production:        San Francisco, CA     September 5-17, 1938
                     (Alcazar Theatre)

Subsequent Productions: Oakland, CA       Sept. 19-Oct. 1, 1938
                     (12th St. Theatre)
                     Seattle, WA       Sept. 19-Oct. 1, 1938
                     (Federal Theatre)

Sing For Your Supper
    Author: Project Staff
    Director: Harold Hecht
    Designer: Herbert Andrews; Lighting, Abe Feder
    Other: Music, Lee Wainer and Ned Lehac; Lyrics, Robert Sour;
        Choreography, Anna Sokolow

First Production:        New York, NY     Mar. 15-June 30, 1939
                     (Adelphi Theatre)

Subsequent Productions: none

"Snickering Horses"
    Author: Em Jo Basshe
    Director: Maurice Clark
    Designer: Samuel Leve
    Other:

First Production:        New York, NY    May 13, 1936
                     (Experimental Theatre)

Subsequent Productions: none

"Spring Afternoon"
    Author: W.A. Kimball
    Director: Clarence H. Talbot

346

Designer: not available
Other: Presented in an evening of one-acts with "All My Life"
  and "Men at Work"

First Production:          Tacoma, WA              June 12-13, 1936
                           (Little Theatre)

Subsequent Productions: none


## The Sun and I
Author: Barrie and Leona Stavis
Director: Edward Goodman
Designer: Tom Adrian Crascraft
Other: Music, Thomas K. Scherman

First Production:          New York, NY            Feb. 26-May 22, 1937
                           (Adelphi Theatre)

Subsequent Productions: Salem, MA                  March 7, 1938
                        San Francisco, CA          February 2-27, 1938


## The Sun Rises in the West
Author: Donald A. Murray, Theodore Pezman and Rena Vale
Director: Mary Virginia Farmer
Designer: Jon Blanchett
Other: Original score, Eddison von Ottenfeld

First Production:          Los Angeles, CA         July 1-17, 1938
                           (Mayan Theatre)

Subsequent Productions: none


## Swing Parade
Author: Book, Max M. Dill and Richard Melville
Director: Max M. Dill
Designer: Sets and Lights under direction of Scott McLean
Other: Music, Nat Goldstein; Lyrics, Richard Melville and

Del Foster; Choreography, Yvonne Matjcik

First Production:    San Francisco, CA    April 15-Jun 30, 1937
                     (Alcazar Theatre)

Subsequent Productions: none


They Too Arise
   Author: Arthur A. Miller
   Director: not available
   Designer: not available
   Other:

First Production:    Detroit, MI          October 23, 1937
                     (Jewish Comm. Center)

Subsequent Productions: none


This Pretty World
   Author: Converse Tyler
   Director: Michael Andrew Slane
   Designer: Sets, C. Gilbert Erickson
   Other:

First Production:    Denver, CO           March 16, 1938
                     (Baker Theatre)

Subsequent Productions: none


Timberline Tintypes
   Author: Yasha Frank
   Director: Margaret Barney
   Designer: Scenic artist, Franya Prudhomme
   Other: Dance direction, Jack Biles

First Production:        Mt. Hood, OR         Aug. 12-Sept. 3, 1938
                         (Timberline Lodge)

and Portland, OR      Aug. 12-Sept. 3, 1938
(WPA Theatre)

Subsequent Productions: none

Tobias and the Angel
    Author: James Bridie
    Director: Ellen Van Volkenburg
    Designer: Scenic designer, Samuel Leve
    Other:

First Production:      New York, NY      April 28, 1937
    (Provincetown Play-
    house)

Subsequent Productions: none

Too Lucky
    Author: Glenn Hughes
    Director: Clarence H. Talbot
    Designer: Blanche Morgan
    Other:

First Production:      Tacoma, WA      July 17, 1936
    (Federal Theatre)

Subsequent Productions: none

Two-A-Day
    Author: Gene Stone and Jack Robinson
    Director: Jack Laughlin
    Designer: Scenic designer, Frederick Stover
    Other:

First Production:      Los Angeles, CA      Oct. 29, 1938-May 14,
    (Hollywood Playhouse)      1939

Subsequent Productions: San Francisco, CA    May 18, 1939
(Alcazar Theatre)

## Whom Dreams Possess
Author: Barbara Ring and Rudolph Elie, Jr.
Director: Roy Elkins
Designer: not available
Other:

First Production:     Miami, FL     June 14, 1937

Subsequent Productions: none

## Within These Walls
Author: Martin L. Bach
Director: Kay Ewing
Designer: not available
Other:

First Production:     Chicago, IL     Jan. 28-Feb. 13, 1937
(Blackstone Theatre)

Subsequent Productions: Indianapolis, IN    Mar. 29-Apr. 3, 1937
New Orleans, LA    April 16-30, 1939

## Woman of Destiny
Author: Samuel Jesse Warshawsky
Director: Edward Vail
Designer: Scenic designer, Cleon Throckmorton
Other:

First Production:     New York, NY     Mar. 2-Apr. 11, 1936
(Willis Theatre)

Subsequent Productions: none

BIBLIOGRAPHY

Books

Aaron, Daniel. Writers on the Left. New York: Octagon Books, 1960; reprinted., New York: Octagon Books, 1974.

Bentley, Eric. The Playwright As Thinker. New York: Meridian Books, Inc., 1960.

Bernstein, Irving. The Lean Years: A History of the American Worker (1920-1933). Boston: Houghton Mifflin and Co., 1960.

Brown, Lorraine, and O'Connor, John, eds. Free, Adult, and Uncensored. Washington, D.C.: New Republic Books, 1978.

Brustein, Robert. The Theatre of Revolt. Boston: Little, Brown & Co., 1964.

Burns, James MacGregor Roosevelt. The Lion and the Fox. New York: Harcourt, Brace and World, 1956.

Buttitta, Tony, and Whitham, Barry. Uncle Sam Presents: A Memoir of the Federal Theatre 1935-1939. Philadelphia: University of Pennsylvania Press, 1982.

Clurman, Harold. The Fervent Years. New York: Alfred A. Knopf, 1957. Conlin, Joseph. The American Radical Press 1888-1960, vol. 1. Westport, CT: Greenwood Press, 1974).

Craig, E. Quitta. Black Drama of the Federal Theatre Era. Amherst: Amherst University Press, 1980.

Famous American Plays of the 1930s. The Laurel Drama Series. Introduction by Harold Clurman. New York: Dell, 1959.

Famous American Plays of the 1970s. The Laurel Drama Series. Introduction by Theodore Hoffman. New York: Dell, 1981.

Flanagan, Hallie. Arena. New York: Duell, Sloan and Pierce, 1940; reprint ed., New York: Benjamin Bloom, 1965.

Friedel, Frank, ed. The New Deal and the American People. Englewood Cliffs: Prentice Hall, 1964.

Galbraith, John Kenneth. The Great Crash. 3rd ed. Forward by the Author. Boston: Houghton Mifflin and Co., 1972.

Gassner, John. Form and Idea in Modern Theatre. New York: The Dryden Press, Inc., 1956.

_____. Masters of the Drama. 3rd ed. New York: Dover Publications, 1951.

Glazer, Nathan. The Social Basis of American Communism. New York: Harcourt, Brace and World, 1961.

Goldstein, Malcolm. The Political Stage. New York: Oxford University Press, 1979.

Himmelstein, Morgan. Drama Was A Weapon: The Left-Wing Theatre in New York, 1929-1941. Foreword by John Gassner. New Brunswick: Rutgers University Press, 1963.

Houseman, John. Run-Through. New York: Simon & Schuster, 1972.

Kirby, Michael. Futurist Performance. New York: Dutton & Co., Inc., 1971.

Krutch, Joseph Wood. The American Drama Since 1918. New York: George Braziller, Inc., 1957.

Mathews, Jane DeHart. The Federal Theatre 1935-1939: Plays, Relief, and Politics. Princeton: Princeton University Press, 1967; reprint ed., New York: Octagon Books, 1980.

Mitchell, Lofton. Black Drama. New York: Hawthorn Books, Inc., 1967.

Nothing to Fear: The Selected Addresses of Franklin D. Roosevelt and the New Deal. Edited by B.D. Zevin. Boston: Houghton Mifflin Co., 1946.

Penkower, Monty Noam. The Federal Writers' Project: A Study in Government Patronage of the Arts. Urbana: University of Illinois Press, 1977.

Rabkin, Gerald. Drama and Commitment: Politics in the American Theatre of the Thirties. Bloomington: University of Indiana Press, 1964.

Rice, Elmer. The Living Theatre. New York: Harper and Brothers, 1959.

Schlesinger, Arthur M., Jr. The Crisis of the Old Order. Boston: Houghton Mifflin Co., 1956.

Shannon, David A., ed. The Great Depression. Englewood Cliffs: Prentice Hall, 1960.

Whitman, Willson. Bread and Circuses. New York: Oxford University Press, 1937; reprint ed., Ithaca: New York Books for Libraries Press, 1983.

Wittler, Clarence J. Some Social Trends in W.P.A. Drama. Washington, D.C.: Catholic University of America Press, 1939.

Williams, Jay. Stage Left. New York: Charles Scribner's Sons, 1974.

## Interviews

(All tapes at George Mason University.)

Barber, Phillip. By members of the Federal Theatre Collection Staff, George Mason University. Interview, 11 November 1978.

Bentley, Eric. By Mae Mallory Krulak. Interview, 22 May 1976.

Blankfort, Michael. By Lorraine Brown. Interview, 22 July 1977.

Fishel, H.L. By Lorraine Brown. Interview, 26 October 1976.

Gilder, Rosamond. By John O'Connor. Interview, 19 February 1976.

Koch, Howard. By John O'Connor. Interview, undated.

Lavery, Emmet. By John O'Connor and Mae Mallory Krulak. Interview, 5 January 1976.

Rhodes, Irwin. By Lorraine Brown. Interview, 26 February 1977.

Rosten, Norman. By John O'Connor. Interview, 14 January 1977.

Russak, Ben. By Lorraine Brown. Interview, 19 February 1976.

Sundgaard, Arnold. By John O'Connor. Interview, 5 September 1976.

Talbot, Clarence. By Karen Wickre. Interview, 21 July 1977.

Tyler, Converse. By John O'Connor. Interview, 15 December 1975.

Welles, Halsted. By John O'Connor. Interview, 17 November 1978.


## Letters

Flanagan, Hallie, to all State and Local Administrators. 4 November 1936. At George Mason University.

Kreymbourg, Alfred, to Hallie Flanagan. 16 February 1936. Billy Rose Collection.

Klebba, Victor, to Robert Dunham, Illinois WPA Director. 4 January 1936. Record Group 69, United States National Archives. Cited by John Charles Koch, "The Federal Theatre Project: Region IV--A Structural and Historical Analysis of How It Functioned and What It Accomplished." Ph.D. dissertation, University of Nebraska, 1981.

## Press Releases

"Death of An American." Press Release from Department of Information. 15 May 1939. Record Group 69, United States National Archives.

"Exclusive to Sunday Worker." Press Release from Department of Information. 30 August 1936. At George Mason University.

"It Can't Happen Here." Press Release from Department of Information. 17 February 1937. At George Mason University.

"Native Ground." Press Release to Brooklyn Daily Eagle from Department of Information. Undated. Record Group 69, United States National Archives.

"New Production Board Operation." Press Release from Department of Information. Undated. Record Group 69, United States National Archives.

"On the Rocks." Press Release. 16 June 1938. At George Mason University.

"Play Contests." Press Release from the National Service Bureau. At George Mason University.

"Prologue to Glory. Press Release written by George Kondolf, Department of Information. 10 November 1937. At George Mason University.

## Production Bulletins

Production bulletins are sometimes referred to as "Production Notebooks." The following are all at the Federal Theatre Collection at George Mason University.

African Vineyard
Battle Hymn
Captain-What-the-Devil
Girl Wants Glamour
The Great Gay Road
I Confess
O Say Can You Sing

Ready! Aim! Fire!
See How They Run
The Sun Rises in the West
Swing Parade
This Pretty World
Timberline Tintypes

## Programs

All programs are located at George Mason University.

The Cherokee Night
Created Equal
Dance of Death

Mr. Jiggins of Jigginstown
The Sun Rises in the West

## Memorandums

"Attendance Figures for Professor Mamlock." General memorandum. Undated. At George Mason University.

Bosworth, Francis, to Playreading Department. 29 June 1936. At George Mason University.

Glaspell, Susan, Kondolf, George, and McGee, John, to Hallie Flanagan. 6 November 1936. Record Group 69, United States National Archives. Cited by John Charles Koch, "The Federal Tehatre

Project: Region IV--A Structural and Historical Analysis of How It Functioned and What It Accomplished." Ph.D. dissertation, University of Nebraska, 1981.

Lavery, Emmet, to Converse Tyler. 17 August 1938. At George Mason University. (Regarding FTP productions.)

Lavery, Emmet, to all Supervisors of National Service Bureau. "Redefinition of Policies and Procedures." 10 January 1939. At George Mason University.

Loving, Pierre et al, to Philip Barber, et al. Undated. Record Group 69, United States National Archives. (Contains a synopsis of Native Ground.)

Tyler, Converse, to Francis Bosworth. 28 July 1936. At George Mason University. (Recommendation for American Wing.)

Welles, Halsted, to Joseph Moss. 15 February 1939. At George Mason University.

Welles, Halsted, to Reference Department. 5 April 1936. At George Mason University.

## Playreaders' Reports

All Playreaders' reports are at George Mason University.

American Holiday.
    Kuttner, Alexander. 21 September 1936.

American Wing.
    Munson, Fleet, Bureau of Research and Publication, FTP. Undated.
    O'Donnell, Judson, Bureau of Research and Publication, FTP. Undated.

Around the Corner.
    Bennett, Henry. 12 March 1937.

Harrett, Lee. 19 March 1937.

Captain-What-the-Devil.
Armstrong, E. 1 October 1936.
Bond, Arthur. 14 October 1936.

Created Equal.
Bennett, Henry. 31 October 1937.
Tyler, Converse. 14 January 1938.

Feet on the Ground.
Motherwell, Hiram. 30 November 1937.
Rimassa, John. 27 February 1937.
Tyler, Converse. 1 November 1937.

The Gallows Gate.
Ayres, Ann Grosvenor. 5 April 1937.
Steinhardt, Samuel. Undated.

The Great Gay Road.
Luban, Milton. 3 September 1936.

I Confess.
Solomon, Louis. 15 July 1936.

If Ye Break Faith.
Bosworth, Francis. 1 November 1937.
Cutner, Alexander. 19 October 1937.
Munson, Fleet. 16 November 1936.
Solomon, Louis. 3 November 1936.

It Can't Happen Here.
Fishel, H.L. Undated

M.D.
Beyer. 15 January 1937.
Lake, Paul. 18 February 1937.
Murray, M. 16 February 1937.

The Man in the Tree.
Silver, J. Edward. 2 August 1937.

Me Third.
        Fuller, Edmund. Undated.
        McCann. Undated.

Monsignor's Hour.
        Caully, Zachary. 19 September 1938.
        Morris, Ruth. 28 December 1936.

A Moral Entertainment.
        Tyler, Converse. 10 January 1938.

Native Ground.
        Andromeda, Nicholas. 21 December 1936.
        Feinberg, Charles. 19 June 1936.
        Malkin, Fanny. 23 December 1936.
        Rimassa, John. 21 July 1936.

One More Spring.
        Levine, Morris. 7 September 1938.

Path of Flowers.
        Bosworth, Francis. 14 April 1936.
        Vittes, Louis. 10 July 1936.

Precious Land.
        Greenberg, J.A. 2 October 1936.
        Lake, Paul. 28 October 1936.
        Malkin, Fanny. 2 October 1936.
        Munson, Fleet. 30 November 1936.
        Solomon, Louis. 2 October 1936.

See How They Run.
        Druce, Jeannette. 9 November 1937.
        Portner, M. 18 August 1937.
        Russak, Ben. 6 December 1937.
        Tyler, Converse. 5 November 1937.

They Too Arise.
        Fuller. 9 February 1937.
        Malkin. 4 January 1937.
        Lipschutz. Undated.

Ressler; Benjamin, Lee; and Schmeltsman, Leo. Undated.
Schmeltsman, Leo. Undated.
Unsigned. Undated.


## Periodicals and Newspapers

Anderson, John. 18 March 1935.

Atkinson, Brooks. New York Times, 24 March 1936; 16 May 1936; 25 April 1939.

_____. "Something of What Has Been Happening in Federal Theatre." New York Times, 2 May 1937.

Bentley, Eric. "Writing for the Political Theatre." Performing Arts Journal 1x-2-3: 47.

Bliss, H. Bond. Review of Whom Dreams Possess, undated. Clipping file at George Mason University.

Borden, Gail. Chicago Daily News, 29 January 1937.

Boston American, 28 December 1938.

Boston Globe, 28 December 1938.

Boston Herald, 14 June 1938.

Boston Post, 11 June 1938.

Boston Record, 29 December 1938.

Brooklyn Citizen, 14 April 1937; 1 May 1937.

Brooklyn Eagle, 18 May 1936.

Brooklyn Times Union, 1 May 1937.

Brown, John Mason. New York Post, 30 March 1936.

Call Bulletin, 1 August 1935.

Cambridge, John. Daily Worker, undated. Billy Rose Collection.

Casey, Lee. Rocky Mountain News, undated. Quoted in Hallie Flanagan, Arena. New York: Duell, Sloane and Pierce, 1940; reprint ed., New York: Benjamin Bloom, 1965.

Cassel, Gould. Brooklyn Eagle, 29 April 1937.

Cassidy, Claudia. Journal of Commerce [Chicago], 5 July 1938.

Chicago Daily News, 22 August 1936.

Chicago Herald Examiner, 17 May 1937.

Cincinnati Enquirer, 8 March 1936; 23 November 1938.

Cohen, Eddie. Miami Daily News, 2 June 1938.

Collins, Charles. Chicago Tribune, 5 July 1938.

Commercial Recorder, 12 May 1937.

Cope, Eddie. San Antonio News, 20 May 1937.

Dabney, Thomas Edwin. New Orleans States, 12 March 1937; 15 December 1937.

Daily News, 29 April 1937.

Daily Worker, 21 September 1936; 22 May 1939.

DeBernardi, A. Denver Post, 28 November 1936.

Denver Democrat, 2 April 1938.

Denver Monitor, 18 March 1938.

Detroit Times, 17 October 1937.

Dexter, Charles. Daily Worker, 24 May 1936.

Drake, Harold. Herald Tribune, 18 September 1936.

Garland, Robert. "Virgil Geddes Talks on Federal Theatre." New York World Telegram, 6 November 1935.

Gassner, John. "Federal Theatre Plays." New Theatre (July 1936: 6,27.

_____. Foreward to Morgan Himmelstein, Drama Was A Weapon. New Brunswick, NJ: Rutgers University Press, 1963.

Geddes, Virgil. "Data for Experimental: Notes on One of the WPA's Recently Proposed Trial Theatres." New York Times, 3 November 1937.

Federal One I-3 (August 1976): 1; II-1 (August 1977): 1; III-1 (April 1978): 1; V-1 (February 1980): 1-5; II-1 (December 1985): 5. (Newsletter of the Institute on the Federal Theatre Project and New Deal Culture.)

Flanagan, Hallie. "Federal Theatre Tomorrow." Federal Theatre Magazine II-1 (May 1936): 26. Cited in Jane DeHart Mathews, p. 62. The Federal Theatre 1935-1939: Plays, Relief and Politics. Princeton: Princeton University Press, 1967.

_____. "A Report of the First Six Months." Federal Theatre Magazine (March 1936): 8-9. Cited in Jane DeHart Mathews, p. 61. The Federal Theatre 1935-1939: Plays, Relief and Politics. Princeton: Princeton University Press, 1967.

Henderson, Mary. "Federal Theatre Project Records." Performing Arts Resources VI (Theatre Library Association, 1980): 24-25.

Herald Tribune, 28 October 1936; 7 May ?; 29 January 1938.

Hobart, John. San Francisco News, 7 September 1938.

Hollywood Citizen News, 7 November 1938.

Hollywood Life, July 1938.

Hollywood Variety, 2 July 1938.

Hughes, Elinor. Boston Herald, 28 December 1938.

"Inside of a Murder." Daily Worker, 23 December 1940.

Jones, Charles P. Times-Picayune, 12 March 1937; 15 December 1937.

Kane, Harnet T. Item, 23 March 1938.

Knoblock, K.T. Item, 15 December 1937.

Kolodny, Irving. "Footlights, Federal Style." Harpers (November 1936): 633. Cited in Jane DeHart Mathews, p. 52. The Federal Theatre 1935-1939: Plays, Relief and Politics. Princeton: Princeton University Press, 1967.

Krutch, Joseph Wood. "Drama." Nation (7 November 1936): 557-58.

Labor New Dealer, 26 August 1938.

Le Baron, Howard. San Antonio Light, 2 April 1937.

Lee, Robert. San Francisco News, 7 September 1938.

Lockridge, Richard. New York Sun, 18 March 1938.

Los Angeles Evening News, 15 January 1938.

Los Angeles Examiner, 2 July 1938.

Los Angeles Journal, 2 July 1938.

Los Angeles Times, 23 October 1937.

Mantle, Burns. Buffalo Courier Express, 25 June 1938. (Includes partial quote from George Bernard Shaw's Preface to On the Rocks.)

_____. Daily News, 18 March 1938.

_____. New York Times, 25 April 1937.

364

_____. "The People's Theatre Grows Stronger." New York Times, 24 May 1936.

McDonald, Hazel. Chicago-American, 29 January 1937.

Miami Daily News, 1 March 1938; 2 June 1938; 17 April 1939.

Munk, Erika. "New York to the Arts: Drop Dead!" Village Voice, 27 May 1986, p. 18.

Neri, Ed. San Antonio Light, 20 May 1937.

New Theatre Magazine (12 December 1934).

New York Daily News, 23 May 1936; 24 March 1937.

New York Evening Journal, 20 May 1939.

New York Evening Post, 21 May 1936; 20 May 1939.

New York Herald, 28 October 1936.

New York Herald Tribune, 24 March 1936.

New York Home News, 3 March 1936.

New York Morning Telegraph, 4 March 1936; 6 March 1936.

New York Post, 4 March 1936; 29 January 1938.

New York Sun, 5 March 1936; 23 May 1936; 20 May 1939.

New York Telegraph, 4 March 1936; 6 March 1936; 21 May 1936.

New York Times, 2 October 1935; 10 October 1935; 13 November 1935; 14 November 1935. Cited in Jane DeHart Mathews, p. 50. The Federal Theatre 1935-1939: Plays, Relief and Politics. Princeton: Princeton University Press, 1967.

New York Times, 21 March 1936; 27 March 1936; 14 April 1936; 28 April 1936; 23 May 1936; 28 October 1936; 17 December 1936; 24 March

1937; 7 May 1937; 9 May 1937; 16 June 1938; 29 January 1939; 20 May 1939.

New York World Telegram, 22 February 1936; 3 March 1936; 21 July 1936; 24 October 1936; 18 December 1936; 16 April 1937; 7 May 1937.

Oklahoma City News, 13 October 1936.

Oklahoman, 10 August 1936.

Pell, Walter. "Which Way the Federal Theatre." New Theatre (April 1937): 7. Cited in Gerald Rabkin, p. 103. Drama and Commitment: Politics in the American Theatre of the Thirties. Bloomington: Indiana University Press, 1964).

Peoria Star, 3 May 1937.

Pike, Alberta. Denver News, 28 November 1938.

_____. "WPA Theatre Gets Credit of Revival of the Road." Rocky Mountain News, 4 April 1937.

"Popular Theatre Reviews Six-Month Career." New York Post, 4 August 1936.

Reading Times, undated. Cited in Hallie Flanagan, p. 248. Arena. New York: Duell, Sloan and Pierce, 1940; reprint ed., New York: Benjamin Bloom, 1965.

Rice, Elmer. "Federal Theatre Hereabouts." New York Times, 5 January 1936.

Soanes, Wood. Oakland Tribune, 20 September 1938.

"Spirit of New York Workers Praised by National Director." Federal Theatre Magazine (28 November 1935). Cited in Jane DeHart Mathews, p. 61. The Federal Theatre 1935-1939: Plays, Relief and Politics. Princeton: Princeton University Press, 1967.

Stanleigh, Lee. Daily Worker, 24 December 1936.

Sunday Worker, 26 July 1936.

Sun Telegraph-Riverside News, 30 April 1936.

Tacoma News Tribune, undated. Press Clippings in Production Bulletins for Girl Wants Glamour, The Leading Man, and Too Lucky. At George Mason University.

Tacoma North End News, undated. Press Clipping in Production Bulletin for In His Image. At George Mason University.

Tacoma Times, undated. Press Clipping in Production Bulletin for In His Image. At George Mason University.

Telegram, 15 April 1937.

Unidentified newspaper article, 29 April 1937. Located in Billy Rose Collection.

Variety, undated. Cited in Hallie Flanagan, p. 228. Arena. New York: Duell, Sloan and Pierce, 1940; reprint ed., New York: Benjamin Bloom, 1965.

Variety, 23 October 1935. Cited in Jane DeHart Mathews, p. 50. The Federal Theatre 1935-1939: Plays, Relief and Politics. Princeton: Princeton University Press, 1967.

Variety, 20 May 1936; 27 May 1936; 3 February 1937.

Viertel, Jack. "Theatrical Life Far from Broadway." New York Times, 1 June 1986.

Watts, Richard. New York Herald Tribune, 15 July 1936.

"WPA Takes over the Selwyn." Variety, 29 June 1938.

## Unpublished Manuscripts

Bain, Frank Reginald. "The Federal Government and Theatre: A History of Federal Involvement in Theatre from the End of the Federal Theatre Project in 1939 to the Establishment of the National Foundation on the Arts and Humanities in 1965." Ph.D. dissertation, University of Minnesota, 1972.

Berman, Harold. "The Playwriting Department." In Katharine Clugston, "Reorganization of Play Bureau," 9 September 1936. At George Mason University.

Billings, Alan Gailey. "Design in the Works Progress Administration's Federal Theatre Project (1935 to 1939)." Ph.D. dissertation, University of Illinois, 1967.

Bosworth, Francis. "Playwrights' Laboratory Theatre." In Katharine Clugston, "Reorganization of Play Bureau," 9 September 1936. At George Mason University.

Clugston, Katharine. "Reorganization of Play Bureau." 9 September 1936. At George Mason University.

Dycke, Marjorie L. "The Living Newspaper." Ph.D. dissertation, New York University, 1947.

"Experimental Theatre." FTP. Record Group 69, United States National Archives.

Flanagan, Hallie. "Federal Theatre Instructions." October 1935. At George Mason University.

Geddes, Virgil. "Reorganization and Plans for the Experimental Theatre Unit." Undated. Record Group 69, United States National Archives.

Gorelik, Mordecai. "On the Meaning of Experimental Theatre." 3 January 1936. (Report of an address made by Gorelik at the first personnel meeting of the Experimental Theatre.) At George Mason University.

"Instructions for Federal Theatre Programs of Works Progress Administration." 10 October 1935. At George Mason University.

Johnson, Evanmarii Alexandria. "A Production History of the Seattle Federal Theatre Project Negro Repertory Company: 1935-1937." Ph.D. dissertation, University of Washington, 1981.

Koch, Jon Charles. "The Federal Theatre Project: Region IV--A Structural and Historial Analysis of How It Functioned and What It Accomplished." Ph.D. dissertation, University of Nebraska, 1981.

Korn, Marjorie Susan. "It Can't Happen Here: Federal Theatre's Bold Adventure." Ph.D. dissertation, University of Missouri, 1978.

Kreizenbeck, Alan Dennis. "The Theatre Nobody Knows: Forgotten Productions of the Federal Theatre Project, 1935-1939." Ph.D. dissertation, New York University, 1979.

Kreymbourg, Alfred. "Plans for the Poetic Theatre." Undated. In Billy Rose Collection.

Kuttner, Alfred B. "Translation Department." In Katharine Clugston, "Reorganization of Play Bureau," 9 September 1936. At George Mason University.

_____. "Production Report for No More Peace." 4 June 1937. At George Mason University.

Lavery, Emmet. "The Flexible Stage." At George Mason University.

Lord, Ann. "Federal Theatre Accounts for Its Audience." Undated. (Report of an Analysis made by the Research Department, National Service Bureau.) At George Mason University.

Mardis, Robert Francis. "Federal Theatre in Florida." Ph.D. dissertation, University of Florida, 1972.

Miller, M. Lawrence. "Original FTP Protest Plays." Ph.D. dissertation, University of California, Los Angeles, 1968.

"Monthly Reports of Experimental Theatre." May 1937; July 1937; November 1936-June 1937 (inclusive). Record Group 69, United States National Archives.

"Play List." Bureau of Research and Publication, National Service Bureau, 12 December 1935. At George Mason University.

"A Review of the Productivity and Services of the Play Bureau from January 1936-December 1936." Undated. Play Bureau publication number 9. At George Mason University.

Ross, Ronald Patrick. "Black Drama in the Federal Theatre." Ph.D. dissertation, University of Southern California, 1972.

Ross, Theophil Walter, Jr. "Conflicting Concepts of the Federal Theatre Project: Critical History." Ph.D. dissertation, University of Missouri, 1981.

Swiss, Cheryl Diane. "Hallie Flanagan and the Federal Theatre Project: An Experiment in Form." Ph.D. dissertation, University of Wisconsin, 1982.

Tyler, Converse. "A Report of the Activities of the Playreading Department for the Period October 1, 1937-April 1, 1938." Undated. At George Mason University.

John W. Crawford

# EARLY SHAKESPEAREAN ACTRESSES

American University Studies: Series IV (English Language and Literature).
Vol. 8
ISBN 0-8204-0099-8          205 pages          hardback US $ 25.00*

*Recommended price – alterations reserved

One of the innovations of the Restoration in England was to introduce publicly the female actor on stage, with the reopening of the theatres. Charles II not only created two companies with this return to England, but promoted the concept of females as actors. It took courage for the first ones to enter this questionable vocation, considering the history the stage had achieved in Elizabethan and Stuart times, a history that demonstrated much criticism about the morality of dramatists and actors. Restoration actresses like George Anne Bellamy and Dora Jordan, as well as early eighteenth-century actresses like Catherine Clive and Peg Woffington proved that much individuality did indeed exist among the first; and even though the theatre had gained a much better reputation by the early nineteenth century, still actresses like Ellen Terry and Julia Marlowe were often the talk of the town because of their personal lives. Yet, these women proved that there is a place for the actress in modern drama.

Contents: 1. Brief background of the world of actors of the sixteenth century – 2. Individual sketches of various early actresses of Shakespearean roles – 2. Summary essay of certain actresses and their influence on Shakespearean drama.

PETER LANG PUBLISHING, INC.
62 West 45th Street
USA – New York, NY 10036

Hanna Scolnicov

# EXPERIMENTS IN STAGE SATIRE
An Analysis of Ben Jonson's *Every Man Out of His Humour, Cynthia's Revels* and *Poetaster*

European University Studies, Series XIV (Anglo-Saxon Language and Literature), vol. 131
ISBN 0-8204-8149-4                                            paperback $ 25.70*

*Recommended price – alterations reserved

This book analyses the problematic structure of Ben Jonson's three comical satires, and shows them to be an adaptation of Roman verse satire for the stage. Jonson was a self-conscious classicist writing with an eye to both classical literature and theory.

The plays are read in the light of Jonson's own precepts, as expressed in the plays themselves, rather than from any external perspective, such as that of the traditional unities. From the existing classical models. Jonson was trying to create a new dramatic genre, suitable for his own age. These plays constitute an exciting experiment in dramatic form, from which much can be learned about Jonson's development as an artist.

PETER LANG PUBLISHING, INC.
62 West 45th Street
USA – New York, NY 10036

James C. Burge

# LINES OF BUSINESS
Casting Practice and Policy in the American Theatre, 1752–1899

American University Studies: Series IX (History). Vol. 19
ISBN 0-8204-0312-1          307 pages          hardcover US $ 34.00*

*Recommended price – alterations reserved

The tradition of «lines of business» – the possession of a part by an actor – had its genesis on the English-speaking stage in Elizabethan times and was well established by the mid-eighteenth century. In this highly original study, James Burge investigates the use of «lines» in eight major American theatre companies. Burge sees in the impact of lines of business on the chief dramatic form of the nineteenth century – the melodrama – a demonstration of the power of this incipient trade unionism in casting and in the choice of repertory. With the rise of the director at the end of the century, lines of business ceased to be a controlling factor in casting practice and policy in the American theatre.

Contents: Development of casting policy and practice in the American theatre from 1752–1899 – Influence of the practices of the English-speaking stage of Elizabeth times and changes in American practice that came with the rise of the director in the theatre of the end of the eighteenth century.

PETER LANG PUBLISHING, INC.
62 West 45th Street
USA – New York, NY 10036